Buckingham's Reminiscences.

ANECDOTES,

PERSONAL MEMOIRS,

AND

BIOGRAPHIES OF LITERARY MEN,

CONNECTED WITH

NEWSPAPER LITERATURE,

FROM 1690 TO 1800.

BY JOSEPH T. BUCKINGHAM.

With Fine Steel Portraits of

ISAIAH THOMAS AND BENJAMIN RUSSELL.

VOL. II.

BOSTON:
REDDING & CO., 8 STATE STREET.
1852.

Your affectionate fellow citizen

Benj Russell.

SPECIMENS

OF

NEWSPAPER LITERATURE:

WITH

PERSONAL MEMOIRS, ANECDOTES,

AND

REMINISCENCES.

BY

JOSEPH T. BUCKINGHAM.

VOL. II.

BOSTON:
REDDING AND COMPANY.
1852.

CONTENTS OF VOL. II.

APPENDIX.

SPECIMENS

OF

NEWSPAPER LITERATURE.

MASSACHUSETTS CENTINEL.

A MEMOIR of the gentleman, who was one of the original proprietors of this paper, and who was the sole owner and conductor of it for more than forty years, may very properly precede any notices of the paper itself. It is regretted by all, who knew that gentleman, that he left no manuscript record of any of the incidents of his variegated life. The scanty materials, from which the following biographical sketch has been compiled, are chiefly recollections of things stated by himself, at various times, in the course of social and familiar communication. In the Centinel itself, however, may be found the most faithful portrait of its editor, as a public character. His private virtues are laid up in the memories of the friends and familiar acquaintances, who have survived him, and will be forgotten only when friendship, memory, and reflection shall have become extinct.

BENJAMIN RUSSELL was born in Boston, in the month of September, 1761. His father was John Russell, —

a descendant from the Rev. John Russell, who was born in England, came to Massachusetts when quite a youth, and was afterwards pastor of the First Baptist Church in Boston. Benjamin was also related, on the maternal side, to Ezekiel Cheever, celebrated as a master of the Boston Latin School, and to the Rev. Jeremy Belknap, the accomplished historian of New-Hampshire, and the author of "American Biography." His father was a mason by trade. He died in 1778, when the subject of this memoir was seventeen years old.

When quite a child, Russell was noted for a remarkably retentive memory and more than ordinary facility in learning the tasks prescribed by his teacher. He was placed at the public school taught by Master Carter, whose aptness in teaching and mildness of discipline were somewhat celebrated. Nothing was then taught in the common schools of Boston but the simplest elements of education. The tasks, that Russell had to perform, embraced nothing but easy lessons in reading, writing, and arithmetic. While yet a school-boy he was in the habit of frequenting the printing-office of Isaiah Thomas, where he acquired considerable facility in setting types, and where, probably, he learned quite as much as at school.

I have heard Russell relate many anecdotes of his boyhood, of which the following is one, and, as near as can be recollected, in his own words: —

It was a part of my duty as an assistant in the domestic affairs of the family, to have the care of the cow. One evening, after it was quite dark, I was driving the cow to her pasturage, — the common. Passing by the burial-ground, adjoining the Stone Chapel, I saw several lights that appeared to be springing from the earth, among the graves, and immediately sinking again to the ground, or expiring. To my young imagination, these lights could be nothing but ghosts. I left the cow to find her way to the common, or wherever else she pleased, and ran home at my utmost speed. Having told my father the cause of my fright, as well as I was able, while in such a state of terror and agitation, he took me by the hand and led me directly to the spot, where the supposed ghosts were still leaping and playing their pranks near the surface of the ground. My hair rose on end, and seemed to lift my hat from my head. My flesh was chilled through to my very bones. I trembled so that I could scarcely walk. Still my father continued rapidly marching towards the spot that inspired me with so much terror. When lo! there was a sexton, up to his shoulders in a grave, throwing out, as he proceeded in digging, bones and fragments of rotten coffins. The phosphorus in the decaying wood, blended with the peculiar state of the atmosphere, presented the appearance that had completely unstrung my nerves, and terrified me beyond description. I was never afterwards troubled with the fear of ghosts.

On the morning of the memorable Nineteenth of April, 1775, it became known throughout the town that a detachment of the British troops had crossed the ferry the night before, and were on their march to Concord, intending to destroy the military stores at that place. About eight o'clock, another detachment, under Lord Percy had paraded in Tremont-street, and were immediately in motion, towards Roxbury. The whole town was in agitation. As soon as the customary morning prayer had been offered in the school, (the school-house near the head of School-street,) Master Carter said, — "Boys, the war 's begun, and you may run." Russell, with several other boys near his age, followed the detachment through Roxbury and Brookline to Cambridge. The troops proceeded on towards Concord, with the intent of aiding and supporting the detachment, which preceded them the night before. The boys spent the day, amusing themselves, on Cambridge common, intending to follow the soldiers into Boston on their return.

The bridge over Charles River in Cambridge was taken up, or rendered impassable, during the day, and when the British army returned from their expedition about dusk, there was no way of getting into Boston but by the ferry. The boys from Boston attempted to follow them, but found it impracticable, and they were thus shut out from their homes. All intercourse between Boston and the country was prohibited by orders of the British commander, and his orders were rigidly enforced. Russell and his companions were unprovided with the means of subsistence, and had no resource but to solicit food and shelter, which were provided for them by the selectmen and other citizens of Cambridge.

The militia of New-England soon began to assemble from all directions, and several of these vagrant lads attached themselves to the officers, — not by regular enlistment, but informally, as waiters, or errand-boys, performing various services of usefulness and convenience. In this way Russell hung around the army, for more than three months, having no intercourse with his parents.

From the summit of Prospect-Hill he saw the memorable contest of the SEVENTEENTH OF JUNE, on Breed's Hill, and the conflagration, which laid in ashes the beautiful village of Charlestown. He used frequently to describe with a distinctness of detail, for which he was remarkable, the movements of the troops from Cambridge across the narrow neck of land, which it was necessary to pass in order to reach the scene of action, exposed to the raking fire of a British sloop of war, — the undaunted activity of Prescott, Putnam, and other officers, passing from one regiment or company to another, endeavoring to encourage the troops to firmness and perseverance, — and the retreat of the patriot army to Bunker-Hill, after the bloody conflict — the defeat of an ill-provided and undisciplined collection of men, that was hardly worthy to be called an army, — a defeat which proved to be an immortal victory.

About the beginning of August, Russell was passing from Cambridge in company with two or three soldiers, carrying baskets of provisions to Gen. Putnam's encampment on Prospect Hill, when he saw his father and one of his uncles in a chaise. Until that moment his father had known nothing of him since the Nineteenth of April. The meeting was doubtless a joyful one to both parties; but the pleasure was manifested in rather a singular mode. Russell used frequently to say — "My father jumped from the chaise and gave me the hardest flogging I ever had." After a short deliberation as to the course most advisable to adopt, young Russell was taken into the chaise, carried to Worcester, and left there as an apprentice with Isaiah Thomas, who had then recently removed thither from Boston, and resumed the publication of the Massachusetts Spy.

Mr. Thomas was not, at that time, in very affluent circumstances. During the first year or two of his apprenticeship, Russell, with a fellow-apprentice, slept in a garret, over the printing-office, on the rags that were taken in from time to time for the paper-maker. Not only his apprentices, but the master himself, frequently made their meals in the office on bread, and "milk bought by the penny-worth at a time."

When the Declaration of Independence was received in Worcester, it was read by Thomas to an assembly embracing almost the whole population of that and the adjacent towns. It was received with every possible demonstration of joy. In the evening, a numerous company congregated at the public tavern, to exchange congratulations, and to testify their patriotism in a manner, which, at the present day, might not be thought consistent with total abstinence principles. Punch, and other exhilarating beverages, flowed freely, and were partaken of by Russell and other young men without much regard to what the next day might bring forth. In describing the affair to me, Russell said — "We were all so happy, that we did not exactly know all that we did, but we gave full vent to our patriotic feelings, till a late hour in the evening. We were a little surprized in the morning, to find that about a dozen of us, and I among the rest, had enlisted as private soldiers in the army, — a recruiting officer being then in the town. Thomas was very angry, and immediately set about procuring my release. He could hardly go on with his business without me, but his principal plea, and that which proved successful, was, that I was not sixteen years of age, and consequently that the officer had transcended his power by enlisting me. I was taken before a justice of the peace, and being duly sworn, was asked if I was sixteen years old. I was quite willing to leave my employment and join the army, and without giving a direct reply, said that I could not swear to my age, as I had no very exact recollection of the day when I was born, or of any circumstances attending my birth, that could lead me to fix on the precise day. I was discharged, however, on the presumption that the enlistment was not strictly legal."

While he was an apprentice, Russell used to write

paragraphs for the Spy, and slip them under the door of the office, — as some others did, who were averse to being known as "scribblers" for a newspaper. One day, employed in setting up one of his own paragraphs, Russell changed a word or two, for which he received a severe reprimand. He made the best apology he could, by appealing to Thomas's judgement as to the propriety of the alteration. It was admitted that the change was an improvement, but he was threatened with corporal chastisement in case he should ever again dare to alter, in any way, what should be given him to put in type. Russell took the scolding meekly, and kept his secret.

At another time, one of his anonymous paragraphs, reflecting severely and personally on some of the Tories, (of which Worcester had an ample share) was published and caused considerable excitement, with not a few whig compliments for the unknown writer. The authorship was attributed to Mr. Bigelow,* who was questioned, and denied all knowledge of its origin, but

* Timothy Bigelow, who was studying law in Worcester. An intimate friendship was early contracted between him and Russell, which continued unbroken till the death of the former, which happened on the 18th of May, 1821. The Centinel of the next morning had the following

Obituary. It is our duty to announce, that on yesterday morning, at 6 o'clock, the Hon. Timothy Bigelow departed this life at Medford, in the 55th year of his age. We trust we need not say how much our feelings on this distressing event prevent our doing justice to such an obituary notice of our deceased friend, as the public have a right to expect from one who knew him so long and so well. But to all, in any degree acquainted with the history of our Commonwealth, for the last thirty years, it is unnecessary to say any thing of the eminent stations and pre-eminent services, sustained and performed by him. Nearly every page of the records of the towns of Groton and Medford, those of the House of Representatives, (of which he filled the office of Speaker eleven years, — eight of them in succession) those of the Hon. Senate, the Council, and the Boards of Commissioners appointed for important objects; of the Grand Lodge, over which he presided several years; and of the Overseers of Harvard University — all, all contain evidence of his devotion to their interests, and of the constancy, integrity, and efficiency, with which he advocated them, and will hand them down to posterity. At his death, he was a member of the Hon. Council, of the Boards of Commissioners for settling the boundary lines between this State and Connecticut, and for said — "I think Ben wrote it — it looks like him — he is full of the spirit of revolution — his notions are Yankee, all over." Russell was interrogated and acknowledged that he wrote the article. He was dismissed without rebuke, and thought that he afterwards received more favorable consideration.

In relating the reminiscences of his apprenticeship, Russell often spoke of Dr. Franklin, who passed through Worcester several times, and never failed to call at Thomas's office, and hold some conversation with the workmen. "With several other young men (said Russell) I was out in the fields one day, when we were overtaken by a tremendous thunder-shower. Some of the party proposed to take shelter under a large tree — others proposed to go into a barn hard by. I objected to both, and advised that we should shelter ourselves under the projecting cliff of a large rock. My advice was followed. Both the tree and barn were struck by lightning, but the rock remained untouched. I mentioned this incident to Dr. Franklin, who patted me on

the disposition of the public lands in Maine; and of numerous scientific and benevolent societies. Amply as this distinguished statesman and patriot filled his public offices, he was equally pre-eminent for the discharge of all the duties of a provident Father, a kind Husband, a hospitable Neighbor, a liberal and enlightened Christian, and last, not least, a constant and sincere Friend. Other pens, more adequate to the task, will record the numerous traits, which distinguished him in the former of these characters, but that which sketches this article will not omit this melancholy occasion to record its grateful testimony, *That he was* THE FRIEND INDEED. The experience of forty years — during which there was not one moment of alloy or vascillation in the exercise of it — is no common evidence of sincerity and constancy of friendship. For several years, Mr. B. was not insensible of his approaching dissolution; but he ever spoke of it with resignation and without repining. No one knew better how to enjoy and appreciate the blessings and comforts of life; and no one had stronger and more endearing ties to bind him to it: but he discovered no undue reluctance to parting with it. He saw nothing in futurity to make a change to be dreaded. Conscious as he must have been that his progress had been that of integrity, honor, and usefulness, he must have contemplated in them the PATH; in his few though severe bodily sufferings, the PRICE, and in his anticipated transition from this to a better world, the "PROOF, of sublime immortality."

the head, and asked if I was influenced in my judgement by what he had written. I replied that I was. The Doctor smiled, pleasantly, and ever afterwards recognized me when he visited our office."

Some time in the spring or summer of 1780, Thomas was *drafted* as a "continental soldier," and was obliged either to join the army or procure a substitute. He had no desire to serve as a private recruit in an army that was then in a forlorn condition. Russell was ambitious of distinction, and readily consented to take the place of his employer. He joined the army at West Point, and was present at the execution of Major Andrè — an account of which all his familiar acquaintance will remember to have heard from his own lips. He was one of the guard, that attended Andrè to the place of execution. In a letter, which Russell wrote to the late Dr. James Thacher of Plymouth,* he has given a minute account of Andrè's appearance and deportment, and of some of the circumstances incident to the occasion.

Soon after this event, the time for which Russell was enlisted expired. He was honorably discharged, and returned to Worcester to serve out the remainder of his apprenticeship. His term of service in the army was only six months. He was never in any engagement with the enemy. Though bound by indenture till he should be twenty-one years old, when he returned to Thomas, Russell insisted upon a release from apprenticeship at twenty, which he contended was a fair consideration for his having acted in the army as a substitute for his employer. His claim was allowed, but not without some backwardness on the part of Thomas.

*In the year 1834, Dr. Thacher published a pamphlet concerning the arrest, trial, and execution of Andrè, of which the letter here referred to makes a conspicuous part.

In November, 1783, having worked some time as a journeyman, Russell was anxious to be in business, and to exert himself in the profession, to which he had been educated. There was then no foundery for casting types in the country, and to procure them from Europe was not an easy matter. With a letter of credit in his pocket, Russell traveled on foot from Boston to New-York, with an intention of buying the printing apparatus of a tory printer, who was about to suspend his business in that city. When he was near the boundary between Massachusetts and Connecticut, he was overtaken by Gen. Putnam, who was on horseback, with a daughter behind him on a pillion. He made himself known to the General,* and they held several conversations, passing each other frequently on the road, till they reached Pomfret. The General invited him to his house, where he spent one night and then renewed his journey. He was eight days walking from Boston to New-York, and lived chiefly on pudding and milk at the houses of the farmers on the road. He arrived in New-York on the morning of the 25th of November, just as the American army took possession of the city, and while the British army and the Tories were getting on board the fleet, that was to take them to Halifax.

The scene, which New York at this time presented, Russell often described with great enthusiasm. "So great was the feeling of hostility and hatred towards the

* "The first time I saw Gen. Putnam (said Russell) he was on the Neck, leading from Cambridge to Charlestown, on the day of the Battle on Breed's Hill. There were British ships of war on either side of the Neck, stationed there to prevent reinforcements from going on to the Hill. All was consternation and excitement, — till Gen. Putnam was seen coming from Cambridge on a full gallop, with his cocked hat on side-ways, cheering up and encouraging the men. We boys, myself and companions, as well as the men, gave loud and hearty cheers for *Old Put.* I did not see him again till he overtook me on my way to New-York."

Tories, that Gen. Washington placed sentinels at the doors of many of them to prevent outrages from our men. I could not get into the office of the person who owned the printing materials, that I was in pursuit of, till I had obtained a pass. I saw the ceremony of lowering the British flag and hoisting that of the United States. The American army with Gen. Washington at its head, came down Broadway and filed into the Park. After the line was formed, the British flag was seen to descend slowly and the American to rise. When they met on the staff, they were stopped for a few minutes. The Yankees felt a little uncomfortable at this delay, fearing that all was not right. But the flags were soon in motion again. The American ensign floated proudly from the top of the staff, and that of the British sunk among the mass of heads at its foot. The air was rent with the most enthusiastic acclamations. I suppose the two flags were stopped when they met each other on their passage, to give them a chance to shake hands and kiss."

Before Russell arrived in New-York, the press and types, which he had intended to purchase, were sent off to Halifax by their owner. The object of his journey being thus defeated, he returned to Boston, and renewed his attempts to procure the materials necessary for the printing of a newspaper. He succeeded in procuring a small fount of Long Primer and another of Pica, with a few alphabets of a larger size, and immediately issued a proposal for the publication of the "Massachusetts Centinel." Before that publication began, an incident occurred, that developed a prominent trait in his character, — namely, the irresistible impulse to do what he thought was right, and the readiness to retract his steps whenever he was convinced that he had done wrong.

Samuel Adams, the renowned and proscribed patriot of the revolution, it is well known, was strongly opposed to the institution of the Society of Cincinnati. Like many other good patriots and honest men, he thought he saw in it the germ of an order of nobility, that might tend eventually to the establishment of a military despotism. Knowing that Russell was about to publish a paper, he called on him, stated his views of the subject, and urged him to take a decided stand against the organization of the society. Russell, ever ready to follow the advice of men, whose character and experience had given them influence, listened to the representations and arguments of Mr. Adams; and, without waiting to unburden his mind in his contemplated journal, forthwith issued a pamphlet, embodying the views of his venerable monitor, with such comments and remarks as his own imagination suggested. The pamphlet had hardly made its appearance in public, when Russell was visited by three or four gentlemen, who took a different view of the matter, to remonstrate against the publication. To their inquiry, "*Who wrote the pamphlet?*" he replied, "*Nobody wrote it.* I stood at the case, and composed it, mentally as well as mechanically." An explanation followed, in which he frankly disclosed the conversation, in which the idea of the publication originated, and the motive, that induced him to make it. His visiters assured him that the information, on which he had acted was erroneous, — that the object of the society was not merely harmless but patriotic and benevolent, — and told him (what it seems he had no suspicion of before) that Gen. Washington was one of its original members and its first officer. This was quite enough for Russell, whose veneration of Washington was little less than adoration. He could not believe that any thing of evil character or tendency could proceed from an institution with Washington at its head, or that aught but good would result from any proceeding, that had the sanction of that immortal name. He ran to every place where his pamphlet had been left for sale, and recalled every unsold copy. But very few had been sold, and those, where the purchaser could be found, were bought up and the whole edition was destroyed. It is not known that a single copy escaped. He was ever afterwards a strong and able defender of the society.

At length, on the twenty-fourth of March, 1784, the proposed paper made its appearance, entitled

THE MASSACHUSETTS CENTINEL,

AND THE

REPUBLICAN JOURNAL.

Uninfluenced by Party, we aim to be just.

The lines which form the title, motto, and imprint, were separated in the centre by the device here given, but which is not any where explained; perhaps the design is too apparent to need explanation. The form was impressed on a half sheet of demy paper, and was made up in four pages, quarto, with three columns on a page. The type was Pica and Long Primer. The head lines of the various departments, which marked the character of the miscellaneous materials, that filled up those several portions, as well as some important lines in advertisements, were displayed in larger letters; but nothing smaller than Long Primer appeared in the paper for more than two years. The title, including the cut, occupied nearly a third of the first page; and the following Address filled the remainder: —

A Free *uninfluenced* Newspaper.

To the candid Public.

When the benign and cheering influence of the cherub PEACE is daily spreading her delectable blessings over this New World: — When arts and sciences, (its ever attending guests) the foster-parents of liberty, are dispelling the gloomy atmosphere of war, and enlightening mankind with liberality of sentiment, every vehicle propitious to the design should be put in motion, and every exertion strained to second the undertaking.

The liberty of the press is the surest bulwark of the people's rights: A privilege to mankind which tyrannical monarchs have beheld with horror, and often attempted to annihilate. Superstition and ignorance have dissipated into obscurity, as the balmy rays of this institution have shed their benignity over the civilized world: In short, its utility is so well known and experienced by the freemen of these United States, that it would be passing an ill compliment on the judgement were we to enter into lengthy panegyrics on its usefulness.

These considerations — an inclination to be useful in the business we profess — and a desire to obtain a competency for our support, have induced us to lay before a candid and judicious public, the following proposals for publishing, every *Wednesday* and *Saturday*, The

MASSACHUSETTS CENTINEL:

AND THE

REPUBLICAN JOURNAL.

CONDITIONS.

I. This paper shall be printed with a legible type, on good paper, to contain four quarto pages, demi.

II. The price of this paper [will] be *Twelve Shillings*, the year, one quarter to be paid on subscribing. If agreeable to the custom in the cities of London, New-York and Philadelphia, the subscribers should choose to pay *per* number, the price will be *Two Pence.*

III. The papers in the town of Boston, shall be delivered to the subscribers as early as possible on publication days.

IV. Advertisements shall be inserted at as low a price as is demanded by any of their brethren in the art, and continued, if desired in Six Numbers.

V. Gentlemen in the country may be supplied with this paper at the above price, (postage excepted) which is cheaper than any other papers, if the advantage of receiving them twice in the week is considered.

The publishers engage to use every effort to obtain, and the most scrutinous circumspection in collecting whatever may be thought of public utility, or private amusement: Variety shall be courted in all its shapes, in the importance of political information — in the sprightliness of mirth — in the playful levity of imagination — in the just severity of satire — in the vivacity of ridicule — in the luxuriance of poetry — and in the simplicity of truth. We shall examine the regulations of office with candor — approve with pleasure — or condemn with boldness. *Uninfluenced by party, we aim only to be just.*

The assistance of the learned, the judicious and the curious is solicited: Productions of public utility, however severe, if consistent with truth, shall be admitted; and the modest correspondent may depend on the strictest secrecy. Reservoirs will be established in public houses for the reception of information, whether foreign, local, or poetical.

Anxious to deserve, they hope a display of that patronage and assistance, which the people of these States are celebrated for bestowing on the exertions of young beginners. And finally, if their abilities should be inadequate, it will at least be some recompense, that such as they have shall be exerted with candor.

W. WARDEN,
B. RUSSELL.

On the last page of the paper, is the following article, which, if the words "Poetical Correspondence" were not placed over it, would be attributed to Russell as the author. If not original, it was subjected to the process of adaptation: * —

To preserve a similitude of publication in our introductory numbers, we have inserted the following: —

THE NEWSPAPER.

Did you ne'er see a Hawk or Kite,
With rapid wings first take its flight?
Then hovering round the field or spray,
Souse down at once and seize his prey.

The Politician thus you spy,
Tripping to Coffee House just by;
And fixing on the NEWS his eyes,
With greediness enjoys the prize;
Then home return with head quite full —
Extremely wise — extremely dull,
Assumes political capacity,
And deals out news with great sagacity:
Of all the senates of the States,
He tells their motions and debates:
Tells where the Congress will remain,
And who 's the President from Spain;
How New-York whigs the tories plague,
Who 's our Ambassador at the Hague.
His hearers all admire his sense,
And wonder at the intelligence.
At night the Club enjoys his gleanings,
Assertions, observations, meanings:
The fearful shrug — the knitted brow —
The *fact* — the *place* — the *when* — the *how.*

We (say with def'rence to the college,)
News-Papers are the spring of knowledge;
The general source throughout the nation,
Of every modern conversation.
What would this mighty people do,
If there, alas! was nothing new?
We tell you *Patrons* what relates
To make us formidable States:

* A part of this article was published in the Massachusetts Mercury, more than ten years after its appearance in the Centinel, as "From an English Paper."

We tell how Europe's balance stands,
How Russia's Queen the Turks commands
How Popish power hath dissipated,
And Frederick just annihilated.

Our services you can't express,
The good we do you hardly guess;
There 's scarce a want of human kind,
But we a remedy can find.
If any gentleman wants a wife,
A partner (as 'tis term'd) for life,
An Advertisement does the thing,
And quickly will the party bring.
Lands may be had; if you would buy,
We tell you where you may apply:
Goods of all sorts where bought, where sold:
Houses to purchase new and old.
Ships, Shops, of ev'ry shape and form,
Carriages, horses, servants swarm.
No matter whether good or bad,
We tell you where they may be had.

If you want money you 'll be serv'd,
And strictest secrecy observ'd.
The sum you ask will strait be lent,
At the small sum of cent per cent.

A News-Paper is like a feast,
Some dish there is for ev'ry guest.
Some large, some small, some strong, some tender,
For ev'ry stomach, stout or slender:
Those who roast beef and ale delight in,
Are pleas'd with trumpets, drums and fighting.
For those who are more puny made,
Are arts, and sciences, and trade;
For fanciful and am'rous blood,
We have a soft poetic food;
For witty and satiric folks,
High-season'd, acid, bitter jokes;
And when we strive to please the mob,
A jest, a quarrel, or a jobb.

The inside pages contain an article of news from a London paper of December 21, — an article on Filial

Piety, under the head of "Food for Sentimentalists," — an extract of a letter from Port Roseway, — "Marine matters," making about a square, — an official Notice from the Secretary of the Commonwealth, — an advertisement of a dealer in Painter's oil and colors, — and three or four paragraphs under the Boston head, of which the following is the first: —

The general topics of political disquisition in the several States, are the commutation, or five years pay of the officers of the army — and the admittance of the refugees. The former, as it is consistent with justice, must be certainly adopted: — The latter occasions various speculations, and much division — while some are very strenuous against their re-admittance, from political principles — others assert that it will be sound policy in permitting them to return, as the wealth they will bring will more than counterbalance the detriment they can possibly be of. Whether the discussion will be of public benefit, or not, time, the great revealer of things, must determine. As the citizens of one Sate have a right to resort to, and settle in any in the confederation — their being naturalized in *any one* State, will entirely frustrate the intentions of those who declare against their admittance, and must produce animosities. Though monarchical government is never to be wished, the above shows the weakness of democracy.

In another paragraph, the editors said, — "The excellent Legendary Tale of Armine and Elvira, a most exquisite repast for Sentimentalists and the Lovers of poetical numbers, will be begun in our Saturday's Centinel, and continued numerically. We shall devote a corner to their amusement, and the Centinel being printed in a form, which, when bound, will make a handsome volume, we doubt not our kind customers will find that the matters in them are well worth their money, as a year's papers will contain, besides intelligence, what, printed separate, would sell for two guineas." There was nothing here promised, that was not performed. Beside the Legendary Tale, alluded to, which filled nearly two columns in each of six papers, most of the poems of Goldsmith, Cunningham's Pastorals, extracts from Cotton, Gray, Cowper, and a large portion of the Narrative of Cook's Voyages, were published in the course of the first year. At first, and for many subsequent years, the Centinel of Saturday was always supplied with an article of a moral and religious character, — sometimes original, but generally selected, — under the head of "Preparation for Sunday." The department appropriated to poetry, was called "Sentimental Repast," "Heliconian Reservoir," and sometimes "Sentimental Sustenance." Occasionally the contents of this column, — the first column on the fourth page, — were described by a single word, in large capitals, significant of their character; as Moral, Prophetic, Descriptive, Sentimental, &c. Another department, consisting of selections of prose articles, was entitled "Food for Sentimentalists." A collection of short anecdotes appeared as "Entertainment for the Disciples of Zeno," and extracts or communications of a didactic or scientific character, were placed under "Food for Enquiring Minds." In short, every thing, whether original or selected, was supposed to be placed in its appropriate column, and every article seemed to wear its appropriate and descriptive title, except the editorial paragraphs under the Boston head. These were all huddled together without regard to subject. An item of news, foreign or domestic, an accident, a death, a marriage, a note to a correspondent, an advertisement, and an arrival of a ship, were often thus thrown together in half a column, and no one would imagine, till he should have made some progress in the reading of it, that it embraced more than one topic.

In the second number of the Centinel the editors published a paragraph, — the first, under the Boston head, saying, — "The talk of the day is Cincinnati. Whatever may be the intention of the orignal design — or whatever consequences may *possibly* result from the continuance of that institution, one circumstance that greatly recommends it, is, that His Excellency GEORGE WASHINGTON, Esq. is *President-General* of that Society." Soon after, Washington's Circular to the state societies, and the Constitution of the parent society, were published in the Centinel, — indicating that the advice and opinion of Mr. S. Adams, had no power to produce in Russell's mind any prejudice unfavorable to the Cincinnati.

The advertising patronage of the Centinel was not large during the first year, notwithstanding that it was solicited in the standing imprint, which declared — "Advertisements are inserted at the usual price in the Centinel, which, from its portableness and circulation, is rendered very advantageous: They will likewise be set off with taste, adorned with conspicuity, and inserted 6 Numbers." The Ship News, which is now so prominent a feature in all commercial papers, ordinarily occupied about a square. The arrivals and clearances seldom numbered more than five or six in each paper.

The correspondents of the Centinel were numerous, and many of their contributions, especially those on politics and morals, were written with strength and propriety. The editors took a noble stand in favor of protection to all domestic manufactures and the products of agriculture and the mechanic arts. As a matter of course they were opposed to the importation of British goods, by British factors and agents, many of whom attempted to establish themselves in Boston, and to push off the products of their manufactories, to the injury of the American producer and importer. The editors and several of their correspondents attempted, both by ridicule and serious argument, to discourage this trade. During the years 1784 and 1785, several public meetings were held to deliberate on this subject and to adopt measures of relief. A meeting of merchants, mechanics, and traders at Faneuil Hall, voted, "That we do pledge our honor, that we will not directly or indirectly, purchase any goods of, or have any commercial connections whatever, with, such British merchants, agents, or factors, as are now residing among us, or may hereafter arrive," &c.: and voted, also, "That we will not let, or sell, any warehouse, shop, house, or any other place, for the sale of such goods, nor will we employ any persons, who will assist said merchants, factors, or agents, by trucks, carts, barrows, or labor, (except in the reshipment of their merchandize) but will *discountenance* all such persons, who shall in any way advise, or in the least degree help or support such merchants, factors, or agents, in the prosecution of their business; *as we conceive all such British importations are calculated to drain us of our currency, and have a direct tendency to impoverish this country.*"

Notwithstanding measures of this description, and the strong appeals to the good sense and patriotism of the people, made in the newspapers, there were many persons who disregarded them, and persisted in practising on the free trade doctrines of that day. The Centinel raised its warning voice in the following manner: —

Commerce has extended her *blessings* upon us, in a manner unprecedented in history; and had she not been so liberal, her votaries perhaps would have found it more to their advantage. Though these productions of foreigners may be purchased at very low prices, yet as they are mere superfluities, every one, possessed of republican principles, must feel anxiety, at seeing such vast hoards of specie daily leaving the continent as remittances. Will we impoverish ourselves? Or will we part with that which can be of no advantage to us?—Are questions that ought to be weighed in the impartial scale, that should ever occupy the breast of a friend to the prosperity of his country. The fair American, conscious of the service she can do her country by a little self-denial, will, we doubt not, dispense with that ostentatious pageantry, now so much in vogue, when they consider likewise, that they are calculated only to give a *fashionable grace* to the want of beauty. For

The beauteous female, unadorn'd and plain,
Secure to please, while youth confirms her reign,
Slights every borrow'd charm, that dress supplies,
Nor shares with art the triumph of her eyes.

The softer sex did, during the revolution, display virtues, honorary as they were useful: And shall it ever be said that meagre want, and cold-handed poverty stalked through our country, occasioned by the inordinate desire of its inhabitants for foreign gewgaws.

[June 12, 1784.]

That no nation can ever be rich or powerful whose imports EXCEED their exports, is a fact not to be controverted. It is a melancholy truth that at present our imports far exceed our exports; and should this continue to be the case, cold poverty will soon stare us in the face, and the gaudy trifles we now import from Britain (which we are foolishly fond of, and for which we pay solid coin) will leave us, and vanish like a vapor before the rising sun. Rags, or nakedness must supply their place, and we too late must mourn our folly.

[January 5, 1785.]

At the close of the first volume, September 18, 1784, the subscribers to the Centinel were again addressed in rhyme thus:—

The CENTINEL, *to its Patrons of every Denomination.*

With plays it hath been long in vogue
To finish with an epilogue,
To bring in view the many clauses,
They wish may gain the best applauses,
And show, by dint of magic art,
The various virtues they impart.

The Centinel, you well might say,
Should try to shun this oft-trod way;
And so it would, if it could find
One, that would better suit its mind;
Or else adopt the part, that 's best,
And partly throw aside the rest;
With modest truth to partly shew
Its matters to the public view,
And let the whole be judged by them —
They must *applaud*, or else *condemn*.

The patrons of the Centinel
Its origin remember well.
" *To captivate the curious mind,*
" *And make the funny more refined*;
" *To amuse the pensive — and the sad,*
" *And make those merry, that are mad.*"
With these in view, it first began,
(And these continue still its plan,)
Strove ardently in many a strain,
ALL its kind readers' praise to gain,
With various themes, — some wise, — some dull, —
Some serious, — some with satire full, —
Some things for those in merry mood —
And copious sentimental food:
For sober lives and conversation,
We give our Sunday's preparation;
State politics of each degree,
Advertisements, *et cetera.*

Whene'er a bowl of punch we make,
Four striking opposites we take;
The strong, the small, the sour, the sweet,
Together mix'd, must jointly meet;
And when they happily unite,
The bowl is *pregnant with delight.*
Thus in the Centinel you find
Its matter variously inclined;
The parts, by properly sustaining,
May all prove highly entertaining.

Be this its boast, it strove to gain
Success, (nor hath it strove in vain;)
The Centinel asks leave to give,
And begs its patrons to receive,

Its thanks; and only will observe
Its inclination still to serve;
Requests, e'en though its merits few,
That it may still receive its due.

Soon after the commencement of the second volume, the second title, "Republican Journal," was taken from the head. The motto was also omitted. The title was now simply

THE MASSACHUSETTS CENTINEL.

At each end of the line was a device, which is thus explained : — "The first represents the Genius of America, seated on a Pyramid of Thirteen Ascents, supporting the Cap of Liberty on a Ball, (emblamatic of her having gained it by war) holding in her hand the Olive Branch, and treading on the Crown and Sceptre, the ensigns of monarchy. The second shows the Sun, breaking through and dissipating a cloud, approaching a serene sky, and shedding its influence on Arts, Commerce, and Agriculture." Here is an exact copy of these devices, the design of which, it must be confessed, could hardly be imagined without the original explanation.

The editors of the Centinel were not disposed to favor the return of those persons, who, during the war, had left the country and resided in England, or her provinces. Many of these "refugees" petitioned the Legislature for restoration to their forfeited privileges of

citizenship, and of their confiscated property. On the propriety of granting these petitions, public opinion was divided. Some writers were in favor of adopting lenient measures towards them, while others were disposed to treat them, — as in fact, they really were, — as outlaws and renegades. The Centinel of May 12, 1784, mentions that near one hundred of the persons included in the act of confiscation and banishment in South-Carolina, had returned and been admitted to citizenship after being "amerced 12½ per cent.;" and adds, that, "as other legislatures of the United States must ere long take into consideration this important matter, we hope the citizens of America have, or will, appoint men to determine it, whose wisdom, experience, and interest are adequate to the task." Again, in August, they say, "However the principles of common benevolence, and the desire of curing the calamities of our fellow-citizens, might operate in favor of an act of amnesty and naturalization to the ill-fated body of men, the refugees; yet the antipathies nurtured during the war have taken so deep a root, as will, we are apprehensive, be very difficult to remove." The following paragraph, January 5, 1785, conveys a more decided expression of their own opinion in relation to this subject: —

The joy of the refugees at Nova-Scotia on the arrival of their new governor, Carleton, speaks, in very plain language, the disagreeableness of their situation. They now solicit relief from calamities which they justly merit, and which their crimes deserve. The sanguinary conduct of theirs, respecting the Americans, is sufficient to eradicate from our breasts every sentiment, with regard to them, of pity or commiseration. In vain do they wish to avert the punishment that awaits them. It is the sure consequence of their conduct, and they must submit to it. With respect to redress, in a change of their rulers, duped as they are, we think the following lines not inapplicable: —

The ass may carry brooms or men,
Just at his master's will;
But let him change and change again,
His lot 's a burthen still.

During its first year, the Centinel was the vehicle of an amusing, though rather an angry controversy, in which some pretty severe personal epithets were used by both parties, and which, almost at its very outset produced a personal rencontre with the editors. It appears that early in the winter or in the autumn of 1784, a portion of the gentlemen and ladies of the town had associated, and formed what was called in their advertisements, "The Tea Assembly," to meet at regular periods at Concert Hall. The "assembly" was also known by the name of "*Sans Souci*, or *Free and Easy*." The name, or the reported amusements of the assembly, became the topic of public animadversion, and "The Observer," a periodical writer, in the Centinel, spoke of it as an "assembly totally repugnant to virtue;"—"throwing aside every necessary restraint, those being esteemed the politest who are the most careless;—and the most genteel and accomplished, who can, like the figures at a masquerade, mix in each scene, however devoid of delicacy," &c.; and concluded by hoping that the citizens would unanimously exert themselves to give a check to so injurious an institution. The Centinel of Saturday, January 15, 1785, came out with the following advertisement:—

A new FARCE.
On Monday morning next will be published,

SANS SOUCI, *alias*, Free and Easy:—Or, *An Evening's Peep into a Polite Circle.* An entire new Entertainment, in three acts.

The above publication is designed more to present what is likely to take place, from the institution of the late Assembly held at C——

Hall, designated by the appellation, than what has hitherto existed. The characters exhibited, and the circumstances mentioned, are mostly imaginary, and are intended rather to satirize the measure than to point at particular persons: However, as all publications of this nature, cannot but fall in some degree on certain characters, if this should be considered as too pointed, on any individuals, the author can only plead the apology, that he is sorry that the portrait can not be softened down to a more agreeable likeness.

Printed and sold by the Printers hereof.

The next paper, Wednesday, January 19, had on its first page, an address to the Public, printed in Pica Italic, of which the following is a part: —

A few days since we were requested to publish a small performance on the institution of the Sans Souci. After carefully perusing it, and perceiving it to be only intended to display the dangerous tendency of that society, not the vehicle of personal abuse, (as has been too common) we determined to publish it and advertised our intentions of so doing. This roused the passions of those who conceived themselves deserving the lash of satire, and urged them to endeavor to suppress it in embryo. A variety of injuries was threatened us, if we persisted in our determination of publishing it. In the afternoon of Saturday we were waited upon by Mr. Samuel Jarvis, who desired to speak with one of us in another apartment; being attended thither, he demanded to know whether or not we intended publishing 'A Farce,' and being answered in the affirmative, exclaimed, "By God I 'll kill you if you do," and endeavored to put his threat into execution, but found his efforts inadequate to the task.

To the public we leave it to make what comments they please, on this high-handed affair, but if (as our brother Edes observes on the matter) 'a Printer, for advertising that he intends to publish a certain book for the information or merely the amusement or innocent diversion of his fellow citizens, is to be beset and abused by a set of club men, because the Title-Page does not happen to hit their taste, we may take a farewell of our independence which we have gloriously obtained, not without great expense of our treasure, and the loss of some of our best blood.'

We return our thanks for the assistance that has been offered us by several patriotick gentlemen. They may depend, that avoiding personal scurrility and local scandal, we are determined our PRESS SHALL EVER BE FREE.

The motto we have adopted of being 'uninfluenced by party' &c.

shall be strictly adhered to; and while we keep within the limits prescribed by the laws of our country, the threats of sanguinary assassins, will ever be considered as impotent and innoxious.

WARDEN & RUSSELL.

This rencontre did not stop the publication of the book, nor put an end to the controversy. Several writers came out on both sides, who treated each other with very little ceremony. The Observer was accused of envy, falsehood, bigotry, misanthropy, and malice. He replied, and gave an abstract of the rules of the assembly, to show that "Gentlemen of nineteen, and Ladies of fifteen were admitted," and that "the entertainment was made up of music, dancing, tea, coffee, chocolate, cards, wine, negus, punch, and lemonade." On the whole, he maintained his position with the best temper, and, in the end, appeared to have gained a triumph.

A controversy of a different complexion made some noise in Boston during the winter of 1784–5, and the columns of the Centinel afford some amusing communications on the subject, — which was the removal of the Rev. Peter Thacher from his pastoral charge in Malden to that of the church in Brattle-street, Boston. The removals of ministers from one parish to another were not quite so frequent then as they have since become. Such changes *then* were as rare as divorces of man and wife; — *now*, they are as common, almost, as the exchange of one mercantile commodity for another. The Centinel of December 15, has the following sly hit at its Brattle-street neighbors: —

Christ's *wealthy* church in Br—tle-street,
His *poorer* flock in M—ld—n greet,
With hearts brimfull of Christian love,
They wish them blessings from above.

Dear Sirs, of late we 've lost our pastor,
And mourn sincere the sore disaster;
Because we clearly can foresee
Our sheep much scattered will be,
Unless we should, of God's free grace,
A shepherd get to fill his place.

Now, having sought divine direction,
We thought it fit, on due reflection,
To tempt the parson of your church
To leave his people in the lurch;
Though few have heard him scarcely thrice,
Yet most believe he preaches *nice*,
And is a man, that 's fitted quite
To make us all in him unite.
On trial *fair*, we plainly find,
Our pious scheme well suits his mind;
Then what remains for us to do,
But settle matters right with you?
Sure, if you cannot him maintain,
Of us you ought not to complain;
Now therefore send him off to us,
And we will fill his mouth and purse;
The cash you owe him, as 'tis said,
Shall very cheerfully be paid;
Another preacher should you want,
A settlement for *him* we 'll grant;
Thus to the world we 'll *fully* show,
That nought but *honor* we 've in view;
Yet stronger arguments than these
We can produce with greater ease,
And make it *clear* that we are *right*,
And act by help of *Gospel* light.

From best of men, we often hear,
That you 've no *souls* to save, (they fear;)
That parts like *his* in napkin lay,
So long as he shall with you stay;
Much time among you he has taught,
And labored all that while for *nought;*
To church no *single soul could add*,
To make his pious heart "full glad."
But, in *this* place, his talents *five*,
To occupy would make us thrive;

From day to day *our* church would grow,
And make at last a *goodly show.*
These *weighty* reasons, as we trust,
You 'll plainly see are good and *just,*
And freely grant us our request,
Because *we* think it for the best.

And now we *all,* with *one* accord,
Subscribe, *Your brethren in the Lord.*

There were several other articles referring to this subject, written by "A Country Minister," and replied to by "A Country Booby," which are amusing enough to reward the task of looking over the file. The reverend gentleman came out, at length, under his own signature, exonerating the people of his parish in Malden from some of the charges of injustice that had been made against them, and declaring, — "although I have suffered great inconvenience by my salary's not being punctually paid me, yet (for aught I know) the people here have been as punctual in their payment as other parishes in the country generally are."

The project of building a bridge across Charles River between Boston and Charlestown, was renewed in the Centinel, in the winter of 1785. It occasioned a "terrible clashing of opinions," among the correspondents of that paper. Another subject, which makes a conspicuous figure in the Centinel, was the plan of incorporating the town as a city. The *bridge* succeeded, but the *incorporation* failed.

A question still more exciting in its character, sprung up near the close of this winter. Governor Hancock resigned his office in the month of February, on account of ill health. James Bowdoin, a distinguished gentleman of Boston, seemed to be pointed out by the common consent of the people as the proper person to succeed him. The editors of the Centinel do not appear to have taken a very active part either for or against him; but they allowed some of their correspondents to abuse him in a most outrageous style. There was no choice of a Governor by the people, and the election of course, devolved upon the Legislature. The opponents of Mr. Bowdoin, exulting in the belief that he would not be chosen, got up a lampoon, that was published in the Centinel, and which, for coarseness of invective and vulgar ribaldry, was quite equal to any political pasquinade of later years. It was published in the Centinel the day on which the Legislature assembled.* But the triumphant mockery was altogether premature, and produced no other effect than mortification to its projectors. For although the House of Representatives, in selecting the two constitutional candidates, gave to Mr. Cushing about thirty votes more than they gave to Mr. Bowdoin, the Senate, in the exercise of its constitutional prerogative of selecting one of two candidates, chose Mr. Bowdoin by a large majority.

At the close of the second volume, March 19, 1785, the editors again addressed their friends and customers in rhyme, as follows: —

A year 's revolved, Time's tablets tell
Since first you viewed the Centinel;
As volume second 's at a close,
In justice to 't, it must suppose,
You 'll just permit it to rehearse
Its (some call 't usefulness) in verse.

* It is quite too long, and exhibited in typography too inconvenient to be placed in this work; but the curious may be gratified by referring to the paper that contains it, and see with what bitterness political animosity could then assail its victim.

First News — but sure, you 've often read
When little 's done, there 's little said.
Though *Peace* proclaims her quiet sway,
And *War*, with us, is done away,
Yet still the Centinel explores
Remotest climes and distant shores,
Through cities stalks, peeps in at courts,
Mingles with business and with sports,
Listens to every word that 's told,
Reads every paper, new or old,
From the crude mass selects the best
For use, and throws aside the rest.

For Entertainment — *The Collection*
Presents each number for inspection:
Anecdotes droll, the bon mot queer,
The carper's snarl, the critic's sneer,
A smart reply, the goose-quill scar, —
Blest trophies of a paper war —
An essay, or a pretty pun,
Or hint, to make a little fun,
And other matters, as you see,
In the uproar, 'bout the *Sans Souci*.

Oft times, when in a sober mood,
It deals out some things that are *good*:
A sober, moral observation,
Prefaced with "Sunday's Preparation;"
Something to suit the great, the small;
In fact, it fain would please you all,
And in its Miscellany gather
Instruction, news, and scraps, for pleasure,
Resolves of Congress, Proclamations,
With *Strictures on the Law of Nations;*
Changes of empires, fate of kings,
Of statesmen, culprits, and such things,
Of great and general concern,
From it you twice a week may learn:
Tell who are pilloried, hanged, or cropped,
Who runs away, or who gets shopped,
What lucky swain has found a bride,
And last, tell who have lately died.
— Here sense and virtue must inspire
In moral mood, to touch the lyre, —

When it proclaims your neighbor 's dead,
Know, this will soon of you be said;
And, strange to think, when you are gone,
The busy world will still go on
In the old track, nor miss you more
Than you have those, who went before.
Your death they 'll read, without a thought, —
Next week, perhaps, you 'll be forgot:
They 'll feast, sport, sing, and laugh as hearty,
As if you still were of their party:
But, though so small in other's view,
Your death 's no trifle, friend, to you.

Here stop — the Centinel will still
The task endeavor to fulfill
To captivate the curious mind,
And make the fancy more refined, —
To instruct, to entertain, and show forth
What 's good, or comical, and so forth.

In March, 1785, the Legislature passed an "Act imposing duties on licensed vellum, parchment, and paper," which laid a duty of two thirds of a penny on every newspaper, and a penny on almanacks, — all which were to be stamped. The act was exceedingly unpopular. The people had not forgotten the British stamp-act of 1765. The fearless independence of the editors of the Centinel was not quite so conspicuous in their comments on this impolitic law, as on some other measures of the government. For example: —

The STAMP ACT, passed the last session of the General Court, meets opposition throughout every part of the Commonwealth; that part laying a duty on newspapers particularly so. The cloven foot in it appears too visible to escape notice. To clog the currents of information, — and to shackle the means of political knowledge and necessary learning, — are discordant notes to the general ear. But its danger is not the whole of its evil consequences. It is deemed *impolitic* and *unequal*, — *impolitic*, as it will encourage our sister States to send their papers into this commonwealth cheaper than they can possibly be afforded here, to the ruin of a set of artizans, whose exertions in the late revolution deserve a more liberal fate: — *unequal*, as the revenue arising from newspapers must (while but a mite in the general treasury) operate, in a great degree, to the destruction of the present printers of these publications. *May* 4, 1785.

In mentioning the disapprobation, which we are certain is generally given to the Stamp Act, by the citizens of this commonwealth, we feel a peculiar diffidence. Ill-nature, we are conscious, will suppose the information as originating in self-interest. But as it is our duty, *in all cases*, to convey whatever may be deemed of public benefit, we shall observe that it is in agitation in several towns, to instruct their representatives to bring in an act to repeal certain clauses in the above-mentioned one. Should there be no alteration, and the act remain as it is, *we are certain* that it must operate to the *impoverishment* of many of the publishers of newspapers in this state; and could the community at large derive any considerable advantage by the sacrifice, we doubt not but they would meet their doom with a becoming satisfaction. But this will not be the case — in their fall, if they must fall, will *close* the *duty*, and every friend to *equal liberty* need not be informed, that the duties arising from the *tax* on the *vehicles* of *political information* will be in no proportion to the impoverishment of a single individual; — consequently it will be *unequal* and *hard*. If we would assume the confidence of dictating our rulers, *we* should suppose that the articles of foreign luxury, for which our cash is constantly bidding adieu to our country, were objects more deserving restrictions and duties, especially when it is considered that Newspapers are the principal support of one capital branch of AMERICAN MANUFACTURY — paper-making.
May 11, 1785.

The offensive act was repealed by the Legislature, the next June, but another was passed, laying a duty on advertisements, — *six-pence* on each insertion. This measure was censured and ridiculed in most of the papers in all the states; but the Centinel thinking it *no infringement on the liberty of the press*, approved its passage, on the ground that it "contributed thousands to the exigences of the state."

A few paragraphs, taken without much regard to order or subject, from the Centinel while in its youthful days, will exemplify the talent, the taste, and the degree of acquirement in the critical use of language, which the editors could then bring to the field of their labors. It has always been understood and believed that the duties of the editorial department devolved, almost wholly, upon Russell, while Warden conducted the mechanical operations. The supposition is doubtless correct, as the same ambitious style of composition characterized the editorials of the paper after the death of Warden. The reader will also meet with some facts, not now generally known, — curious and interesting as connected with the customs and habits of life in Boston, in the last century.

The taste for Air Balloon matters has grown to such an extraordinary pitch, that nothing can pretend to have any intrinsic value in it, unless it has this *name* as an appendage. The gentlemen and ladies upon *bon ton* are not the only objects that can boast of this aerial bombastic insignia to their ornaments; as a countryman was heard to say one day last week, — "*Fine balloon String Beans!*" *July* 14, 1784.

Every man may learn the elements of geography, which is the noblest science in the world, from an attention to the temperature of his own mind. Melancholy is the *north pole;* Envy the *South;* Choler the *torrid zone;* Ambition the *zodiac;* Joy the *ecliptic;* Justice the *equinoctial;* Prudence and Temperance the *arctic* and *antarctic* circles; Patience and Fortitude the *tropics.*

The Rev. Mr. Hazlitt is now delivering a course of Lectures on the Evidences of the Truth of the Christian Religion. This learned and ingenious gentleman, by a happy and insinuating style, blends instruction with amusement. Those of a Deistical turn of mind would, we doubt not, reap much benefit from an attendance on these Lectures, as the perspicuity of his arguments strike conviction into the most obdurate hearts. *January* 19, 1785.

The general complaint in the coffee-houses for some time has been that *there is nothing in the papers.* The *politician,* who looks for the accounts of battles and sieges, marches and encampments, ambuscades and surprizes, rails vehemently at the barrenness of our prints, and the want of spirit and enterprize in the sovereigns of Europe. He is angry at the Emperor and the Dutch for not going to loggerheads at once, if it were only for his entertainment. Commend me, says he, to those glorious times, when 40,000 men were killed in one engagement. This was a feast at one's breakfast table in the morning! but now, there is nothing to amuse, nothing to entertain, nothing to exhilarate;—in short, through the whole four pages, he can see *nothing in the papers!*

The *old women*, who relish nothing but the relation of fatal accidents, providential escapes, broken legs and arms, and fractured skulls, complain too grievously of the present want of news. Not above one dog in a week runs mad, nor two scaffolds in a month fall down for their gratification. The dullness of the times is intolerable—*there is nothing in the papers!*

Those who are curious in physic and philosophy have equal cause to complain. We hear nothing at present of hurricanes in the West Indies, or earthquakes in Italy; no plagues either at Smyrna or at Constantinople; *all patients are in perfect health*, and the face of nature is uniform tranquillity: In short, all is dead, and *there is nothing in the papers.* *June* 29, 1785.

Died at Nesqueunia about three weeks since, the woman, who has been at the head of the sect called Shaking Quakers, and has assumed the title of the Elect Lady. What is extraordinary, a brother of hers, who was one of their principal elders, died the same week and of the same disorder: They were taken with inward bleeding, and died suddenly. It is not improbable that the manner of worship, practised by those extravagant enthusiasts, might conduce to a rupture of the vessels, and occasion this mode of dissolution; as many of their ceremonies require such unnatural distortions, and continued agitations of every limb and muscle, as must shock the strongest constitution; and the texture of the human body is too delicate to render it a fit habitation for such violent and disorderly spirits. We hope these instances of untimely death, in those who deemed themselves immortal, will induce others, who adopt this gymnastic religion, to compare the danger of ruining their constitutions with the benefit which may arise to their souls from such violent exercise. *October* 2, 1785.

The death of the Elect Lady, so called among the Shaking Quakers, has given a universal shock to her poor deluded adherents. Certain it is—they believed her to be immortal; that Christ, in person, was making his second appearance on earth, and that he would continue till all who were to be saved should be called in, and join the church. Their faith in this strange personage, (or, as they used to term her, *Holy Mother*) was such, that they believed she sat daily in council with the Deity; and that things past, present, and future, were ever open to her view. But alas! this *feigned immortal*, who has long *made the simple drunk with the cup of her fornications*, is no more! Her followers now begin to find they have been duped by an impostor. Some few, still thirsting for the poison of *Satanic delusion*, avail themselves by saying, *She is not dead, but sleepeth.* Others, *that she is gone to prepare a place for them in glory.* *October* 23, 1785.

It must afford pleasure to every ingenious mind, when it reflects on the avidity with which the experiment on Balloons is seized by almost all ranks and denominations. The advancement of philosophy will most assuredly receive the assistance and applause of every friend to science, which will stimulate our enterprizing geniuses to exert their abilities in the execution of some capital performance in this way, that will do honor to the invention, and add reputation to the town.

March 30, 1785.

Human nature has received another blot — and the laws of God have again been violated by the cowardly crime of suicide. Capt. Isaac Gleason of Waltham, we are told, on Wednesday last, impiously put an end to an existence he could not make. Like the villain, who destroyed the temple at Ephesus, the memories of suicides ought to be held up to the execration of posterity, and their bodies exhibited *on a stake, to blacken in the sun*, that the traveler may point at it and say, There hangs the coward fool — and meets a fate he justly merited.

January 7, 1786.

Sometime in the summer of 1785, a British ship of war, Capt. Stanhope, was in Boston harbor. The officers were often in the town, and had an altercation with some individuals, the precise nature of which is not to be learned from the notices in the papers. It appears that the Captain published an account of it in the Halifax papers, with a correspondence he had had with Governor Bowdoin relating thereto, on which the Centinel, September 17, made the following remarks: —

Insolence and ignorance never appeared in a more striking light, than they did in the letters lately sent by Capt. Stanhope to our worthy chief magistrate. Although those published in the last Thursday's papers were much altered in Nova Scotia, yet even those are enough, if there had not been enough before, to stamp his character with ineffable contempt — and hold him up to the abhorrence and detestation of every one in whose breast one spark of honor is resident. . . . . The subterfuge of Mr. Stanhope's, in ushering his late correspondence, *corrected and revised*, to the public, under the cover of an Extract of a letter from Boston, is a proceeding worthy of so piddling a *genius.* However, as we wish some of that gentleman's *original* productions may be seen, we shall endeavor to obtain a copy of the correspondence for our next Centinel.

The correspondence was published in the Centinel of September 28. The editors introduced it by saying, they should not comment much on the letters, and add, — "Insolence is a quality British officers generally lay claim to, but where ignorance and folly join hand in hand with it, the character *they* compose is too contemptible to deserve any other notice than personal chastisement. Whether *these* three qualities do not compose Mr. Stanhope's character the world may judge — and whether he does not merit the punishment, let the candid determine from his letters — they need no comment — vengeance is satisfied when *they* appear to the world as he first wrote them — and if even *his* 'senses' are not *agitated* by the reflection of their public appearance, we must pronounce him *really* '*dead*' to every principle of shame."

It was not without great difficulty that the Centinel was sustained, for several years. Money was scarce, and the collection of newspaper bills was no easier than it has been in later years. The publishers, on every fitting opportunity, expressed grateful acknowledgements to their customers, but these were generally accompanied by calls similar to the following: —

A LOUD CALL.

☞ That "times are hard" is the general complaint of all ranks of people; but that they are peculiarly so with the Printers hereof, is a certain truth, which must apologize for their now earnestly requesting those, whose accounts with them are of more than one year's standing, to make payment. *Dunning* is an unthankful business; and glad would they be, had they no occasion for it; but really the want of the money due them, while it sickens the *whole heart*, will urge them to a conduct disagreeable in the extreme.

The effect produced by this appeal, if any, may be estimated after reading their address, six months after, namely, in March, 1786, in which they express in suitable terms their gratitude "for the very liberal encouragement, and even partiality, shown their endeavors to serve the public in the line of their profession;" and pay "their warmest thanks in a particular manner" to their advertising friends for *their* favors. They venture to "hope that they shall profit by the experience they have acquired," and to *enlarge* and *improve* the Centinel "at its present price." They conclude, — "In regard to the *wherewith*, little need be said. Having experienced the public generosity, they only observe, that a display of it *now*, would positively be very timely."

The Centinel of Wednesday, March 22, 1786, — the first number of the fifth volume, — announces the death of the senior editor, WILLIAM WARDEN, on the Saturday preceding, in the 25th year of his age. The annunciation is unaccompanied by any obituary notice, or any remark of the surviving editor. The imprint was changed to "Printed by Benjamin Russell, near the State-House, Boston."

Agreeably to notice in the last preceding number, the Centinel was enlarged to a "Crown Folio." The small cuts or devices were removed from the ends of the head line, and one of them, — that which represented the Genius of America on a pyramid — was placed in the centre of the line, between the words Massachusetts and Centinel. There was no other change in the typography.

It was in this year, that *the Rebellion* broke out in Massachusetts — an event which has consigned to infamy the name of Daniel Shays, the most prominent leader in that atrocious attempt to overturn the government of the state. The Centinel was a faithful watchman on the side of the constitution throughout the whole of that interesting and trying period, and exerted all its influence to quiet the fears of the timid, to stimulate the courage of the faithful, to keep down the clamor of the discontented and factious, and to uphold the cause of patriotism, order, and law. Sometimes it soberly and earnestly appealed to the good sense and judgement of the honest opponents of the measures of the government; at other times, it assailed the mob with wit and ridicule, in sarcasm and lampoon. The latter mode was not, probably, less effectual than the former. Here are a few stanzas of

A SONG, *dedicated to the Lovers of Wit, the Friends to Truth and good Government.*

Come rouse, my bold boxers, 'tis Liberty calls;
Hark! hark, how she lustily bawls, and bawls!
It is high time, — if ever for mobbing 'twas time, —
To mobbing, ye chicks of Dame Liberty, run,
Scour up the old *whinyard* and brush up the *gun;*
Freedom we'll chime,
While Tag, Rag, and Bobtail
Lead up the decorum, — Huzza!

Sure these are the plaguiest of all plaguy times,
When *villains* must hang for their crimes, their crimes,
And *debtors* a guantlope of bailiffs must run;
When *rulers* must *govern* and *we* must *obey,*
And *law* down our gullets is crammed every day —
Rap, rap! — 'tis a dun! —
The sheriff's behind him,
We'll gag him and bind him — Huzza!

* * * * *

The senates and courts to our friend Beelzebub
We'll drive with the musket, and club, and club,
  And in *apron* and *jerkin* our governor dress:
To sit in the saddle, we've men that know how,
And make all your *ruffle shirts* foot it and bow;
    The world shall confess
    We've spirits in *hogsheads*,
    And cunning in *foxheads*, — Huzza!

Thus no longer with *stocks* and with *pillories* vexed,
Nor with work, jail, or sheriff perplexed, perplexed,
  The mob men shall rule and the great men obey;
The world upon wheels shall be all set *agog*,
And blockheads and knaves hail the reign of King Log:
    Under his sway,
    Shall Tag, Rag, and Bobtail
    Lead up our decorum, — Huzza!

The following, — not a bad imitation of the pastoral style of the English poets, — appeared about the time when the Rebellion was suppressed, and when Shays and his colleagues were seeking refuge in other states, or hiding themselves from the officers of the law in Massachusetts: —

SHAYS:

A REBEL ECLOGUE.

JEDIDIAH. JONAS. TIPPLE.

Two young Insurgents (where the sign-post high
Stands at the road, and speaks the tavern nigh)
Agreed to try, by song, which most could praise
Rebellion's influence, and the name of Shays:
With umpire Tipple, seated by their side,
Thus Jedidiah spoke, and Jonas thus replied.

JEDIDIAH.

Hear how the whirling winds around us blow!
And see the country buried deep in snow!
Why should we joyless doze away our time?
Come, let's begin, and waste the morn in rhyme

JONAS.

Of Shays and liberty then let us try —
I'll wage you cannot sing so well as I.

JEDIDIAH.

Ho ! that's a pity ! thou shalt judge and see,
O cousin Tipple ! and the umpire be.

TIPPLE.

Make haste, my boys — I'll judge of what you sing,
For see ! 't is sunrise, and I want a sling.

JONAS.

See this junk bottle, once my joy and pride,
With all these curious letters on its side;
Once it was often filled ! — Now, by my heart,
I'll bet this bottle, and it holds a quart;
I'll wage my mare — bring you an equal stake —

JEDIDIAH.

— That should be seen, if I had one to make.
Father and I, and all hands labor sore,
And hope in time to pay the tavern score.
We 've four years grievous taxes yet to pay;
An hundred mugs of flip to wipe away;
But since you will be mad and wage — here, take
This great tobacco-box — 't is all I stake.

JONAS.

Give us but rum, our pleasure and our pride;
A rebel cares not how the world may slide.
Though all our evils overspread the land,
And vengeful justice should our wiles withstand,
Unawed by law, and uncontroled by sense,
Nobly we join to drive the vagrant hence.

JEDIDIAH.

What is rebellion ? grievances redressed,
Tis Policy, to most advantage dressed —
Sheriffs and duns could ne'er but conscience fret,
We clamor rather at the public debt:
Or like a bull to belch — we grieve and groan —
For public interest, and mean our own.

JONAS.

Still firm and steady let each rebel stand,
Nor dread the weight of Justice' heavy hand;
Secure from brother Shattuck's iron box,
From whipping-posts, and pillories, and stocks;
See from all countries hosts of rebels spring !
Hear through the ranks the martial music ring !

In cause so great let every country raise
Her fresh supplies, and aid our General Shays.

JEDIDIAH.

A little tumult is a dangerous thing —
Drink deep, or taste not, of Sedition's spring;
These mobbing draughts but gently turn the brain,
And bold Rebellion sobers us again.
Fired at the name of Shays and war's alarms,
Fierce in the cause, we tempt the heights of arms;
While from the level of our narrow mind,
Short views we take, nor see the length behind;
But more advanced, behold, with strange surprize,
New scenes of tumult and sedition rise!
So when at first Wachusett hill we try,
Mount o'er the vales, and seem to tread the sky,
One part attained, we tremble to survey,
The groaning labors of the crooked way;
The increasing prospect cheats our wondering eyes,
For still Wachusetts on Wachusetts rise.

JONAS.

Where carrion lies, the hungry crows abound;
Where plunder is, Insurgents will be found.
From laziness what cheerful pleasures come!
Sweet of a morning is New-England rum!
In all these blessed gifts no sweets there be —
For dearer than the whole is Shays to me.

JEDIDIAH.

I'll weave a garland for my darling Shays;
I'll twigs of hemlock and of dog-wood raise;
There the green bough of Rebels shall be seen
With sprigs of hemp and devil's-weed between.

JONAS.

The mighty wolf is baneful to the sheep;
Storms in the spring will make the farmer weep;
The lagging frosts to blossoms prove unkind,
And county courts disturb a debtor's mind;
Of Lincoln's sword more ills does Fame report,
Than of the wolves, and storms, and frosts, and county court.

TIPPLE.

Cease to contend — so well, so long you sing,
You must be dry — and I, too, want a sling.

But hark! what noise is this insults my ear,
Which strikes my trembling heart with rebel fear,
A troop of Lincoln's horse! — in yonder field! —
Lord! — run! — run! — run! or we shall all be killed.

Some, who read these sketches, may be gratified to see the following "Protest, or Excommunication" which was published in the Centinel, January 2, 1780, at the request of the Rev. James Freeman, minister of the Stone-Chapel, Boston: —

Whereas a certain congregation in Boston, calling themselves the first EPISCOPAL Church in said town, have, in an irregular and unconstitutional manner, introduced a Liturgy essentially differing from any used in the Episcopal Churches in this Commonwealth, and in the United States; and have also assumed to themselves a power, unprecedented in the *said* Church, of separating to the work of the ministry, Mr. *James Freeman*, who has for some time past been their Reader, and of themselves have authorized, or pretendedly authorized him to administer the Sacraments of Baptism and the Lord's Supper; and, at the same time, most inconsistently and absurdly take to themselves the name and style of an Episcopal Church:

WE, the ministers of the Protestant Episcopal Church, whose names are underwritten, do hereby declare the proceedings of said congregation, usually meeting at the Stone Chapel in Boston, to be irregular, unconstitutional, diametrically opposite to every principle adopted in *any* Episcopal Church; subversive of all order and regularity, and pregnant with consequences fatal to the interests of religion. And we do hereby, and in this public manner, protest against the aforesaid proceedings, to the end that all those of our communion, whenever disposed, may be cautioned against receiving said Reader, or Preacher, (Mr. *James Freeman*,) as a clergyman of our Church, or holding any communion with him as such, and may be induced to look upon his congregation in the light, in which it ought to be looked upon by all true Episcopalians.

Signed by EDWARD BASS, NATHANIEL FISHER, SAMUEL PARKER, THOMAS FITCH OLIVER, WILLIAM MONTAGUE, JOHN C. OGDEN, ministers of Episcopal Churches in Newburyport, Salem, Boston, Marblehead, and Portsmouth.

The Constitution of the United States was adopted in the Convention on the 17th of September, 1787. It was published entire in the Centinel on the 26th of the same month, together with the Resolve and the Circular addressed to the State Conventions. From that time till its ratification by all the states, Russell devoted all his powers to secure its adoption. Every argument in its favor was strenuously urged by him or his correspondents, and every objection was answered or refuted. A series of essays in favor of the constitution, — first published at Hartford, and supposed to be written by Oliver Ellsworth, — were republished in the Centinel, and many articles of the same character from other intelligent and influential sources, were commended to public consideration. Russell was one of the Boston Mechanics, who held a succession of meetings at the "Green Dragon Tavern," in Boston, to represent the sentiments of that respectable class of citizens in a Memorial to the State Convention of Massachusetts — a document, which had great influence with that body, and which (as Governor Hancock is reported to have said) turned the scale in favor of the constitution.

While the several State Conventions were deliberating on the proposed constitution, Russell kept the account of their progress "posted up," in detail, with scrupulous fidelity. When the news arrived in Boston that Delaware had ratified the constitution, the Centinel added to the intelligence, a remark in the peculiar vein of the editor: — "The State of Delaware being the first to adopt, ratify, and confirm the American Constitution, argues well. It is a good maxim, which inculcates the practice of '*entering at the little end of the horn;*' — as, at every step we take, our circle is increased, and our basis progressively growing broader and broader."

"Ten States (he continues,) have called Conventions. South-Carolina we have not heard from — New-York, as yet, could not, — and Rhode-Island, (*shame come upon her rulers for it!*) will not. The call of conventions is tantamount to the final adoption of the constitution — as, in these assemblies, such unanswerable arguments will be given, as must convince every member, disposed to hearken to truth, of the expediency of the measure, whatever may have been their former sentiments respecting it."

Again, in his next paper, — "Three pillars of the great Dome of Federal Empire are reared, — and, as the convention of Georgia has been in session, and that of Connecticut will sit next week, — we hope soon to have it in our power to felicitate our readers on the better half of the pile being completed." A few weeks after, on the 9th of January, 1788, the editorial department leads off with the following supplicatory paragraph: —

This day the Convention of this state are to meet for the purpose of assenting to and ratifying the Federal Constitution. May the GREAT IDEA fill the mind of every member of this honorable body, that Heaven, on this auspicious occasion, favors America with an opportunity, never before enjoyed by the sons of men, of establishing a form of government, *peaceably* and *deliberately*, which will secure to these states all those blessings which give worth to existence or dignity to man, PEACE, LIBERTY, and SAFETY! — And may the guardian God of our "dear country" inspire the convention of this Commonwealth with *wisdom*, *disinterestedness*, and *patriotism* equal to the display of those virtues in our sister states, who have already erected Three Pillars of the glorious Fabrick of the Federal Republick.

In the next Centinel, the proceedings of the Convention are reported, briefly, in detail. Here is the *editorial* description of the body; —

THE CONVENTION.

Concentered HERE, the united wisdom shines
Of learned JUDGES and of sound DIVINES;
PATRIOTS, whose virtues searching times have tried;
HEROES, who fought where BROTHER HEROES died;
LAWYERS, who speak as TULLY spoke before;
SAGES, deep read in philosophic lore:
MERCHANTS, whose plans are to no realms confined;
FARMERS, the noblest title of mankind;
YEOMEN and TRADESMEN, pillars of the state;
On whose decision hangs COLUMBIA'S fate.

Thus, the various orders, which constitute the great Family of the Commonwealth, concur to form the august, the honorable Convention, now sitting in this metropolis. To this enlightened and respectable body, the eyes not only of their *constituents*, but of AMERICA, and the world, are turned. And, from the rays of intelligence, which beam from every quarter of the assembly, we fondly anticipate the most learned, candid, and patriotic discussion of the great subject of the Constitution.

Next came the information that Georgia and Connecticut had ratified the Constitution, and the Centinel thus announced the intelligence: —

States, like the generous vine, supported live —
The strength they gain is from the embrace they give.

THE FEDERAL PILLARS.

UNITED THEY STAND — DIVIDED THEY FALL.

A vessel from Georgia confirms the pleasing intelligence, that that state has unanimously ratified the Federal Constitution. Thus is a FIFTH PILLAR added to the glorious Fabrick. May Massachusetts erar the SIXTH.

As we predicted in our last, so it happened. Monday morning was ushered in with the ringing of bells in this metropolis, on account of the pleasing intelligence received by Saturday night's mail, that the State of Connecticut had added a FOURTH PILLAR to that GRAND REPUBLICAN STRUCTURE, the FEDERAL CONSTITUTION.

Similar announcements were made as the states successively adopted the constitution, — a new pillar was added to the device in the Centinel, — and the intelligence was given in language of the same jubilant character. In August, 1788, when eleven states had adopted it, the eleven corresponding pillars in the cut stood perpendicular: that representing North-Carolina was raised to an angle of about forty-five degrees; that for Rhode-Island was broken, just above the base, which stood firm, while the shaft was in a sloping posture, and at the capital was this inscription, "☞ *The foundation good — it may yet be* SAVED." Over the whole range of pillars, in large capitals, were the words, — "REDEUNT SATURNIA REGNA." Under it was the following: —

THE FEDERAL EDIFICE.

ELEVEN STARS, in quick succession rise,
ELEVEN COLUMNS strike our wondering eyes;
Soon, o'er the *whole*, shall swell the beauteous DOME,
COLUMBIA'S boast, and FREEDOM'S hallowed home.
Here shall the ARTS in glorious splendor shine,
And AGRICULTURE give her stores divine;
COMMERCE refined, dispense us more than gold,
And this new world teach WISDOM to the old;
RELIGION here shall fix her blest abode,
Arrayed in *mildness*, like its parent, GOD;
JUSTICE and LAW shall endless PEACE maintain,
And the "SATURNIAN AGE" return again.

Russell was a constant attendant in the Massachusetts Convention, and reported the debates for the Centinel. These reports he afterwards revised, with the aid of the principal speakers, and published in a duodecimo volume. Very few copies of this book are now in existence, and those few are highly valued by their owners. The sittings of the Convention were held in the old meeting-house, which stood on the site now occupied by the Rev. Mr. Gannett's meeting-house in Federal-street. This street was then known by the name of Long Lane, a name, which was changed for that, which it bears now, immediately after the adoption of the constitution. In a memorandum, now before me, Russell says — "I had never studied stenography, nor was there any person then in Boston that understood reporting. The presiding officer of the Convention sat in the Deacon's seat, under the pulpit. I took the pulpit for my reporting desk, and a very good one it was. I succeeded well enough in this my first effort to give a tolerably fair report in my next paper; but the puritanical notions had not entirely faded away, and I was voted out of the pulpit. A stand was fitted up for me in another place, and I proceeded with my reports, generally to the acceptance of the Convention. The doubts that still existed as to whether enough of the states would come into the compact to make the constitution binding, made the proceedings of the Convention intensely interesting. When the news arrived of the acceptance of it by the State of Virginia, there was a most extraordinary outbreak of rejoicing. It seemed as if the meeting-house would burst with the acclamation."

Soon after the ratification by Massachusetts, Russell gave utterance to his exultation in the following Song: —

THE RAISING:

A NEW SONG FOR FEDERAL MECHANICS.

Come, muster, my Lads, your mechanical tools,
Your Saws and your Axes, your Hammers and Rules;
Bring your Mallets and Planes, your Level and Line,
And plenty of Pins of American Pine.
For our roof we will raise, and our song shall still be —
A government firm, and our citizens free.

Come, up with the *Plates*, lay them firm on the wall,
Like the people at large, they 're the ground-work of all;
Examine them well, and see that they 're sound;
Let no rotten parts in our building be found.
For our roof we will raise, and our song shall still be —
Our government firm, and our citizens free.

Now hand up the *Girders*, lay each in his place;
Between them the *Joists* must divide all the space;
Like Assembly-men, *these* should lie level along,
Like *Girders*, our Senate prove loyal and strong.
For our roof we will raise, and our song shall still be —
A government firm, over citizens free.

The *Rafters* now frame — your *King-Posts* and *Braces*,
And drive your Pins home, to keep all in their places;
Let wisdom and strength in the fabric combine,
And your Pins be all made of American Pine:
For our roof we will raise, and our song shall still be —
A government firm, over citizens free.

Our *King-Posts* are Judges — how upright they stand,
Supporting the *Braces*, the laws of the land —
The laws of the land, which divide right from wrong,
And strengthen the weak by weakening the strong.
For our roof we will raise, and our song shall still be —
Laws equal and just for a people that 's free.

Up! up with the *Rafters* — each frame is a State!
How nobly they rise! their span, too, how great!
From the North to the South, o'er the whole they extend,
And rest on the Walls, while the walls they defend.
For our roof we will raise, and our song shall still be —
Combin-ed in strength, yet, as citizens, free.

Now enter the *Purlins*, and drive your Pins through,
And see that your *Joints* are drawn home, and all true;

The *Purlins* will bind all the *Rafters* together,
The strength of the whole shall defy wind and weather;
For our roof we will raise, and our song shall still be —
United as States, but as citizens free.

Come raise up the *Turret,* — our glory and pride,
In the centre it stands, o'er the whole to preside;
The Sons of Columbia shall view with delight
Its PILLARS and ARCHES, and towering height!
Our roof is now raised, and our song shall still be —
A Federal Head o'er a people still free.

Huzza, my brave boys! our work is complete,
The world shall admire Columbia's fair seat;
Its strength against tempests and time shall be proof,
And thousands shall come to dwell under our ROOF.
Whilst we drain the deep bowl, our toast shall still be —
Our government firm, and our citizens free.

The Song, which follows, published in the Centinel of January 31, 1789, — after twelve states had adopted the constitution, chosen a President, and Representatives to the first Congress, — is not distinguished as original; but it partakes so liberally of the spirit and style of Russell, that, if it was not written by him, I must believe it was composed from his dictation: —

MECHANICS' SONG.

BY ABRAHAM AIMWELL, ESQ.

Ye merry Mechanics, come join in my song,
And let the brisk chorus come bounding along;
Though some may be poor, and some rich there may be,
And yet all are contented, and happy, and free.

Ye *Tailors*, of ancient and noble renown,
Who clothe all the people in country and town,
Remember that Adam, your father and head,
Though lord of the world, was a *Tailor* by trade.

Ye *Masons!* who work in stone, mortar and brick,
And lay the foundations deep, solid and thick,
Though hard be your labor, yet lasting your fame,
Both Egypt and China your wonders proclaim.

Ye *Smiths*, who forge tools for all trades here below,
You have nothing to fear, while you smite and you blow;
All things you may conquer, so happy your lot,
If you 're careful to *strike while the iron is hot.*

Ye *Shoemakers!* nobly, from ages long past,
Have defended your rights with *awl* to the *last*,
And *Cobblers* all merry, not only stop holes,
But work, night and day, for the good of our *soles.*

Ye *Cabinet-makers!* brave workers in wood,
As you work for the ladies, your work must be good;
And *Joiners*, and *Carpenters*, far off and near,
Stick close to your trades, and you 've nothing to fear.

Ye *Hatters!* who oft, with hands not very fair,
Fix hats on a block, for a blockhead to wear,
Though *charity* cover a sin, now and then,
You cover the heads and the sins of all men.

Ye *Coach-makers!* must not by tax be controlled,
But ship off your coaches, and bring us home gold;—
The roll of your coach made Copernicus reel,
And fancy the world to turn round, like a wheel.

Ye *Carders*, and *Spinners*, and *Weavers!* attend,
And take the advice of Poor Richard your friend;
Stick close to your looms, and your wheels, and your card,
And you never need fear of the times being hard.

Ye *Printers!* who give us our learning and news,
And impartially print for Turks, Christians, and Jews,
Let your favorite toast ever sound through the streets—
The freedom of press, and a volume in sheets.

Ye *Coopers!* who rattle with *driver* and *adze*,
And lecture each day upon hoops and on heads,
The famous old ballad of *Love in a tub*,
You may sing to the tune of your rub-a-dub dub.

Ye *Ship-builders! Riggers*, and *Makers of Sails!*
Already the New Constitution prevails;
And soon you shall see o'er the proud swelling tide,
The ships of Columbia triumphantly ride.

Each *Tradesman* turn out with his tool in his hand,
To cherish the *arts*, and keep peace through the land;
Each *'prentice* and *journeyman* join in my song,
And let the brisk chorus come bounding along.

I must introduce one more article as a specimen of Russell's jubilant style of announcing the progress of federal principles. It appeared soon after the inauguration of Washington in 1789. There can be no doubt as to the authorship of this article. The *allegory* is one which Russell always delighted to introduce, and in the indulgence of which he was generally successful and happy: —

THE FEDERAL SHIP.

Just *launched* on the *Ocean of Empire*, the Ship COLUMBIA, GEORGE WASHINGTON, Commander, which, after being thirteen years in *dock*, is at length well *manned*, and in very good condition. The Ship is a *first rate* — has a good *bottom*, which all the Builders have pronounced *sound* and *good*. Some objection has been made to parts of the *tackling*, or *running rigging*, which, it is supposed, will be *altered*, when they shall be found to be incommodious, as the Ship is able to make very good *headway* with them as they are. A *jury* of *Carpenters* have this matter now under consideration. The *Captain* and *First Mate* are universally esteemed by all the Owners — Eleven * in number — and she has been *insured*, under their direction, to make a good *mooring* in the *harbor* of Public Prosperity and Felicity — whitherto she is bound. The Owners can furnish, besides the Ship's Company, the following materials: — *New-Hampshire*, the Masts and Spars; *Massachusetts*, Timber for the Hull, Fish, &c.; *Connecticut*, Beef and Pork; *New-York*, Porter and other Cabin stores; *New-Jersey*, the Cordage; *Pennsylvania*, Flour and Bread; — *Delaware*, the Colors, and Clothing for the Crew; *Maryland*, the Iron work and small Anchors; *Virginia*, Tobacco and the Sheet Anchor; *South-Carolina*, Rice; and *Georgia*, Powder and small Provisions. Thus found, may this *good Ship* put to sea, and the prayer of all is, that GOD *may preserve her, and bring her in safety to her desired haven.*

In February, 1789, as the time drew near for the organization of the government under the constitution, Russell published the Pasquinade, which follows. Some

* Only eleven States had then adopted the Constitution. North-Carolina and Rhode Island are not recognized as owners of the Ship.

allusions contained in it are not readily understood ; and perhaps the application of its satire, in some instances, may, at the present day, be deemed hardly justifiable; but *that* was not the day when newspaper editors and their correspondents hesitated to speak their thoughts freely, and with a freedom, which was afterwards *dignified* with the epithet *libelous,* and attributed to the *licentiousness of the Press :* —

Notwithstanding the medical exertions of a *celebrated Physician* — the prescriptions of three *gubernatorial* Esculapians — and the endeavors of the whole fraternity of *State Quacks* and *Mountebanks* to prolong its existence — in convulsions the most violent — in contortions and wreathings the most painful, on *Wednesday* last, finished its wicked career,

The Genius *of* Antifederalism.

It was born in August, 1787 — was aged 17 months. Though thus cut off in its childhood, it still lived to do much mischief; and to have grown so detestable, that even its friends — its foster-parents, shewed the utmost resentment whenever called by its name: It has, however expired, a striking instance of the truth of the adage, — "*The wicked shall not live half their days.*"

On WEDNESDAY, MARCH 4th, the funeral obsequies will be consummated — when a GRAND PROCESSION will be formed.

ORDER OF THE PROCESSION.

The DEMON of REBELLION,

drawn in a flaming Car, by *Ignorance*, *Knavery*, and *Idleness*.

DANIEL SH–YS, and JOHN FR–NKLIN,

armed with *levelers* in their right, and halters in their left hands.

DAY, SHATTUCK, &c. &c. their followers, two and two, each with *caps* and *bells*.

Several "*great men*" their abettors, in *disguise*.

CHIEF PHYSICIAN —

Supporters,		*Supporters,*
Injustice,	The BODY.	Knavery,
Abuse,		Defamation,
Prevarication,		Falsehood.

His SATANIC MAJESTY — Chief Mourner.

His standard — motto — "*The prop of my Empire is fallen.*"

A KNOW-YE Rhode-Islander — and a *pine-barren* Carolinian, in sackcloth, with brazen helmets — crest "*A Highwayman robbing by law,*" motto — "'Tis power which *sanctifies* a crime."

A cart drawn by *Fraud* — with Paper-Money, Tender-Laws, &c. the sides painted, "*Be it enacted,*" &c.

The GODDESS of DISCORD — in weepers.

— In her right hand a torch expiring — in her left a bloody sword broken.

BENEDICT ARNOLD, SILAS DEANE, &c. with swords embossed, "*In '75 we were right.*"

A standard, motto, "*Birds of a feather flock together.*"

Hon. PATRICK H–NRY, of Virginia,

Bearing a scroll, with the words, "*In the creation of* TWO *Confederacies are all my hopes of greatness.*"

His Excel. G. CL–NT–N, Esq.

In both hands a Purse, tied up. The words thereon, "*If New-York loses the Impost, I lose thee.*"

The GENIUS of IMBECILITY,

In a car — painted on both sides with hieroglyphicks. "*A ship rotting in the harbor. — An English Crow picking the Eagle's eyes out — the Eagle asleep; his talons cut — an American fort, with English colors — a rusty sword — a broken ploughshare — starving mechanics — broken merchants, &c.*"

200 Wrongheads, two and two.

"*While we're in, let's keep in.*"

A WOLF, covered with the golden fleece of a LAMB, marked 4000l. per ann.

The Geniuses of the Philad. Gazetteer — New-York Journal — Boston Gazette, &c. in their original *blackness;*

"*The days of our years are evil and few.*"

A cart, with antifederal Pamphlets, Essays, Protests, &c. in reams, marked "*waste-paper.*"

GALEN and the Junto — two and two.

The GODDESS of POVERTY — in tatters —

"*Follow me, my sons,*" she cries,

"*We do,*" each scribbler replies.

A dray with stumps of pens, broken inkstands, &c.

Antifederal Scribblers, in dishabille, two and two, chaunting the following lines: — *Who will close the Procession.*

Our prospects how fleeting, how feeble our cause,
Engag'd as we 've been, in subverting the laws:
Though we 've spread far and wide our libels and lies,
And *Anties* at heart, assum'd *Freedom's* fair guise.
Tho' WASHINGTON, and FRANKLIN, each scribbler defames,
And slanders with malice their actions and names;
Though ADAMS, and JAY, and your HAMILTON too,
Are libel'd and black'd by each cur of our crew;
Tho' we 've slander'd you much both abroad and at home,
And strove to demolish the FEDERAL DOME,
Yet finding our *Genius* to *Erebus* fled,
And in its disease all our prospects lie dead,
The time of contrition 's assuredly come —
And we wait from the Feds our sentence and doom.
But with truth we can say, what we fear to deny,
That we 've felt *heretofore*, as if telling a lie.
While engag'd in this cause we seldom had rest,
For the gnaw-worm of conscience has tortur'd our breast —
Then forgive us, ye Feds, though we ask it thus late —
Our grief is sincere as our crimes have been great.

It was in the course of the following winter that a series of essays over the signature of LACO * appeared in the Centinel, intended to affect the re-election of Governor Hancock — against whose administration some dissatisfaction had manifested itself. These essays were written in a style not unworthy of a Junius. They were severe, but not unmannerly. Many were startled at the exposure of the Governor's faults and weaknesses, who had never before indulged a thought that he was not as perfect as a created man could be. Laco was attacked, by several writers in the Centinel, and most ferociously abused in the Chronicle, both by the editors and their correspondents. The real author of these essays was not immediately known, and the bitterness of

* Stephen Higginson, an eminent merchant of Boston.

his opponents seemed to increase with every baffled attempt to discover him.

Russell was a great stickler for honorary titles. Soon after the constitution went into operation, a newspaper discussion sprung up on the question whether any, and if any, what titles should be given to the President, Vice-President, Members of Congress, and Cabinet Ministers. The Centinel made a hard push for high-sounding titles — the Chronicle and Boston Gazette fought as boldly against them. A correspondent of the Centinel proposed that the President should be addressed as "His Majesty the President of the United States," and to this proposition Russell yielded his cordial assent. He also proposed that the address of the Vice-President should be "His Excellency;" — that of a Senator "Most Honorable;" — and that of a Representative "Honorable." In accordance with this scale of dignity, these different degrees of honor were sometimes used, but the practice was not ratified by the public sentiment. The Centinel, on some occasions, would say — "Yesterday the Most Honorable ———, Esq. set out on his journey to New-York," "The Honorable ———, Esq. yesterday took his seat in the House of Representatives," &c. Whatever title was placed before a name, Russell always put "Esq." at the end of it; and this was his uniform practice. No man, who had ever been a member of the Senate of Massachusetts, was spoken of in the Centinel, while Russell was its editor, without these additions to his name.*

* It is still common in Massachusetts, to address our Senators as "Honorable Mr. ———," though they have no more claim to the distinction, either by law or courtesy, than any other individuals. The custom is ineffably ridiculous, and is a legitimate subject for the pen of the satirist.

THE COLUMBIAN CENTINEL.

On the 16th of June, 1790, the Centinel was published with this new title on an enlarged sheet, with improved typography, and containing the following address

To the Patrons of the Centinel.

The multiplicity of political events, which are daily augmenting as the *United States progress* as a Confederated Republic, has induced the editor to increase the Centinel to the respectable size, in which it this day appears; without any immediate advance of price. At two dollars *per annum*, the Centinel is the cheapest paper ever printed in this or any other part of America; and the Editor wishes long to be able to adhere to that price: If, however, Experience should make him *feel* that it is too low; and cruel *Necessity* should oblige him to raise it — the principle of gratitude for past favors will constrain him not to increase the half-yearly charge more than *Eight Pence;* and in this *small addition*, he doubts not his liberal Patrons will cheerfully acquiesce. Due notice will be given of the period when the rise, if *necessary*, shall take place. — At present, *Calculation* designates the middle of *September*, when the *semi-annual* accounts of the Centinel are usually made out — Hope points to a period more remote.

At all times, the Editor has *felt* the liveliest emotions of gratitude for the patronage he has received — and he has embraced every opportunity of acknowledging that such have been his impressions: On the present occasion he presents his Patrons the renewed tribute of unfeigned thanks for their friendship and partiality.

Benjamin Russell.

From this date the Centinel took a decided and high rank among the newspapers that were springing up in every part of the country. The advertising custom rapidly increased, and the income soon became sufficient to insure a pecuniary independence to the proprietor. It took strong ground in support of Washington, and all the measures of the federal administration. Washington was accused by the persons, who had opposed the constitution, of entertaining an undue partiality for England, and wanting in gratitude to France. Mr. Adams, the Vice-President, and Mr. Hamilton, Secretary of the Treasury, were also placed under the ban of the opposition, and pursued with relentless ferocity. The Centinel, as the leading journal of the Federalists of Massachusetts, ably defended the administration, and pushed the war most vigorously into the ranks of the opposition.

While Congress was holding its first session, Russell wrote to the Department of State, and offered to publish gratuitously, all the laws and other official documents — the country being then almost or quite bankrupt. All laws and other papers emanating from the various departments of the government, were accordingly transmitted to him and were published "by authority." At the end of several years, he was called upon for his bill. It was made out, and in compliance with his pledge, was receipted. On being informed of the fact, General Washington said, — "This must not be. When Mr. Russell offered to publish the laws without pay, we were poor. It was a generous offer. We are now able to pay our debts. This is a debt of honor, and must be discharged." A few days after, Russell received a check for *seven thousand dollars,* the full amount of his bill.

About this time began the warfare between the Centinel and the Chronicle, which lasted till after the close of the war of 1812. The Centinel being the organ of the Federalists, and the Chronicle that of the Jacobins, — as the opposition was then called, — the columns of both papers teemed with hostility and invective, and frequently with not a little of vulgar abuse. Persons, who have a taste for this sort of reading, by referring to the files of these papers for twenty-five years following 1790, will find abundant matter for its gratification. Irritating personal reflections and altercations were frequent, and some times led to rencontres of a disagreeable nature. These mutually exasperating remarks upon the editors and their correspondents produced an affray, which will be best learned from the annexed article, which appeared in the American Apollo. Russell never alluded to the affair in his paper until after the trial for the offence he was alleged to have committed; nor would he even then, probably, had he not been prompted by some of his friends. The report appeared in the Apollo of March 29, 1793, and undoubtedly embraces an authentic statement of the facts in the case: —

In the month of January, 1792, the inhabitants of the town of Boston were assembled for the purpose of passing a final determination upon a question, which had been long in agitation, and upon which they all felt interested in the highest degree. The meeting was very numerous, and the hall in which they were assembled much crowded. When the question was taken, the moderator declared himself unable to determine, by the show of hands, which side had prevailed; it was therefore agreed to adopt another method of ascertaining the majority: that those who were on one side should all go out of the hall, and that the selectmen, together with two persons then to be chosen, one from either side, should stand at the door of the hall, and count the voters as they should pass; after which those of the other party should go out and be counted in the same manner. In pursuance of this agreement, Benjamin Austin, jun. was chosen as the teller on one side, and accepted the office. Dr. Jarvis, Dr. Eustis, and Mr. Lucas were then successively chosen for the other side, and declined serving; upon which Benjamin Russell was chosen and accepted the trust. Immediately upon which, Mr. Austin, who was near the middle of the hall, and had been making his way towards the door, turned round, addressed the moderator, and said, he must decline serving; that he would cheerfully serve with Dr. Jarvis, Dr. Eustis, *or any other gentleman*, but not with *such a fellow as Ben Russell.*

The next day after this Mr. Russell, upon being asked whether he did not intend to resent the insult he had received the day before, said he would ask him whether he meant it as a personal affront to him, or as a general reflection upon him as a tradesman; and if he should answer the former, he would spit in his face and wring his nose. Accordingly he sought Mr. Austin upon the exchange, and when he had found him, asked the question just mentioned; to which Mr. Austin answered that he would have nothing to do with Ben Russell; and afterwards added, that he did not choose to put himself upon a par with Ben Russell. Upon this denial of satisfaction, and repetition of insult, Russell did as he had threatened, spit in his face, and reproached him with virulent and abusive language.

Such, as appeared in evidence, was the transaction upon which the action was grounded, in which the plaintiff laid his damages at one thousand pounds; and, by way of aggravating the offence, he had alleged that, at the time when it happened, he was a Senator for the county of Suffolk, and that the Senate was then in session.

The defence made by Mr. Russell's counsel upon the trial, was of two kinds. First, they denied the fact. Upon this, however, they laid but little stress. They were sensible of its weakness: for it was supported only by the acknowledgement of the plaintiff himself. It was proved that Mr. Austin had, in conversation with several members of the Senate, denied that Russell had spit in his face; but it was also proved that, at another time, he had said his agitation of mind was so extreme at the time, that he did not know whether he had been spitten upon or not. In common cases, the confession of the party is the best evidence that can be offered against him; but, in the present instance, where it was variant from itself, incredible in its own nature, and contradicted by positive and credible evidence, it could not be expected to have any weight with the jury, and the defendant's counsel, therefore, placed but little reliance upon it. Their second and substantial point was, in mitigation of damages; they contended that although the jury, as the organs of the law, must pronounce Mr. Russell guilty, yet they could not consider the injury in any other than a very trivial light as it respected the plaintiff. He had drawn it upon himself. In the presence of twelve hundred of their fellow-citizens, he had outrageously insulted a man, whose situation in life was very far from being disreputable: he had thus insulted him, without assigning any reason whatever for so doing, and at a moment when the object of the insult had received a mark of respect from the inhabitants of the town, by an appointment to execute a duty, in their opinion, of considerable importance. When called upon by this injured man, to explain himself, and to avow the principle upon which he had treated him so contemptuously, instead of giving the satisfaction so justly required, he had repeated the insult, with circumstances of additional aggravation. It was an injury, which no man of common spirit could endure; yet it was of such a nature, that the laws of the country had not provided any remedy for the sufferer. If, under a sense of indignation at such treatment, Mr. Russell's resentment had hurried him beyond the limits of moderation, and led him to take his own satisfaction, by retorting upon the offender, an insult of a still higher nature, he could not indeed be justified for his violation of the rigid letter of the law, but surely the disgrace inflicted upon the plaintiff could not entitle him to any considerable compensation in damages: that, as to his Senatorial capacity, the respect and veneration of the people, in a free republican government, was due to the public offices themselves, not to the men who hold them: That it was ridiculous to suppose the honor or reputation of any man could be the more or the less precious to him, from the circumstances of his being in a public character; and that, as he was not, at the time when the affair occurred, in the execution of his office, he could not be considered in a different light from any other citizen under similar circumstances.

Upon this defence, the opinion of the Court was unanimous, that the previous insult offered by the plaintiff was a proper subject of consideration by the jury, in mitigation of damages. As to the point whether his Senatorial character was a legal circumstance of aggravation, there was some diversity of opinion. Judge Dawes thought it was a principle, upon which every man must judge for himself; and therefore left it altogether to the jury. Judge Sumner inclined to the supposition that it was not any subject of aggravation except when the plaintiff is in the actual execution of his official duties. Judge Paine and the Chief Justice were clear and decided, that it was a circumstance of aggravation, and that it ought to have great weight with a jury in the estimation of damages; at the same time, they expressed, in as full and unequivocal a manner, the sentiment that no official rank or dignity whatever could authorize the man invested with it, wantonly to insult the feelings of even the humblest member of the community; that, if a man clothed with authority would descend from his eminence to injure a private citizen, he ought not to be allowed to draw after him the atmosphere of his elevation for his protection.

The jury, after retiring for a few minutes, returned with a verdict, finding guilty, and assessing damages for the plaintiff in the sum of twenty shillings.

Of the political doggerels that were published in the Centinel, in this early stage of the party strife, the following is a specimen: —

SONG.

To be sung at the Quarterly Meeting of the Jacobin Club in this town: Stanzas by the President and Officers, — Chorus by the united voices of the whole Fraternity. The taste of the Society would rather have preferred the music of *Ca Ira*, but as that respectable body loves to turn things topsy-turvy, it finally agreed upon a perversion of the old "Rule Britannia."

When first CONFUSION'S tattered train
From Night and gloomy Anarch rose,
This was the measure of the strain,
And this the matchless theme they chose: —
Rule, Confusion, rule the Free;
Order shall submit to thee.

'Tis ours to bid Ambition drop,
To bid the germ of Genius fade,
To clip the golden wings of Hope,
And scorn the Hero's sainted shade: —
Rule, Confusion, &c.

While peaceful Virtue joys to find
Protective *Law's* pacific reign,
Ours is the bold unbiased Mind,
And ours the War-exciting strain: —
Rule, Confusion, &c.

So from the dread volcano's breath,
The mingling elements are driven,
That blast the yellow-waving heath,
And dim the sparkling eye of Heaven: —
Rule, Confusion, &c.

No son of science e'er shall tread
With classic step this ritual ground;
Ne'er shall the ray of Genius shed
Its visionary light around: —
Rule, Confusion, &c.

But Gallic counsels shall preside,
And Gallic hopes inspire the soul
To trample on the statesman's pride,
And give to Anarchy the whole: —
Rule, Confusion, &c.

Dear Goddess of the Gorgon Eye!
'Tis thine to bid the Arts decay,
To bid the Child of Genius die
And tear his laureled crown away: —
Rule, Confusion, &c.

So when the bickering flame extends
To earth, the trophied marble bows;
No more the sculptured dome ascends,
No more the breathing canvas glows:
Rule, Confusion, &c.

With equal passion, equal power,
Around each jetty brother stands;
For equal Wisdom guides the hour,
And equal Honesty commands.
Rule, Confusion, rule the Free,
Vanquished Order bows to thee.

April 9, 1794.

In 1795, the Spirit of Federalism began to manifest the maturity of its strength in the Centinel. It was in that year that the ratification of the commercial treaty with Great-Britain, (generally called Jay's treaty) created great popular excitement. The Jacobin societies, which had then become numerous throughout the Union, were violent in their opposition. Mobs were frequent in the large cities and towns, and Boston was rather infamously distinguished by these popular demonstrations of dissatisfaction. For several nights in succession, companies of mischief-loving individuals paraded the streets, carrying an effigy of Mr. Jay, and other emblems of mobocracy, making night hideous with their shouts and brawls. One of the devices carried in these nocturnal processions, was an illuminated shell of a water-melon, representing a man's face, accompanied by a scurrilous label. The Centinel, as usual, was on the side of order and law, and denounced the mobs and their leaders in terms like the following: — "The laws prostrate, — the magistrates literally trodden under foot — women and children frightened — bonfires made in the centre of the town — oaths and imprecations, united with threats *to tear the hearts of magistrates from their breasts,* and roast them at a fire:" — *such,* it said, was a sad picture, but a true one. Application was made to Governor Adams for the exercise of his authority to put a stop to these outrages; but he excused himself from any interference, and turned off the applicants, it was said, with a declaration, that *it was nothing but a water-melon frolic.* After the actors in these scenes had become tired of their sport, and the excitement had in some degree passed away, some one wrote for the Centinel a series of communications, entitled "A brief History of the Rise and Progress of the recent Mobs and Riots," which contain many facts, valuable to those who seek to be familiar with the early history of the two great political parties, which, for half a century, struggled for *the balance of power.*

It was about this time (perhaps a little earlier) that the celebrated Monsieur Talleyrand, who, afterwards acted so prominent a part in the negotiations between the French Directory and the Envoys of the United States, was in Boston, and frequently visited the editor of the Centinel. Louis Philippe and one of his brothers were also there at the same time. Louis was introduced to Russell by Talleyrand. The French exiles lived with another French exile, or emigrant, a tailor, by the name of Amblard, who kept a shop at the corner of State-street and Wilson's lane, where the Globe Bank now stands. They were frequent visiters at the Centinel office, and especially on the occasion of every fresh arrival from Europe, to learn the news from their country. Russell had regular files of the *Moniteur*, the official journal of the Directory, which to these exiles was peculiarly interesting. At one of these visits, they observed Russell taking snuff from a parcel in a bit of brown paper, and asked him if he had no other snuff-box. He replied, he could not afford a better. The next day Talleyrand brought a gold one and presented to him. "This, (said Russell,) I kept many years. It suddenly vanished; by what agency I never *knew;* but *suspected* that my better half popped it into the crucible." While he resided in Boston, Louis Philippe opened a school for teaching the French language, and received his pupils at the house of Amblard. As an acknowledgment of the civilities he had received from Russell, he presented to him an *Atlas,* and a French work on Geography. The Atlas was of great service to Russell. It was always on his table, and he seldom wrote or published an article concerning the movements of the hostile armies in Europe, without referring to it to authenticate the intelligence.

In 1796, the bills making appropriations for carrying into effect the treaty with Great-Britain, were subjects of long, interesting, and angry debate in the House of Representatives. The bills were reported in the early part of the session, but met with powerful and obstinate opposition in both houses of Congress. In many towns in Massachusetts, the people held meetings, and adopted petitions to Congress, praying for a speedy determination of the business; but the bills were not finally passed till the fourth of May. On announcing their passage, Russell let out his enthusiasm in strains like these: — "The Public Spirit of Massachusetts never before accorded so truly with the finest chords of Federalism, as it has done, in the late rising *en masse* of THE PEOPLE, to make known their wishes and expectations on the subject of the treaty. Their voice has been heard and has had its due influence. The CRISIS, at which the Peace, Happiness, and Prosperity of our country stood suspended, has passed by; *Confidence* has assumed its wonted security; and *Business* again trips lightly to the music of the *sledge*, the *hammer*, and the *axe*. On the great question now decided, we congratulate our Country. It will be a memorable era in the history of the United States."

Again, before the end of many days, his extatic emotions broke out in the following manner: —

ALL 'S WELL!

Is still the watchword of the Centinel, notwithstanding all the croakings and abuse of the Ravens of the Chronicle. Let us trace the truth.

"ALL IS WELL"

With America's guardian friend, THE PRESIDENT. He is now satisfied in seeing the great end of all his toils and sufferings attained — the Peace and Independence of his country secured.

"ALL IS WELL"

With the constituted authorities of the Union — the first and second branches having given being to the *Instrument of Peace;* and a majority of the "*immediate* Representatives" of the People have confirmed its existence by making for its support the most ample appropriations.

"ALL IS WELL"

With the *State Governments.* Their duty is *easy*, and the taxes of their constituents *light.*

"ALL IS WELL"

With the *Yeomanry* of the United States. They have prayed for the continuance of peace, and their prayers have been heard. The labors of their hands prosper and flourish. They have no burdens but those they wish to bear, as men interested in the support of good government and order. They have borne the *toils* of *war;* they are now reaping the *fruits* of *peace.*

"ALL IS WELL"

With the *Merchants.* They have, as with one voice, prayed as the Farmers have prayed, and have been heard as they have been heard. *Peace* still continues to heap blessings on their enterprize. Every tide wafts them riches. Every gale in every climate swells their canvas.

"ALL IS WELL"

With the *Mechanics.* They, too, with the Farmers and Merchants have prayed for Peace, and been heard. The sound of every instrument of *handicraft* and *industry* is heard from the rising to the setting sun, from the St. Croix to the St. Mary's. The reward of their laborious toils is sure; and the industrious man now sees the yearly accumulation of his property with redoubled satisfaction, for he *knows* that under the reign of good order, law, and government, it will be *secured* to him.

"ALL IS WELL"

With the honest American *Seamen,* maugre all the *lies* of the *lying Aurora* and *copying Chronicle.* * * * * *

"ALL IS WELL"

With the *Great Body of the People of the United States.* Nine tenths of them have given their voice for Peace. Peace is secured to them, and under the reign of Peace their skill, industry, and enterprize, will tell the world that with them "*all is well.*"

"ALL IS WELL"

With the fair *Daughters of America.* Their boding fears of war are dissipated. Their husbands, fathers, sons, and sweethearts will not now be called from domestic life to encounter the perils of warfare. Each hour shall bring them fresh enjoyments, and in every instance of the prosperity of their country, they will tell truly that "*all is well.*"

When General Washington, at the close of the year 1796, declined a re-election to the office of President, the Centinel warmly and zealously advocated the election of John Adams, and was a faithful supporter of his administration. With the commencement of that administration, the war between the two political parties grew more intensely hot and bitter. The conduct of the ruling powers in France, — the attempts of the French diplomatic agents in our sea-ports, to fit out vessels of war to prey on the commerce of Great-Britain, — their insulting opposition to the laws of the country, — and, above all, the spoliations committed by French privateers on our merchant vessels, and the indignities offered to our envoys in Paris by the French Directory, were topics which had excited the most acrid feelings of the federal party; while, if not directly approved, they were viewed with great lenity by the opposite party. In 1797, the subject of permitting American merchant vessels to arm and defend themselves, was agitated in the public newspapers, and petitions, from various quarters, were sent to Congress in favor of the measure. The editor of the Centinel was among the foremost to urge the fitting out of an armed force for protection. Several articles were furnished by correspondents; the following is one of his own, and may serve as a specimen of its numerous kindred: —

ARM! OR STARVE! The Jacobins to a man are opposed to *arming* our vessels, or fitting out a single ship of war. They well know, that owing to French *gun boat piracies*, our mechanics and artificers are almost starving; and that the moment Congress gives leave to our merchants to arm, and orders our naval yards to commence building new ships, that they will find full employment — THIS IS FACT! The moment the news arrives that the merchants shall have liberty to arm their vessels, not an axe, hammer, or mechanic implement will be idle. Business will assume its activity: and the music of the cunning workman will be heard on all our wharves. The French have broken down every barrier of the treaties made "*in the name of the most holy and undivided Trinity:*" They have declared, in the teeth of those treaties and the laws of nations, that the ships of all countries, kindred, and climes, shall be a good prize to them, if they have a bale of *English Goods* on board, and bound from or to any port. Those treaties and the laws of nations give belligerent powers the right to search neutral vessels. But as the French have declared by their late decree, that they were null and void, we have no right to be governed by them, as they respect France; but to treat their citizens as we would pirates.

The ninth of May, this year, by appointment of President Adams, was observed as a national fast. The Centinel, issued on the morning of that day, contained the editor's recommendation to an observance of the day in a strictly religious manner. "There is surely, (said he,) at this moment, a peculiar fitness and propriety in this solemn act of public devotion. When the mad ambition of a foreign nation threatens our liberty and independence, — when, notwithstanding the repeated efforts of our Executive, to continue to us the inestimable blessings of peace, we have too much reason to dread that war, with all its train of calamities is at hand; — it highly becomes us to offer up our supplications, that our country may be protected from all the dangers that threaten us, and that the American people may be united in those bonds of amity and mutual confidence, and inspired with that vigor and fortitude, by which they have, in times past, been so highly distinguished. And although we have abundant cause to humble ourselves before the throne of Heaven, to acknowledge our dependence on the blessings of Providence; we would not be unmindful that we have also ample reasons for rendering our devout and fervent Thanksgivings for the unrivaled happiness and prosperity which we have hitherto enjoyed. While the old nations of Europe have been daily witnesses of the most horrid scenes of bloodshed and devastation, we have been suffered in peace and tranquility, and under the best constitution of government enjoyed by any nation on earth, to arrive to a point of national strength and opulence, never before attained by any country in so short a space of time."

If any discrepance should be thought to exist between the sentiments here expressed and those of the last preceding extract, it must be accounted for by that fervency of patriotism which avails itself of various and sometimes conflicting arguments, to effect a favorite object.

As an offset to the "Psalm for Fast Day," which had been published in the Chronicle,* the Centinel gave the following as

THE JACOBIN'S PSALM,

For Fast Day — *to the tune of Psalm* 148*th.*

Ye tribes diminished join,
With Jacobinic prayer,
To curse the powers divine,
And earthly powers that are:
And let, this day,
All Democrats,
And owls, and rats,
Shout heaven away.

Thy voice, oh! J——n, †
Oft tried in wicked wiles,
Raise loud, with G——n, †
And noted, simple G——s, †
Thou V—n-m too, †
Half wise as G—s, †
Whose wit beguiles,
The tempest brew.

The French Republic stands
On drunken pillars five,
Upraised with palsied hands,
And scarcely kept alive.

* See vol. i. p. 283. † Jefferson, Gallatin, Giles, Varnum, Giles.

Directory speaks—
And justice flies,
And honor dies;
The bubble breaks.

They move the crazy wheels•
Of governmental jar:
Plunder their coffers fills,
And plunder prompts the war.
Ye few who 've chains,
Join heart and hand,
And firmly stand
By Gallic chains.

Let our ignoble race,
A patriotic few,
When Satan's arms embrace,
Loud shout the cry and hue.
For *France*, for *France*,
We'll boldly bawl,
And, one and all,
We'll join the dance.

O praise our Gallic friends,
However vile they are:
Lo, now our party ends,
Let us for *France* prepare.
The honest tribes
We cheat no more;
Our day is o'er;
And gone our bribes.

Columbia's guillotine
Will find each patriot head:
We'll go, by night unseen,
Glide o'er the ocean's bed.
Our hopes are gone,
Our Dev'l forsakes,
Destruction takes,
For Heaven we've none.

Ye Gallic Printers, strain
Your last, your languid cry;
You've curst both God and men,
Now curse yourselves and die.

Quick off we'll creep,
  Or stony gaol
  Won't surely fail
Our limbs to keep.

Congress, your wrath forego;
  We're punished now enough;
Nor send, in gondalo,
  Our patriot bodies off.
    We'll drive full well
      Our honest selves,
      Like subtle elves,
    To *France* or hell.

Ye clouds of dust and smoke,
  Ye lightnings, in your ire,
Our sorry gullets choke,
  And blast us with your fire.
    Our game is up;
      Our shame and sin
      Shall settle in
    Oblivion's cup.

The year 1798 has been signalized by the opponents of Adams's administration as the *Era of the Black Cockade;* — perhaps not inappropriately, as that badge was generally worn by the Federalists of Massachusetts. Russell, it has been said, was the instigator of the fashion. I know not how that may be; but the first allusion to it, that I remember, was in the Centinel of July 4, as follows: —

It has been repeatedly recommended, that our citizens wear in their hats on the day of Independence, the American Cockade, (which is a *Rose*, composed of black ribbon, with a white button, or fastening) and that the Ladies should add to the attraction of their dress (the Ladies' cockade should be a *white rose*,) this symbol of their attachment to the government, which cherishes and protects them — either on their breasts or in their bonnets. The measure is innocent; but the effect will be highly important. It will add cement to the *Union*, which so generally and so happily exists. Every cockade will be another edition of the *Declaration of Independence*, and the demonstration of it, by this national emblem now, will be as highly laudable as the display of the immortal instrument of 1776 was then: Those who signed the Address to the President are pledged to display this evidence of it to the world—and they may be assured, that the influence of their example in this measure will be productive of as great good, as the influence of their names was on the paper. All those, who have not had opportunity to sign the address, and who feel themselves Independent Americans, cannot hesitate to show by some outward mark, that they love their country better than any other in the world; this mark ought to be the black cockade. The Ladies, we understand, are universally in favor of the measure; and if they lead, who will not follow?

To those who object, (if there be any,) on account of singularity or novelty, it is only necessary to say, that the custom is sanctioned by antiquity, and has met the approbation of the great, the wise, and the good, in all ages.

The next Centinel says,—"The Jacobins have the impudence to say, that the people of Boston were really divided, and they give as a proof, that not more than half of them wear the American Cockade. This being the case, let every Bostonian, attached to the constitution and government of the United States, immediately mount the COCKADE, and swear that he will not relinquish it, until the infamous projects of the external and internal enemies of our country shall be destroyed." A few days afterward, the editor again touches on his favorite project, thus:—"The Cockade is generally worn by every class of citizens in almost every town in the United States. It is considered as a token of patriotism and union. It will enliven our commencement at Cambridge this day. It will receive the smiles and approbation of the Fair Daughters of Columbia; and will convince the Gallic spies, now in our country, that we are not a divided people."

It was in this summer that the President appointed Washington to the office of Commander-in-Chief of the army, which Congress had authorized to be raised, in consequence of the troubles with France. Russell must have ransacked the English vocabulary to find all the superlatives, which he used in praise of Washington's patriotism, as manifested in accepting the appointment. He published three thousand copies of the letter of acceptance, and distributed them in various parts of the commonwealth. A writer in the Salem Gazette complimented him on this "act of patriotism and liberality," to which Russell replied, — "The editor of the Centinel has but a small claim to the act of patriotism acknowledged in this article. He has on former occasions made sacrifices ; but a number of federal patriotic gentlemen have superseded him. They have, by liberal subscriptions, voluntarily defrayed the expense of circulating several thousand pamphlets in the interior, where the people are less in the habit of reading newspapers. These gentlemen directed the publication of General Washington's immortal letter, in hand-bills ; above three thousand of which have been sent into the back towns, the eastern and southern shores ; and we are happy in hearing that they have added fuel to the patriotic fire of the times, and that numbers of the reverend clergy, never weary in well-doing, have read them to their congregations after divine service. It is second only to inspiration."

On his way from the seat of government to his residence in Massachusetts, during this year, President Adams was, in all the principal towns, greeted with tokens of love and approbation. Addresses, fraught with patriotic feeling and federal principles, and his replies to them, make an imposing display in the Centinel, and are frequently accompanied with an editorial note. Russell said, in one of his congratulant paragraphs,—"President Adams may be denominated the American Herschel. He certainly discovered the baleful *comet* of French perfidy many months before his fellow-citizens, who now see it plainly."

The words "Massachusetts Federalist" had been recently added to the title of the Centinel. The political communications increased in number, and, if possible, were more severe on the opponents of the Federal Administration. It was about this time also, that the Editor began to compile "A Brief Review of the Political State of the World," a task of considerable labor, which was continued annually for a number of years, and which usually occupied two or three columns in each of several successive papers, near the close of each year. As a vehicle of useful and accurate intelligence, the Centinel secured to itself a reputation superior to that of any other American newspaper. Russell had a peculiar mode of condensing and arranging the contents of foreign journals, and presenting, in the most readable shape, all the prominent incidents of the war, that then agitated almost the whole of Europe. The files of the Centinel, from 1790 to 1815 contain the materials for a better history of the French Revolution and of the wars, which grew out of the attempt of other European powers to re-establish *legitimacy* in France, than any that I have had the privilege of reading. The movements and operations of the contending armies are described with a vividness, that brings the reader directly to the scene of operation. We see the roads, in which the armies marched from city to city; the bridges they passed, and then destroyed; and the localities where they encamped. Russell had a *military* taste, and it was as natural for him to take his map and follow the track of an army, and to record all the minute incidents connected with it, as it was to breathe. And he always kept his account *posted up* to the latest moment, so that he was always ready for a new arrival of intelligence, and would, not unfrequently, venture upon predictions of events, which the next arrival would often announce as historical facts.

Through the whole of this period, and for some years afterward, the Centinel was an indispensable source of news for the country printers, — every one of whom relied upon it for matter to fill up the news department of his paper. Subscribers in the country also increased beyond all precedent. It was every where known and every where read; and, if industry in collecting and fidelity in republishing information, that was important to be known, are worthy of credit, never was popularity more honestly earned.

In January and February, 1799, the editor of the Centinel made a severe attack on John Bacon, a senator from Berkshire, who voted against the Report of the legislative committee on the *Virginia and Kentucky Resolutions*: — "The Hon. Mr. Bacon (he said) the solitary *Nay* of our Senate, the advocate of Alien Legislators, the Gallatins of Geneva and the Lyons of Hibernia, was once *a preacher of the Gospel.* How well he minded his Bible, which, before the French Revolution, was the rule and guide of his faith, will be seen by comparing his speeches with the injunction in Deuteronomy: — '*One from among thy brethren shalt thou set over thee; thou mayest not set a* STRANGER *over thee* which is not thy brother.' It was certainly in character for the privy counselor of Daniel Shays and Luke Day to vote against Sedition Acts." This was followed by other paragraphs, alluding to the private history of Bacon, in terms adapted to provoke irritating and bitter retorts. Bacon was defended in the Chronicle, and, probably, many of the paragraphs in that paper were written or dictated by him. But Russell was not disposed to let off the object of his political vengeance, without some severer blow than an off-hand paragraph; and, accordingly, he published, in the Centinel of February 27, the following letter, — rather more elaborate and carefully constructed than his ordinary writings: —

The Hon JOHN BACON, Esq.

SIR,

In discharging my Editorial duty, I have been necessitated to notice your public conduct in life, and in the Senate of *Massachusetts;* and to animadvert on your *Speech*, printed in the papers. Your political turpitude in advocating the *infallibility* of *Virginia* and *Kentucky* disorganizers; and your arrogance in attaching unworthy motives to your compeers of the *Senate*, have rendered you a proper mark for censure or ridicule. You have not escaped censure; and you have replied to the observations made on you. For my part, I am not displeased that the cursory notice taken of you in the CENTINEL, has *disturbed* the *Stoicism* which is your boast, and which, in fact, is the *most permanent ingredient* in your composition; and the public really considers your lengthy exculpatory address and certificates in the last *Chronicle*, as the contortions of a *sorely* wounded adder.

In a late CENTINEL you were implicated of inconsistency (or in other words of *Clerical Jacobinism*) when a *Preacher of the Gospel* in this town; — of Toryism in the "times which *tried* men's souls," and of disaffection to the Independence and real prosperity of your country, at the present moment.

Would time permit, I could easily bring a cloud of evidence in support of every one of these imputations. Perhaps it is unnecessary.

The certificate of the *Old South Church*, of 1781, I consider as amply sufficient of itself to satisfy every one of the "*inconsistency*" of your doctrines and creeds on theological subjects. The liberality of the worshipers at that Church, would ever induce them to exercise towards you the offices of *Christian Charity* and brotherly love; but I know from general remark, that such was the "*inconsistency*" of these doctrines arising from the *singular* (not to say *perverse*) bias of your nature, that when the routine of duty called you to the desk, and your *real* sentiments were known, you had the mortification of holding forth to comparatively *empty pews* and *solitary galleries*. Your love for dabbling in *troubled waters* impelled you to seek a *public disputation* in Mr. *Croswell's* meeting-house, with Mr. MURRAY: and there are many living evidences of the miserable predicament your "*inconsistencies*" then placed you in. You plumply denied the *existence* in the Bible of a text quoted by Mr. MURRAY; and you gave ample evidence of your chagrin, when he immediately referred you to the passage in the sacred volume then on the desk. — You left the field of controversy; — and your partizans, mortified at the imbecility of their champion, assailed the victorious disputant with *something more like* ARGUMENT than any thing advanced by you — *brick-bats* and *rotten eggs*: — but to show the contempt in which Mr. M. held your opposition, when one of *those arguments* struck the pulpit just below, he pleasantly said, "*Here we have it, brethren, Bacon and eggs.*"

To the implication of *Toryism* in 1775, you say "*there are too many living witnesses of your character and conduct in this respect, both in and out of the Legislature to leave the least occasion for any reply.*" This is a true *Baconian* flourish to *get under* an allegation. You certainly are not capable of a neutral character; I could, therefore, have wished you had adduced *some* evidence of your *whiggism* at that time; — For my part, I have turned over the public records of those days, when the Pulpits were the Citadels of *Patriotism* as well as *Piety* — and the Clergy the equal champions of both; — for evidence of *your* attachment to any other than the then arbitrary government of *Great-Britain;* and amidst the groves of laurels which encircled the brows of the *Clerical Heroes* of those trying times, I have seen no chaplet whereof the Rev. Mr. BACON has the *least claim* to the *smallest sprig*. You mention the Legislature. — It is perhaps fortunate for you, that during the debates on the *Virginia* Resolutions, the galleries were not open; — as, thereby I have been deprived of the knowledge of some hints of Toryism, which I have been told, were pretty plainly insinuated against you. How well you succeeded in getting rid of them you best know.

That at the present time, you are opposed to the best interests of your country; — that you have betrayed the trust reposed in you by your constituents; and that you appear to be as ill qualified to exercise the office of a *Legislator* as a *Clergyman;* — and to have as little real knowledge of the Constitution of your country, as you appear to have had of the Bible, in your controversy with Mr. MURRAY; — I could adduce your late vote in the *Senate* opposed to the entire body of the *Senators* of *Massachusetts*, and to 117 of the *House of Representatives*, without including those of the minority who declared their detestation of principles you so unblushingly advocated; — Could bring forward the recent election of the Hon. Mr. SEDGWICK to a seat in Congress; and need only to contrast the incongruities and follies of your Speech with the Constitution and Laws of my country. —— But, Sir, attention to other duties will not at present permit me. At another time, I may find leisure, if the subject should acquire adequate importance — to pay some attention to these particulars; to reply to some of your statements of the conversation between us; but never to notice your innuendoes or epithets. As long as your political conduct shall partake of its present qualities, you may depend, Sir, of always finding a surgeon who will probe your wounds to the quick, in

Feb. 26, 1799. THE EDITOR OF THE CENTINEL.

Another specimen of Russell's style in his political controversies is the following, — certainly not the mildest, nor even the most acrimonious, that might be selected: —

THE FRETFUL PORCUPINE

Is sore at the necessary punishment the CENTINEL has inflicted on him for his outrageous abuse of THE PRESIDENT of the United States. It was the first time we recollect to have noticed the "*Blackguard*," — his private personalities we ever deemed beneath attention; but we could not have justified it to our consciences, in passing by the virulent invectives of this incendiary against the Chief Magistrate of the Union. Knowing the ground he had lost by his conduct, and boiling over with diabolical malice towards all who have had any hand in opposing his audacity, and chastising his insolence, he quits the original subject, and indulges his native blackguardism in distorting new ones; and has been reduced to the pitiable necessity of quibbling on an introduction of ours to a French State Paper. We detest the conduct of *France* as much as this alien can pretend to; and we were active vindicators of the cause of Federalism, when this intruder was uttering curses and imprecations against every thing American. Yet even this spurious exotic has the effrontery to call himself a Federalist at the same time he superciliously boasts himself a *subject* of the British monarchy.

Success has made this quill-driving animal vain and conceited. He is so swoln by it as to become totally blind to his own situation:—Nay, he is ignorant, in common with other brutes, of his creation and cause of existence. COBBETT was never encouraged and supported by the Federalists as a solid, judicious writer in their cause; but was kept merely to hunt Jacobinic *foxes*, *skunks*, and *serpents*. The Federalists found the Jacobins had the *Aurora*, *Argus*, and *Chronicle*, through which they ejected their mud, filth, and venom, and attacked and blackened the best characters the world ever boasted; and they perceived that these vermin were not to be operated on by reason or decency. It was therefore thought *necessary* that the opposite party should keep, and *feed* a *suitable beast* to hunt down these *skunks* and *foxes;* and "*the fretful Porcupine*" was selected for this business. This imported, or transported beast has been kept as gentlemen keep a fierce *bull Dog*, to guard his house and property against thieves, Jacobins and Frenchmen, and as such he has been a good and faithful dog, and has been *fed* and caressed accordingly. It is true he has sometimes, as most dogs will, growled at his masters, and as "STERNE'S *puppy*" was wont to do, has darted at the venerable PRIESTLEY; but as he has evinced an inveterate antipathy to all Frenchmen, he has been excused. However, as he grows more and more fretful for want of *food*, (as may be seen by his modest, polite, decent, civil, gentlemanlike *dunning*, or rather *bullying* advertisement to his *feeders*) some think we should *shorten his chain;* or send him home again to *England*, to starve, or feed on Jacobin vermin there; or else transport the "*Hedge-Hog*" to *Boston*, where the *Board of Health* would soon order him to be taken by the tail, and thrown into the dock at low tide, as a common nuisance.

We know not what the "*Hedge-Hog*" means by "*Genet-feasting*."

This was followed by others equally *gentle* and equally rich in words of invective.

An event now occurred, which afforded the editor of the Centinel an opportunity of renewing his expressions of admiration for the character of Washington. The publication, which gave an account of his death, was printed with a broad, black border, and to the annunciation was added,—"How shall we express our grief on this distressing event! with what language shall we give vent to the full feelings of our heart! It is true, he had reached the summit of human honor, and was ripe for immortal glory. It is true, he had retired, in a degree, from public office to the rural walks of life. It is true, the government of our country has devolved on wise and faithful men. Yet WASHINGTON was still our guardian, our pride, and our defence. Amidst the threatening storms of foreign violence — amidst the more dangerous convulsions of party rage, it was still our consolation that WASHINGTON lived. His reputation was a bulwark and a shield, under whose broad and protecting shade America reposed with unbounded confidence. He led our armies amidst the perils of revolution to victory. His virtues, his wisdom, his name alone, kept the jarring elements of our confederation from bursting asunder, hushed to peace the voice of discord, and consolidated these States under one firm and fair fabric of government. For these purposes, Heaven kindly *lent* him to us — to make us a nation — and to render us prosperous, powerful, and happy. Having accomplished his high errand, *he* is now recalled and *we* are overwhelmed with grief."

The death of Washington produced a universal expression of regret, and political writers seemed to forget their animosities, while they were paying funeral honors to the greatest man of the age; but when the first week or two of mourning was over, they returned to the war with renewed vigor. The Centinel was liberal and sincere in its lamentations, and for several weeks kept a registration of the funeral ceremonies that were observed throughout the nation.

The approach of an election for governor of Massachusetts, in the spring of 1800, awakened all the slumbering embers of party strife. The Federalists succeeded in electing their candidate. Defeat excited the other party to unwarrantable crimination, and that was, of course, met with federal recrimination, no less fierce and unpolished. An election of a President of the United States was also pending, and the contest between the friends of Mr. Adams and Mr. Jefferson respectively, was conducted with barbarous ferocity. Many of the charges against either candidate were made in language that could hardly be tolerated, even if quoted as a matter of mere curiosity. Epithets of the coarsest character were exchanged, without care and without remorse. The editor of the Centinel was not of a temper to take a blow with meekness, and if force was not added to the returning stroke, his disposition was not in fault. The republican party of the *nation* succeeded in the election, but Massachusetts gave her vote for Adams. After it became known that Mr. Jefferson or Mr. Burr was to be the President from the fourth of March, 1801, and that the choice must be made by the House of Representatives, the Centinel advocated the election of the latter, — in which it was sustained by some able writers.

The following Parody appeared in the Centinel in February, 1801. I have no doubt that it was the offspring of Russell's own prolific imagination, which was always on the look-out, or busy in contriving something, wherewith to annoy his political adversaries: —

THE JACOBIN UNIVERSAL PRAYER.

Parent of ill! in every State,
  In every Club adored —
By small, by wicked, and by great,
  Of mischief sovereign lord, —

Thou great curst cause! but yet obeyed,
  Who all my thoughts confined,
To follow Mischief's wayward trade,
  To Virtue's precepts blind, —

Yet taught me, in this dark estate,
  To choose the wrong from right,
And binding Nature fast in Fate,
  Kept Virtue out of sight; —

What Conscience dictates to be done,
  Or warns me not to do,
That teach me more than Heaven to shun,
  This more than Hell pursue.

What lessons thy free bounty gives
  Let me not cast away,
For thou art paid when man deceives —
  To cheat is to obey.

Yet not to *this* contracted place
  Thy precepts let me bound,
But let me pillage all our race,
  And mischief deal around.

Let then this weak, unknowing hand
  Be taught thy bolt to throw,
And deal damnation round the land
  On each I think my foe.

If I am wrong, O teach my heart
  Still in the wrong to stay;
If I am right, thy grace impart
  To lead my steps astray.

Bless me alike with foolish pride,
  And impious discontent,
At aught Heaven's bounty has denied,
  Or aught its goodness lent.

Teach me to laugh at others' wo;
  To tell the faults I see;
To others hatred let me show,
  They friendship show to me.

Base though I am, not wholly so;
  Since governed by thy will,
O lead me whereso'er I go,
  And be my Mentor still.

This day be noise and strife my lot,
  Be others' wealth my own, —
Thou knowest if best bestowed or not,
  And let thy will be done.

To thee, whose temple is each space
  That 's bad beneath the skies —
One chorus let us Jacos raise,
  One common ruin rise.

The fourth of March arrived, and on that day the Centinel appeared with the following

Monumental Inscription.

" *That life is long which answers Life's great end.*"

YESTERDAY EXPIRED,
Deeply regretted by MILLIONS of grateful Americans,
And by *all* GOOD MEN,
The FEDERAL ADMINISTRATION
Of the
GOVERNMENT of the *United States:*
Animated by
A WASHINGTON, an ADAMS;—a HAMILTON, KNOX,
PICKERING, WOLCOTT, M'HENRY, MARSHALL,
STODDERT and DEXTER.
Æt. 12 years.

Its death was occasioned by the
Secret Arts and Open Violence,
Of Foreign and Domestic Demagogues:
Notwithstanding its whole Life
Was devoted to the Performance of every Duty
to promote
The UNION, CREDIT, PEACE, PROSPERITY,
HONOR, and
FELICITY OF ITS COUNTRY.

At its birth it found
The Union of the States dissolving like a Rope of snow;

It hath left it
Stronger than the Threefold cord.

It found the United States
Bankrupts in Estate and Reputation;
It hath left them
Unbounded in Credit; and respected throughout the World.
It found the *Treasuries* of the United States and
Individual States *empty;*
It hath left them *full and overflowing.*
It found
All the Evidences of Public Debts worthless as rags;
It hath left them
More valuable than Gold and Silver.

It found
The United States *at war* with the
Indian Nations;—
It hath concluded *Peace* with them all.
It found
The Aboriginals of the soil *inveterate
enemies of the whites;*
It hath exercised towards them *justice* and *generosity*,
And *hath left them fast friends.*
It found
Great-Britain in possession of all
the *Frontier Posts;*
It hath demanded their surrender, and
it leaves them in the possession
of the United States.
It found
The American sea-coast utterly *defenseless;*
It hath left it *fortified.*
It found our *Arsenals* empty; and *Magazines* decaying;
It hath left them full of *ammunition*
and *warlike Implements;*
It found our country dependent on Foreign Nations
for *engines of defense;*
It hath left
Manufactories of *Cannon* and *Musquets* in full work.
It found
The American Nation at *War* with

Algiers, *Tunis*, and *Tripoli;*
It hath
Made *Peace* with them all.
It found
American Freemen in Turkish slavery, where
they had languished in chains for years:
It hath
Ransomed them, and set them free.

It found the war-worn, invalid *Soldier starving* from want;
Or, like BELISARIUS, *begging his refuse meat from door to door;*
It hath left
Ample provision for the regular payment of his *pension.*

It found
The *Commerce* of our country confined
almost to *Coasting Craft;*
It hath left it
Whitening every sea with its canvas, and
cheering every clime with its *stars.*

It found our
Mechanics and *Manufacturers* idle in
the streets for want of employ;
It hath left them
Full of business, prosperous, contented and happy.
It found
The Yeomanry of the country oppressed with unequal
taxes; — their farms, houses and barns
decaying; their cattle selling at the
sign-posts; and they driven to
desperation and *Rebellion;*
It hath left
Their coffers in cash; their houses in repair; their
barns full; their farms overstocked; and their
produce commanding ready money,
and a high price.
In short —
It found them *poor, indigent Malcontents;*
It hath left them
Wealthy Friends to Order and Good Government.

It found
The United States *deeply in debt to*
France and *Holland;*
It hath *paid* ALL *the demands* of the former, and
the principal part of the latter.
It found the Country in a ruinous
Alliance with *France;*
It hath honorably dissolved the connexion,
and set us free.

It found
The United States without a swivel
on float *for their defense;*
It hath left
A NAVY — composed of Thirty-four ships of war;
mounting 918 guns; and manned
by 7350 gallant tars.

It found
The EXPORTS of our country, a mere song, in value:
It hath left them worth
Above SEVENTY MILLIONS of Dollars per annum.
In one word,
It found AMERICA *disunited*, *poor*, *insolvent*,
weak, *discontented*, and *wretched.*
It hath left HER
United, *wealthy*, *respectable*, *strong*,
happy and *prosperous.*
Let the faithful Historian, in after times say these things
of its Successor, if it can.
And yet — notwithstanding all these services and
blessings, there are found
Many, very many, weak, degenerate Sons,
who, lost to virtue, to gratitude,
and patriotism,
Openly exult, that this Administration
is no more.
And that
The "Sun of Federalism is set for ever."
"Oh shame, where is thy blush?"

As one Tribute of Gratitude in these Times,
This MONUMENT
Of the Talents and Services of the deceased;
is raised by

March 4th, 1801. The Centinel.

That Russell, and the Federalists generally, believed that the accession of Mr. Jefferson to the Presidency was the forerunner of great national calamity, there can be no doubt. The Monumental Inscription was followed by a note, saying, — "With this day begins the EIGHTEENTH year since the birth of the Centinel — and, at no period, during that time, hath it enjoyed a greater share of patronage and assistance than it now enjoys. We shall demonstrate our gratitude therefor, by the faithful discharge of our duty; without vaulting or tottering: Especially now, when every thing dear and venerable is exposed to be undermined or battered down. As a Centinel, we will sound the alarm, and faithfully make report of our discoveries of the disposition, force, and movements of our country's foes. Further we need not say."

During the whole of Mr. Jefferson's administration, the Centinel was the undeviating opponent of every one of his measures. The reduction of the navy, the non-intercourse scheme, the embargo, and the gun-boat system, — all, — met the decided reprobation of Mr. Russell and the leading Federalists. The embargo law, which was unlimited as to the time of its operation, was disapproved of by many of the Republicans, but the policy was sustained by the Chronicle and the other papers of the party, and this led to further and more virulent attacks and vituperable accusations. The arrival of the law in Boston was announced in the Centinel in the sportive paragraph, which follows. It was afterwards treated in a less gentle manner: —

THE GENERALS. General *Blockade*, General *Resolution*, and even General *War* have not made more noise in Europe, than has been recently made here by General *Embargo*, who arrived last evening from Washington. He has been rather tardy in his movements; some of his *non-commissioned* suite having been in town two days, and his principal Aid, Major *Non-Importation* having taken up winter quarters here some weeks before. We know not who are in the *train* of the General; but it is expected he will be followed by his other Aids, Major *Poverty* and Captain *Starvation*. Several honest folks are much alarmed at his visit, particularly the houses of Messrs. *Codfish & Co.* of Marblehead, Commercial Point, Cape Cod, &c.; Messrs. *Prime Beef, Pork & Co.* a respectable establishment, in the interior; and Messrs. *Drawbacks, Mechanics, Mariners & Co.* of this and other commercial towns. The General is considered as a very unwelcome guest; especially as it has been hinted we shall not probably be rid of him, until he is driven away by General *Peace*.

In consequence, it was said, of some evasions of the embargo law, an additional act was passed, authorizing the absolute detention of all vessels bound coastwise, if any suspicion existed that there was any purpose of evasion. The President wrote a letter to the governor of Massachusetts, empowering him to grant certificates in favor of any merchant, in whom the governor had confidence, to transport flour from one port in the United States to another, in order that the inhabitants might not suffer any inconvenience from a deficient supply of bread. Russell accompanied the publication of this letter, with the following: —

UP TO THE HOB. On our first page will be found an *extraordinary* missive from President Jefferson to Governor Sullivan, appointing him *Dispenser of favors and Minister of Starvation for Massachusetts*. This bold stroke to starve a people into democracy has been received by them as it deserved; and is universally execrated as a decree, which Bonaparte would scarcely dare to issue. We wish the hirelings, who defend this new stretch of power, would inform the public, on what article of the Constitution, or Law of the land, power can be given for such purposes. It seems the new office is not general among the governors. The new *Grand Dignitaries of the Empire* are only the Governors of Orleans, Georgia, South-Carolina, Massachusetts, and New-Hampshire.

In 1811, when Mr. Gerry was governor of the commonwealth, the Legislature made a new division of the districts for the election of representatives to Congress. Both branches had then a democratic majority. For the purpose of securing a democratic representative, an absurd and singular arrangement of towns in the county of Essex was made to compose a district. Russell took a map of the county, and designated by a particular coloring the towns thus selected. He then hung the map on the wall of his editorial closet. One day, Gilbert Stuart, the celebrated painter, looked at the map, and said the towns, which Russell had thus distinguished, formed a picture resembling some monstrous animal. He took a pencil, and, with a few touches, added what might be supposed to represent claws. "There," said Stuart, "that will do for a salamander." Russell, who was busy with his pen, looked up at the hideous figure, and exclaimed, "Salamander! call it Gerrymander." The word became a proverb, and, for many years, was in popular use among the Federalists as a term of reproach to the democratic Legislature, which had distinguished itself by this act of political turpitude. An engraving of the "Gerrymander" was made, and hawked about the State, which had some effect in annoying the democratic party.

The "Berlin and Milan Decrees" of the French emperor, and the retaliatory "Orders in Council" of the British government, had seriously injured the commerce of the United States, and were judged, by many, as good cause for war. Russell, as the organ of the federal party, made apologies for the latter,—considering them as justified by the former, and he was, therefore, opposed to war with England for any of the causes, which then existed, though the impressment of seamen from American merchant ships was a crying evil, often practised with great insolence and injustice. War was declared in June, 1812. With what spirit the Declaration was received, may be seen from the announcement in the Centinel:—

PREDICTIONS VERIFIED. The awful event so often anticipated by us as the inevitable effect of the infatuated policy of the Rulers of the American People has now been realized,—and the worst of measures has emerged from its secret womb in the worst of forms. A naked and unqualified WAR is declared to exist between England, Ireland, and their dependencies, and the President is authorized to use the whole land and naval forces of the United States, "*to carry the same into effect.*" This *Declaration of War* is accompanied by a *Presidential Manifesto*, both of which are given in this day's Centinel. They are now before the American People, who will sit in judgement upon them. We say nothing of the *Law;* but we call upon the freemen of the United States to read the Presidential Manifesto—to read it carefully—and, as they read, to commune with their hearts and understandings on the assertions and conclusions it contains: To compare them with those solemn truths and sober facts, which their eyes have seen and their ears heard: To inquire of the Merchant, the Insurer, the Navigator, touching the truth of the many unqualified assertions in the Manifesto respecting their immediate concerns: To do all this truly, fairly, and impartially: And then, in the presence of that God of truth, who knoweth the heart, pronounce,—and boldly pronounce,—Whether these assertions are Truths, Falsehoods, or Prevarications:—Or, whether, if true, they warrant the naked Declaration of War, in which they and their dearest interests are now involved.

In 1812, the Federalists supported Dewitt Clinton of New-York, for President, in opposition to Mr. Madison. Obliged, as the organ of his party to follow its dictation, Russell gave the nomination his support, but it was not cheerful and hearty. It was a measure that he could never relish, and he really took but little interest in the election.

The progress of the war, though marked by some brilliant exploits of the navy, did not reconcile its opponents to its continuance. On the anniversary of the Declaration, a very able article in the Centinel exhibited the loss and gain in a manner which showed that the losses on our part greatly overbalanced the gain. This article stands as editorial, but internal evidence proves that it was not written by the editor. It is much too elaborate and philosophical to have emanated from his pen. The same paper says: —

MARK WELL. Every hour the WAR grows more vindictive and sanguinary; and the pretended *object*, for which it was waged, more hard to be obtained: — And though a *Pacific Embassy* is said to be on its voyage to Europe, every *syllable* uttered by the administration, and every *act* of its officers, appears intended to augment the ferocity of War, and to put peace at an irrecoverable distance. *People of America*, think on these solemn truths.

This was from the pen of Russell; and there can be no doubt that the following had the same origin: —

OBJECT OF THE WAR. The attention of the people is daily and hourly called to bloody recitals of events of the War, the losses of property, and the progress of loans and taxes to carry it on; and they inquire, What is the object of all this? All the reply that can be made to the inquiry, is, — *That all this waste of blood, property, and money, is to afford encouragement to British, Irish, and Jersey runaway sailors, to enter on board American vessels, and then to be* PROTECTED, *while they are underworking the native born American Seamen and Navigators, and thereby taking the bread from the mouths of their wives and children!* This is the great object of this War! This is what is called fighting for "*Sailors Rights and Free Trade.*"

Again, in a few weeks, a similar objurgatory paragraph says, — "The National Legislature terminated its extra session of ten weeks, on the second instant. This session was *especially* called for the purpose of adopting measures for the prosecution of an unnecessary and unjust WAR; and, by reference to the list of acts, it will readily be seen, that a broad foundation for the further Poverty and Ruin of the people is laid, through direct taxes and other internal taxes, and through loans and other ways and means, to carry on this wicked war. The House has been as subservient as even Bonaparte could wish; but the Senate have, in several instances, acted that independent part, which might have been calculated upon, from the very respectable accession of superior talents and worth to that branch of the Legislature. From a careful calculation and revision, it appears that 58,779,491 dollars is the least sum, which the war will cost to the end of the year 1813. Let the good people of this country seriously reflect upon this subject."

Neither Russell, nor his federal friends, had any confidence in the pacific declarations of the national government. The appointment of Mr. Gallatin as one of the envoys to negotiate a peace with Great-Britain, in 1813, was viewed with indignation. This gentleman had been Secretary of the Treasury from the accession of Mr. Jefferson. The Senate adopted a resolution, declaring his mission as envoy incompatible with his continuance at the head of the Treasury department. In reference to this occurrence, the Centinel said: —

We take no particular concern in the nomination of a Secretary of the Treasury for this appointment. It was within the discretion of the Executive; but we maintain that his holding both offices would be a reproach to the American character, already debased by permitting him to continue in one of them. It establishes the inference, either that the office of the Secretary of the Treasury is useless, and that his duties at the most critical period may be performed by proxy; or that this foreigner is the only man in the nation qualified for a place, which must be kept vacant until his return. No wonder that the American blood in the Senate of the United States was quickened in the veins of many who have generally supported the administration. We rejoice in this salutary hint to the President, and trust it is the precursor of a more important earnest of their determination to fulfill the objects of their creation, by acting as a high and independent branch of the government. . . . . They are in fact at issue, on many points, with a back stairs junto of mad men from the interior, speculators in Indian land, and dreamers of foreign conquest, which forms the *combatant* cabinet at Washington. They will of course be denounced. The court paper hardly preserves a *gossamer covering* over the chagrin and resentment of the palace. But we know the nature of the materials which compose the minority of that body; and we believe there is, among the majority, high-minded and honorable men, who will revere themselves.

In this style and temper, the editorials and communications in the Centinel were continued throughout the whole period of the War. All the successes of the army or navy were related in the language of exultation, and in a tone that showed that the record was made by a patriotic spirit. But it is believed, that not a word of apology or approbation of the proceedings of the government ever gained admission into its columns. The treaty of peace, signed in December, 1814, was hailed with the most joyous words of welcome; but no superfluous gratitude was thrown away upon the administration for its agency in producing it.

It was not long after the close of the war, that the federal party ceased to exist, *as* a party. The organization was kept up until the election of Mr. Munroe as President, but symptoms of dissolution had, for some time been apparent. In the summer of 1817, the President made a visit to New-England. His movements were every where hailed with expressions of satisfaction. His arrival in Massachusetts was signalized by flattering displays of loyalty, and by none more than those, who had been the violent opposers of Mr. Madison, and the rudest in their denunciations of Mr. Munroe as a member of Mr. Madison's administration, and especially in his capacity of Lieutenant-General of the United States army, — an office, which he held while he was also at the head of the Department of State. He was certainly treated with the most flattering attention during his stay in Boston, and by no one in a more distinguished manner than by Benjamin Russell. Let it not be understood, however, that Russell is here charged with exercising more servility than others. Many of the leading Federalists were equally forward in tendering to the President all the hospitality that the chief magistrate of the nation could demand or expect; and seemed resolved to take from the Republicans, or Democrats, all the credit of the civilities, which he received. There seemed, however, to exist a general desire that no party asperities should be manifested on the occasion; and the only indication of it, which appeared, was an Address, presented to the President, signed by seven of the leading Republicans, as a committee appointed for that purpose, by the republican members of the Legislature, which had then recently adjourned.

This union of old political enemies to honor the chief magistrate of the Union, was called, by the editor of the Centinel, the "Era of Good Feelings," — a phrase, which passed into a by-word, and was frequently quoted as a word of reproach, by those who clung to the federal organization. Some of the republican papers, which had been devoted to the Madisonian policy, and had supported the election of Mr. Munroe to the presidency, were a little provoked at the conduct of the Federalists, in bestowing so many attentions on him during his tour, and Russell came in for a full share of their sarcasm. One of them said, —

The President has probably by this time arrived at Niagara, from whence he is to proceed to Detroit, where we presume he will be waited upon by those celebrated Chiefs, *Walk-in-the-Water*, *Split-Log*, One-who-puts-his-foot-in-it, *Big-Elk*, and *Thunder-Storm*, with an address forwarded to them from Boston. Whether there is to be a grand *pap-poose review* we have not learned.

In a notice of this "exhibition of wit," the writer of which Russell thought was "a *sour-cider* carper," he said, — "If it has had no other effect than the mere *elicitation* of these *scintillations*, it were worth all the pains and expense; as it proves the existence of a *raw material* where no one ever dreamed of looking for it."

The course pursued by Russell in this matter, disaffected some, who had been his best supporters and most valuable aids as correspondents, — one of whom, at least, never forgave him, and would never after permit the Centinel to be left at his residence. But the power of the federal party was evidently declining. Russell was chairman of the Central Committee, and, in that capacity, as well as in that of editor, supported the nomination of a representative to Congress, who was an admitted republican in politics, and who was also nominated by the republican party. From this "Era of Good Feelings," the fate of the Columbian Centinel was sealed. Its decline, though not rapid, was perceptible, and it soon came to be disregarded as *authority*, in political circles.

On the President's message, at the opening of the next session of Congress, the Centinel said, — "It will be found to contain much interesting and satisfactory intelligence. . . . . The facts in the message are judiciously arranged; the style is as plain as the alphabet; and its frankness and total exemption from that diplomatic jargon, which so often '*mystified*' other Presidential State Papers, are not among the least of its merits."

I am not aware that Russell ever passed a word of censure upon any act of Mr. Munroe's administration, or upon that of Mr. J. Q. Adams, which succeeded it; but, on the contrary, all their public measures were approved, and some of them made the subjects of inflated encomium. In regard to the politics of the state of Massachusetts, a feeble opposition to the republican leaders was kept up for a few years. Under the advice, or dictation, of Mr. Russell, the Federalists nominated Judge Levi Lincoln as their candidate for governor of the commonwealth. He had previously received the nomination of the Republicans, — with whom, as a party, he had always been identified, — and declined, but accepted the nomination of the Federalists and was elected. I believe this was the last nomination made by the federal *party*. At the commencement of the administration of Mr. Adams, in 1825, an entire new organization of parties took place, and the adherents of Mr. Adams, took the name of "National Republicans," — a name, which a few years after, was discarded, and that of Whig, as a more euphonious and convenient designation, — took its place. The words "Massachusetts Federalist," which had formed a second descriptive title of the Centinel for more than twenty years, were also laid aside, for "American Federalist," as more truly indicative of its editor's attachment to the Union, without regard to party names or organizations. Mr. Russell was a sincere and hearty advocate for the election of John Quincy Adams to the Presidency in 1824, and for his re-election in 1828.

During the twenty years preceding this "Era of Good Feelings," the political communications in the Centinel were numerous, written with great ability, and with unqualified opposition to the administration of Mr. Jefferson, and frequently with implacable severity upon all its advocates and defenders. The editor was backed by gentlemen of the first talent in the commonwealth — gentlemen, who, as a select body, were called, by the Republicans, "the Essex Junto;" but — by whatever name, or whatever might have been the origin of this phrase, intended as an epithet of reproach, — were as honest and high-minded men, as ever lived. The memorable "Hartford Convention," of 1814, had some of these gentlemen among its prominent members; and the character, which Mr. H. G. Otis gave of that assemblage, when he said, that a body of purer and nobler-minded men would never meet again until the general assembly of the spirits of the just made perfect, — may be received as unexaggerated truth.

In the beginning of November, 1828, Mr. Russell sold the Centinel to Joseph T. Adams — a young gentleman, who had been educated for a lawyer, — and Thomas Hudson, — who had served a regular apprenticeship in the office, and had, for some years, been the foreman, and had the sole direction of the printing department. His address "TO THE PATRONS OF THE CENTINEL," was very brief. It merely introduced his successors, with a complimentary assurance of their patriotism, intelligence, and liberality, and added, —

Those, who have been acquainted with the arduous duties, which, with very little relaxation, the editor has performed for near half a century, need not be informed of the necessity, which requires the transfer, now announced.

With heart-felt gratitude and thanks for innumerable and unceasing favors, conferred upon the undersigned in all the mutations of the times, from the dark period of 1784 to the bright days of 1828, by his generous and indulgent subscribers, liberal and constant advertising friends, and highly talented correspondents; with a repetition of his earnest request that the patronage he has enjoyed may be continued to his deserving young successors; and with renewed and sincere wishes for the happiness of all his friends, he tenders them an affectionate Farewell.

BENJAMIN RUSSELL.

A confraternal dinner was given to Mr. Russell, by the printers and editors of Boston, at the Exchange Coffee-House, on the 15th of November. It was attended by several of the printers from Salem and Cambridge. The young, the middle-aged, and the old, were at the table, and all seemed generously intent on showing honor to the guest of the occasion. The editor of the Boston Daily Advertiser, Nathan Hale, Esq. presided at the table. On rising to propose a toast in honor of the venerable guest, he said, —

As they had met for the purpose of paying a tribute of respect and affection to an old friend, who had just taken leave of the profession, in which they had been associated with him, it was a fit occasion to bring to mind some of the services he had rendered, and to express the sense they entertained of his many good qualities. Their veteran friend had been the conductor of a public paper nearly from the date of the acknowledgment of our national independence; and, during that whole period, had taken an active part in the politics of the day. He had never been neutral on any question, in which he conceived the welfare of the country was involved, but had always supported the side, which he believed to be right — boldly, earnestly, and ably. This he had always done with good temper, and with no unkind feelings towards his adversaries. If he was ever found in the wrong, it always gave him pleasure to be set right. It had been the lot of few men to be actors in so many important political events as he. In no one was he more distinguished, than in the great work of rearing the edifice of our national Constitution. The pillars of this fabric, as they were slowly and laboriously raised, were delineated on the print of his paper, to show the progress of the work; and those, who were engaged in the task, were constantly aided, encouraged, and cheered, by the agency of his indefatigable press. His paper, though changed, from time to time, in its outward appearance, with the progress of the arts, and extended in its dimensions, with the growth of the community, has always retained the same spirit — a spirit uniformly devoted to the promotion of the public good. For more than forty years, it has had a most important agency in forming the public mind — in diffusing knowledge and sound principles — in correcting errors — in promoting useful projects — and in advancing the welfare and securing the good order of society. In promoting these objects, he has had the countenance, assistance, and friendship of some of the wisest and best men of the country. He has set a good example to those, who are in a situation to follow his steps; and, in retiring from the occupation, in which we have been associated with him, he is entitled to a hearty expression of our good will and esteem, and to our kindest benedictions.

The Chairman then proposed — "The health of our veteran friend, who, through a long life of useful public services, has been most esteemed by those, who knew him best." In an affecting manner, but somewhat embarrassed by his feelings, Mr. Russell replied, as follows: —

Mr. President and Gentlemen,

In requesting your acceptance of my thanks for the sentiment announced from the Chair, every pulsation of my heart beats with gratitude, for the friendly and fraternal manner, in which my discharge of editorial duties has been viewed, by those, who are the best judges of them, and for the friendly interview now enjoyed. I trust that a formal speech is not expected from me. I could not, if I would, make one; and I would not if I could, detain you for any length of time, from the feast of reason, which you, gentlemen, have known so well how to provide. But, without remaining wholly silent, when called upon by duty, permit me to say, that it has been with regret that I have considered it necessary to dissolve my connection, as far as regards labor and care, with a profession, which needs no general panegyric. Its importance to the world and to civil liberty, and its great utility, are stamped in every step of the march of mind, and every verdict, pronounced by public opinion. And you, gentlemen, are well qualified to make its character as honorable to our country as it is useful to all countries. That the profession of an editor is not, as some have asserted, irksome, and without enjoyment, permit me to inform such gainsayers, as one proof, at least, of their error, that there is an individual, who entered it as a volunteer, pursued it with a steady march more than forty years, and found it, with all its toils by day and watchings by night, not only a source of gratification, but never attended by a single hour of regret or disgust. This individual, Mr. President, could also add, that during the lapse of time, that has been mentioned, and which, it is well known, has been filled up with momentous events, he has not the recollection of a single instance, when, in the most zealous discharge of duty and devotion to the cause he espoused, that he has not recognized a brother in every opponent, and been ready to extend to him the fraternal hand and to reciprocate social feelings. This, Mr. President, is not an ebullition of egotism; and that individual feels, that it is to the knowledge of this disposition, and not for any professional eminence, that he is indebted for the kind attention, that has always been paid to him.

Mr. Russell was evidently much embarrassed by his feelings; for, in the course of his life, he had made many speeches on exciting occasions, from the impulse of the moment, much better as to style and arrangement, than this. To what particular circumstance, — if any, — he alluded, when he said he considered it necessary that he should dissolve his connection with the press, is not known. He had not manifested any failure of physical faculties or of his natural intellectual vigor, that should render such a step indispensable; and he was not so far advanced in life that he might not have continued to conduct his paper for many years. The circulation of the Centinel had diminished, and other papers had sprung into existence, and were gaining popularity with a younger generation. This might have operated unpleasantly on his feelings; and, probably, he foresaw that, without a change in his style of writing and general system of arranging his materials, in order to suit his paper to the taste of the "varying hour," its circulation would continue to diminish, until the establishment might be of little value; and that it would be better to sell it *then,* than to run the hazard of a poorer bargain when a sale would be unavoidable. Many persons had been subscribers to the paper from its commencement, and many others had been its readers and supporters for a long time, — all of whom regretted Mr. Russell's retirement; but it was, notwithstanding, a judicious and fortunate procedure. Neither the talent nor the industry of the new proprietors, — though perseveringly exercised, — was sufficient to place the Centinel on the commanding eminence it had once occupied. Its subscription list was augmented in 1830 by the addition of that of the New-England Palladium, and in April, 1836, by that of the Boston Gazette. From 1830, it was issued daily as well as semi-weekly; but, with all these accessions to its support, it continued to decline, till the first of May, 1840, when it was sold to the proprietors of the Boston Daily Advertiser, and its identity was merged and lost in the more popular traits of character, which distinguished that paper.

While he was editor of the Centinel, Mr. Russell was always ready to promote all projects for public improvement, and all institutions for philanthropic purposes. He was always ready to contribute of his means to public or private charity. Avarice was not one of his failings; if it had been, he might have died worth half a million. The following anecdote, — which, perhaps, many readers may have heard from his own lips, — illustrates the generosity of his disposition, in cases of private necessity: —

About the year 1790, when Russell was in the habit of visiting, personally, all vessels newly arrived in the harbor, for the purpose of procuring intelligence, he went on board of one from the island of Guadaloupe, and examining the list of passengers, he perceived the name of *Udin*, or *Udang*.* Having known a captain of that name, while he was in the army, and knowing that he was an officer, in whom General Washington placed great confidence for fidelity and enterprize in peculiar services, Russell set off in search of him, and, after considerable fruitless inquiry, found him at an inferior tavern in Corn Court, so called, kept by a well-known landlady by the name of Duggan, whose sign was a picture of John Hancock. It was in the winter, and the weather was extremely cold. He found the old revolutionary soldier, thinly dressed in a short Nankin jacket, and trowsers of the same material, hovering over a small pan of coals, destitute of money, or any other valuable property. They recognized each other. The captain was delighted to see an old acquaintance, and after some few ceremonies of recognition, earnestly and affectionately inquired after the health and happiness of the *great commander*, as he was accustomed to call General Washington. Russell, who never suffered himself to be outdone in expressions of love and reverence for Washington, was touched by these tokens of devotion towards the man, whom of all others, he most venerated, and immediately took measures for the relief of the captain from his state of utter destitution. He got up a subscription and raised money enough to purchase for him two suits of clothing, and to enable him to board,

* The orthography of this name is uncertain.

for a time, at a more respectable public house, — the Bunch-of-Grapes tavern in State-street. Russell then set himself to work to get a situation for the captain, that would afford him a suitable maintenance. By application to General Lincoln and some other distinguished men, well known to Washington, an office of some emolument, was secured for him at Albany, where he was respected as a faithful and capable officer and a worthy citizen.

Another incident occurred in the life of Russell, which, though for a time a topic of much abuse from his political opponents, was really so creditable to the good feelings of his heart, and so happily illustrated the natural energy of his character, that it should not be forgotten. One of his cousins, William Russell of Salem, was a prisoner of war on board the British frigate Nymph, which, in 1814, was cruising in and near the harbor of Boston. He entertained a notion that he could get his relative released. Without consulting any of his friends, or making his project known, even to his family, he hired a small fishing-boat, with two men to manage it, and went in search of the frigate. Not knowing exactly at what point she was to be found, nor knowing how long it might take to discover her, he took with him provisions sufficient to last him and his associates about ten days. These provisions consisted of fresh beef and mutton, poultry, bread, butter, and cheese, and a generous allowance of wine. He had the good fortune to fall in with the Nymph about twenty miles from Boston. His boat was hailed from the frigate. The captain was informed that the persons in the boat were anxious to see a relation who was a prisoner in the ship. Russell was permitted to go on board. He represented to the captain the case of his cousin, and prevailed on him to release his prisoner. As the crew of the frigate were rather short of provisions, the commanding officer thought it a good opportunity to lessen the number of prisoners, and released William Russell on condition that four other prisoners, who were on the sick list, should be taken away with him. This proposition was, of course, readily agreed to. Then, *and not till then,* Russell made a present to the officers of the Nymph of the provisions he had on board his boat, — an act of courtesy, which could hardly have been omitted without incurring an imputation of meanness. But it furnished the democratic party with the groundwork of a charge of aiding and assisting the enemy, of treasonable intercourse, &c. No notice was taken of it by the government, though some of the influential newspapers were loud in their censures and denunciations. After an absence of about thirty-six hours from the town, Russell arrived safely with the five released captives as evidence of his address.

Though he made no pretensions to literary scholarship, he was frequently consulted in regard to literary compositions intended for popular effect. When Thomas Paine (afterwards Robert Treat Paine,) had written his celebrated Song, "Adams and Liberty," he showed the manuscript to Russell, who, after casting his eye over it, said, "You have not introduced the name of Washington." Struck with the omission, which was entirely inadvertent, Paine sat down at Russell's table, and wrote the following stanza : —

Should the tempest of war overshadow our land,
Its bolts would ne'er rend Freedom's temple asunder,
For, unmoved, at its portal would Washington stand,

And repulse with his breast the assaults of the thunder.
His sword from the sleep
Of its scabbard would leap,
And conduct with its point, every flash to the deep.

Paine often acknowledged that he was indebted to the suggestion of Russell for the introduction of this stanza, into a composition, which has probably done more to extend his fame than any thing else he had written.

The newspaper poets were proud of seeing their productions in the Centinel, and the editor usually repaid their favors with a compliment. Many of these contributions are as well worthy of preservation, as hundreds and thousands of verses, which are imported, and stamped with the approving seal of British critics. The little epigram, which follows, with Russell's introductory criticism, appears as original in the Centinel of August 2, 1800: —

☞ *We may search far and long before we shall find a more delicate morceau than the following:* —

THE FEMALE GRAMMARIAN.

"A Kiss," said young Charles, "is a *noun*, we allow,
But tell me, my dear, is it *proper*, or *common!*"
Lovely Myra blushed deep, and exclaimed — "Why I vow,
I think that a *kiss* is both *proper* and *common!*"

Several pieces of poetry appeared in the Centinel, the same year, signed "Analaski," of which the following is the best, and which, the editor said, "presents a high-wrought Picture from the Pencil of impassioned Genius and Sensibility": —

ODE,

ON THE FOLLY OF EXULTING ON FOREIGN WAR.

Scenes of sweet peace! our native plains,
Ye wild paths of our airy hills!
Ye *gates of Heaven*, our father's fanes,
Which yet Devotion's fervor fills!

Mid ye should angry murmurs swell?
To tranquil joys the heart rebel?
Exulting when the wrath of war
Hurls its volcanic torrents, dreadfully afar!

To us, indifferent, whether reign
The impious *Gaul*, or zealous *Russ;*
A *silken* or an iron *chain*
Alike, to Honor is a curse.
Our wishes cannot change decrees
Of Heaven's high monarch, as he please
States and their Empires are o'erthrown,
'Tis his commissioned worm that saps the monarch's throne.

The steed in verdant pasture bred
Starts at the martial-rallying choir,
Wild floats the forelock o'er his head,
His nostrils smoke, his eyes are fire;
'Till custom round the martial plain
Guides him with her imperial rein;
Then all impatient for the field
He laughs th' embattled host, and spurns the glittering shield.

Thus hearts that throb'd at fiction's tale,
With battle's shouts familiar grow; —
Mothers, whom *distant* war made pale,
From Glory's carnage learn to glow. —
From them, what daughters shall be led
Shameless, to vex the marriage bed!
Nor joy, nor love, nor soft desire,
Nor heavenly charity, one tender wish inspire!

A single death in times of yore,
Was subject for a nation's tears;
Whole nations weltering in their gore
Will scarcely satiate moderns' ears;
Thus when th' avenging angel hied,
The first-born-hope of *Egypt* died.
Scourges of blood the fountains dry
Of every tender thought of sweet humanity.

Behold *Helvetia's* favored plain,
Ere by the storm of war o'erswept,
There gayly waved the yellow grain,
The child in fearless cradle slept;

The shepherd's pipe was heard at noon,
To rustic revels lit the moon,
The wife's quick shuttle plied the woof,
While bending age, made welcome every humble roof.

Waked by the kine, that at the door
With outstretched neck impatient lowed
Her swelling udder to out-pour
And join the neighboring pasture-crowd,
The youth to active labor sprung,
And jocund up the mountain sung,
Below whose summit crowned with snows,
Fair love, unspotted faith, health, happiness repose:—

Now see! the ox with loosened yoke
Wander deserted hills around!
Behold the cottage ruins smoke!
Behold the indignant peasant bound!
While tottering age, affrighted maids,
Fear the loud sigh mid caverned shades,
And mothers dumb, at terror's cry,
Throw, to the iron-hoof, their infant progeny!

What though on *Alps*, huge *Alps* arise,
And snows eternal fence the coast?
To scale the heavens Ambition hies,
And Havoc urges on the host;
Pale Famine on their steps attend,
Ruin, the desolating fiend;
Starts from the blood-soaked sod the horse,
And screams the affrighted raven o'er the mangled corse!

While Victory high her standard waves
How writhes below the wounded plain!
Along the hills what torture raves!
What thousands envious of the slain!
O'er them the careless victor rides,
Stamping his steed's feet in their sides,
While sullen moves the groaning team,
Plunging their writhing bodies in the bloody stream.

Perversely then shall we exult,
When Glory's shout is borne on air?
What is of war the true result
But silent misery and despair!

Our ardent passions take the rein,
Unless secured by reason's chain,
Pure virtue ne'er exulting flies
From calm humanity and peace to boisterous skies.

Mr. Russell was proud of his character as a mechanic. To the mechanics, as a class, he was strongly and affectionately attached. When, in the brightest day of his political career, when he was associated with men of the highest rank in political circles, and even courted by some of the leaders of his party, he never forgot that he was a mechanic, and would, at almost any time, withdraw from a political committee, or conference, to attend a meeting of mechanics. His agency in the meetings at the Green Dragon, while the Convention were discussing the Federal Constitution, has already been noticed. In 1795, he, with a few other mechanics of Boston, formed a society, afterwards named the Massachusetts Charitable Mechanic Association. Of this association he was President from 1808 to 1817, inclusive. He was always sincerely devoted to its interests, and did more than any other individual to establish it on a permanent basis, and to increase its popularity, usefulness, and reputation. He was also President of the Faustus Association, — a society formed by the printers of Boston and the adjacent towns, for mutual protection and advantage.

Mr. Russell had not only an *ambition* for public employment; he had a *talent* that enabled him to discharge the duties of every employment, that his fellow-citizens saw fit to impose upon him. He filled the important station of President of the Board of Health of the town of Boston, from 1806 to 1810, inclusive. He was a member of the school committee, by election of the people, from 1817 to 1821, inclusive, and, afterwards, held the same office by virtue of his office as an alderman of the city. He was a member of the common council from the organization of the city government in 1822, and was annually re-elected for four successive years. In 1829 he was elected an alderman, and re-elected for three successive years. Probably no other man had ever held the office of a popular representative so many years in succession. He was first elected a member of the House of Representatives of Massachusetts, in 1805, and was re-elected every succeeding year thereafter, including 1821. In 1822 and 1825, he was elected a senator for the county of Suffolk; and again, a representative from Boston in 1828, and each succeeding year, including 1835. In 1836 and 1837, he was a member of the Executive Council; and this, I believe, was the last of his service in any public capacity.

Mr. Russell's retirement from all connection with the Press was sincerely regretted by his professional cotemporaries. Although, during the long period of high political excitement, he had been engaged in many angry disputes, and had not been over-scrupulous in the application of personal reflections, yet, from the day when Mr. Munroe was elected to the Presidency, — when the federal party became virtually dissolved, and gave up its existence as an organized national party, he had been one of the most courteous and good-natured of editors. From the date of that election to the last publication under his name, it would be difficult, if not impossible, to find in the Centinel a severe or bitter remark upon those of the profession, who did not fall in with his views of the policy, which he had adopted. He had hailed that election as the commencement of an "Era of Good Feelings," and he adhered to the principle, indicated by that significant phrase, with entire good faith. As, in his private intercourse, he had never harbored resentment long enough to extinguish his sympathies, except, perhaps, in a single instance, so, when his political relations were changed, his political animosities expired. Socially and politically, he suffered not the sun to go down upon his wrath. He had a fiery and a hasty temper, but it might be aptly and truly said of him, he "carried anger as the flint bears fire, which, much enforced, shows a hasty spark, and straight is cold again."

Being now a man of perfect leisure, Mr. Russell sought public employment, and his fellow-citizens were ready to avail themselves of his experience and willingness to serve them. He was four times elected an alderman of the city, — as before stated, — an office of much labor, and with no compensation. He was again sent to the Legislature as a representative. His election as a member of the Executive Council, was made by the vote of the Legislature. When not engaged in public employment, he was almost daily seen on the Exchange, or in some other public place, where he was wont to relate the incidents and anecdotes of days gone by, and where he always found willing auditors. In 1837, he was severely afflicted by the death of his wife, — a lady, whose many excellent endowments, as a wife, a mother, and a friend, had made his house a paradise for near forty years. By this bereavement he lost a friend and counselor, who had acquired an influence over his heart and understanding, that was discernible in the softening of some of the asperities of his natural temper. Soon after, he broke up his domestic establishment, and took lodgings for himself, an unmarried daughter, and an unmarried sister, in a private boarding-house.

It has been stated that Mr. Russell left no manuscripts in the form of a diary, and hardly a scrap of paper, on which he had made a memorandum of any occurrence. I have not been able to discover any thing that he wrote, after he relinquished the situation of editor, except a very few letters to his intimate friends. The letter, which follows, and which, judging from its date, I apprehend was one of his longest and latest, carries on its face all necessary explanation. The original has many erasures and interlineations. Two or three omissions are supplied by the words in brackets: —

Lincoln-street, June 24, 1840.

My dear friend,

. . . . I am fearful, from the conversation we had today at Ashton's, that you are under a wrong impression respecting the late Whig gathering, in Worcester. It was no mob meeting; but a convocation worthy of the Old Bay State, although a little too noisy in the afterpiece. I refused going, as a regular delegate, because I did not wish to take on myself the responsibility of attending the convention, as such, as I had perfect confidence, that good Whig nominations would be made by those who did go, and my defect of hearing could not have permitted [me] to discharge any duty, which my age, &c. might have induced friends to call me [to perform.] Nor did I make up my mind to go, *as a volunteer*, until Wednesday morning, when, seeing the mighty masses, which were thronging the depot, and wishing to be a mere looker-on, in my second native town, of the largest assemblage ever convened in the Heart of the Commonwealth, I jumped into the car and went. An accident prevented me from seeing the early part of the proceedings; but all I did see, bating the huzzas and salutations, reciprocated between the Whig Ladies of Worcester and their Whig visitors, was done [in] good order, good discipline, cheerful countenance, and not an instance of Intemperance. The business of the

Convention, which I did not see, I am confidently assured, was done as well as at the Conventions we have attended. A large majority of the Deputies elect met the evening before, and made the usual Caucus arrangements. These, and many others, met at an early hour on Wednesday forenoon; were duly organized, and proceeded to the usual nominations, which were unanimously agreed to, and reported to, and confirmed by, other assemblages of Whigs, from all parts of the State and Connecticut, accompanied by many hundred banners and many bands of music. All these were paraded with the utmost regularity, and occupied a cortege of nearly two miles in length. Several hundreds who were in the cars, [by] the accident I have alluded to, were prevented coming on the field till afternoon. But all the business had been finished and confirmed with approbation, and therefore [we] had nothing more to do, than to join in the felicitations, and hearty cheers, which overflowed from all hearts. But for the accident alluded to, which could not be prevented, — the whole gathering would have passed off with as much order and decorum, as that which has ever attended the great Mechanic and Civic Processions, which we have seen in Boston. To this circumstance I attribute the fact, that the loud cheers were made by those who came at the eleventh hour, and who had no other means of becoming known to the convention. The best discipline pervaded all the numerous ranks. The utmost attention was paid to the speakers' addresses, from the numerous hustings, which the great multitude made indispensable; and there was not one mob-like or disorderly movement made during the day or evening. The cheerings were heartfelt, and must have been heard with pleasure by every Whig ear within hearing. I repeat, that all the Business parts of the day were conducted with true Yankee order and decorum; and the cheerings, although loud and hearty, and might have been considered too loud, were not more loud and hearty, than you and I have heard in old Faneuil Hall. The *People* feel the wrongs of their tyrannical Oppressors, — and when they raise the voice to proclaim them, — it is the voice of God. I hate *mobs* in the true acceptation of the term; but I am confident, had you been at Worcester, under the circumstances in which I was placed, you would have contradicted every assertion, that the Worcester gathering was a mob proceeding. I make this statement in the sincerity of my heart, to remove any impressions which you must have had on your mind, in what you remarked to-day.

Your affectionate fellow citizen, BENJ. RUSSELL.

I write in great haste, and hope you will excuse this scrawl.*

* The name under the engraved portrait, which accompanies this volume, is a fac simile of the signature affixed to this letter. It will be observed that at the date of it Mr. Russell was near the completion of his seventy-ninth year.

Mr. Russell was much affected by the death of his wife, and a decay of his intellectual power was perceived by his familiar acquaintance. In 1843, another event had a similar effect. This was the sudden death of a son-in-law, Samuel L. Abbot, an amiable man and highly respectable merchant. To the business talent of Mr. Abbot, Mr. Russell had been indebted for much aid in the management of his pecuniary affairs, and the death of so excellent an adviser and friend, seemed to be the removal of a prop, that supported his house. From this time, the failure of his physical and intellectual faculties became too evident and too rapid to escape the notice of those that knew him. His gait was noticeable for a shuffling motion, as if the machinery, which lifted the feet, was entirely out of order. He seldom visited places of public resort, and his walks for exercise were chiefly on the common. His memory was much impaired. Though he would still relate incidents of his youth and early manhood, — sometimes with surprizing accuracy, — yet, at other times, he lost entirely the order of events, in regard to which he had once been scrupulously exact.

In the month of October, 1844, I sat with him, at his boarding-house, a couple of hours. There was a military review on the common; and, knowing that he had never permitted such an event to pass off without his being a spectator, I asked him if he would like to walk out and see the troops. He said he did not feel quite smart enough to bustle through the crowd. A few minutes afterwards he asked *if they were voting for President.* This confusion of ideas in his mind was a melancholy manifestation of the loss of memory. When I informed him that the election of President would not take place for some days to come, he seemed to be mortified that he had committed such an error. To restore him to cheerfulness, I mentioned the names of some of his old friends in the Mechanic Association. His memory and natural joyousness revived, and he related many anecdotes concerning the past members of that association, and talked much of the difficulties they had to encounter in the early stages of its history. He then reverted to revolutionary times, and repeated the whole of a poem, written by J. M. Sewall, and recited, or sung, at Worcester, in 1776, entitled "The Fiery Devil." It was a parody on a British song — "The Watery God." It contained more than a hundred lines. He had repeated this to me, a few years before, and I then wrote it down from his dictation, not knowing that there was any printed copy of it in existence. Afterwards, I saw it in a newspaper printed in 1784. On comparing the printed copy with my manuscript, taken from his recollection, I discovered the variation of a single word only, and that a very unimportant one.

After this interview I saw Mr. Russell but once. I called on him one morning in November, in company with a gentleman, — a member of the Mechanic Assotion — with whom he had long been familiarly acquainted. We found him rather indisposed to conversation, owing, as I supposed to his sense of hearing being somewhat impaired. I was not then aware that he did not recognize the friend who was with me; and was surprized to learn, the next morning, that immediately after we left him, he inquired *who it was that called with Buckingham.*

The progress of decay was now daily perceptible. He had no sickness. He was sometimes a little nervous, and would send for the doctor; but medical prescriptions were useless, and were seldom given. His physician very frankly told his friends, — what, indeed, was quite evident to them, — that he could be of no service; *for the machine was worn out, and there was not material enough left, to form the basis of repairs.* His appetite was gentle, and satisfied with small quantities of the simplest food. The animal functions of nature continued their operations without artificial aids.

In this manner a month or two passed away. On the morning of the fourth of January, 1845, Mr. Russell was sitting by the fire-side, and rose to go to his bed. He asked his daughter, who was with him, what made the room look so dark. Perceiving that his eyes no longer performed their office, she led him to the bed. He lay down, and, in the course of an hour, ceased to breathe. He suffered no painful struggle in passing from time to eternity. The transition from world to world was so tranquil, that the affectionate watcher noted not the moment of change. The once bright and fervid flame palely and feebly burned till the oil was consumed, and the vital spark went out.

Thus died Benjamin Russell, in the eighty-fourth year of his age. His funeral was honored by the attendance of the members of the Massachusetts Charitable Mechanic Association, members of the Grand Lodge of Freemasons, and a long array of those who had been associated with him in friendly and social relations. The remains were deposited in a tomb in the Old Granary Burying Ground. Unbroken repose to his ashes! Unending happiness to his soul!

THE SALEM MERCURY.

THIS paper was published by John Dabney and Thomas C. Cushing, and began with the year 1787. It was printed weekly on Tuesday, on a demy sheet, four columns to a page, and chiefly on Long Primer type. It was conducted with great care as to the selection of authentic intelligence, and was furnished with communications from able writers. In politics, the editors were ardent friends to the Union of the States, and advocates for the Constitution. On the third of March, 1789, they gave expression to their patriotic feelings, after the following fashion: —

> If ever angels from the sky descend,
> 'Twill be the Federal Structure to defend.

To-morrow, (the great, the important day, big with the fate of these United States,) commences a new era in the politics of our country. May this auspicious day be ever sacred — no mourning, no misfortune happen on it! — The day whereon convenes that august assembly, the NEW CONGRESS, when, it is presumed, that every sincerely honest and independent heart in the Union bounds with joy! especially as the prospect brightens, of the luminary of our hemisphere presiding as Chief — an additional lustre to this truly magnificent Body!

> As *great* in battle, *great* he is in peace!
> He comes again to point our way to fame;
> The FEDERAL PLAN shall bid our evils cease,
> And stamp Columbia with a lasting name.

On contemplating our country, just arrived upon the solid and uniform track of regular, equitable, and effectual government, after having so narrowly escaped the dreadful calamity of anarchy and disunion; while, on one hand, *civil dissension* yawned for our peace and safety, and, on the other, *foreign subjugation* watched, to devour all that was valuable in life, the present pleasing reverse of affairs must yield delight to every beholder. The many happy effects, which will necessarily flow from the motions of this grand system, are, no doubt, in some measure anticipated in the warm imaginations of its uniform friends, who anxiously look up for the future existence and weal of their country, to the united wisdom of the Fathers of the land, in our Supreme Legislature, most judiciously composed of

Patriots, whose virtues searching Time has tried;
Heroes, who fought, where brother heroes died;
Lawyers, who speak as Tully spoke before;
Sages, deep read in philosophic lore;
Merchants, whose plans are to no realms confined;
Farmers, the noblest title to mankind;
Yeoman and Tradesmen, pillars of each state,
On whose decision hangs Columbia's fate.

May the national blessings resulting from this political revolution continue, and continually expand, from generation to generation, till the last shock of time buries the empires of the world in one undistinguished ruin!

The Mercury of October 13, 20, and 27, has no publisher's, editor's, or printer's name in the imprint. That of the 27th, contained an advertisement, stating that the partnership of Dabney & Cushing was dissolved on the 14th; and another stating that the business was to be carried on by T. C. Cushing.

In October of this year, while President Washington was on his tour through New-England, he visited Salem. In a long and circumstantial account of that visit, the Mercury says, — "No particular circumstance of the day seems to have pleased more than the plain and hearty manner in which Mr. Northey, the chairman of the selectmen, received the President. This gentleman is of the society of Friends; and when the President was presented to the selectmen, Mr. Northey took him by the hand, being covered, and said, 'Friend Washington, we are glad to see thee, and, in behalf of the inhabitants, bid thee a hearty welcome to Salem.' "

The first paper issued by Cushing in 1790, had for its title THE AMERICAN EAGLE, and is designated, in the imprint, as "Number 1, in 1790." The next paper, is entitled

THE SALEM GAZETTE,

"Number 2, in 1790," and this mode of reckoning was continued through the year. At the beginning of the year 1791, the usual manner of computing the age of the publication was restored, and the paper of January 4, is designated as "Volume V. number 221," that being the whole number of weekly issues from the first number of the Mercury. The title, Salem Gazette, has remained, without change, to the present day, and the number of each publication has proceeded in order from the same beginning.

In the Gazette of October 14, 1794, "the Editor informs its patrons that he relinquishes the publication to Mr. WILLIAM CARLETON, who will conduct the same after this day. . . . . He recollects, with sensibility, the benefits he has received, since he became (this day five years) the sole Editor of it; and gratitude obliges him to acknowledge, that, notwithstanding the disadvantages, under which it has been published, he relinquishes it with an increase, double to what it possessed when he received it. A more undivided attention to it has now become necessary, than he is able to bestow; and many have thought it expedient that it should be made a semi-weekly paper. He has no doubt that these deficiencies will be amply supplied by Mr.

Carleton, and, in his favor, he solicits a continuance of that patronage to the Salem Gazette, under which it has so long lived."

In assuming the editorial and publishing department of the Gazette, — after the customary expressions of deference and respect, — Mr. Carleton said : —

In the prosecution of this publication, the present Editor does not expect its importance to be increased from an adherence to *any party;* it is, on the contrary, his determination to *continue* it, impartial, independent, and uninfluenced, but by the public good — neither devoting it to the cause of unfeeling Aristocracy, or employing it in kindling the vindictive rage of Democracy, or lighting the destructive torch of Anarchy; but in endeavoring to fix the public eye on the blessings of a free government, constitutional laws, and good order in society. He is persuaded that the political transactions of the day are what always render a Gazette most interesting, and more especially at a period so important as the present — these shall receive all the attention, which the present confined limits of the Gazette will admit — at the same time a due regard shall be paid to those more domestic concerns, which, though not equally important, it may be pleasant and useful to notice, and, on all his youthful exertions, he solicits the candor of an indulgent public.

In the next Gazette we find the commencement of that long series of articles, under the title of "SUMMARY," which gave notoriety to that paper as long as Carleton was its publisher, and afterwards contributed still more to the fame of the Essex Register. These articles, — a most entertaining composition of miscellaneous ingredients, — were prepared by the Rev. William Bentley, one of the ministers of Salem, an eminent scholar, and a man of rather eccentric but unspotted character. Each of these summaries may be considered as an index to all the current news of the period, which intervened between the days of publication. They extended, according to circumstances, from half a column to one or two, and sometimes to three, columns. But no description that I can give will present the character of the Summary, so distinctly as that of the writer himself, namely, — "As a Summary is necessarily miscellaneous, we must be excused, if sometimes we seem to pass abruptly from one thing to another. It is our intention to mention all interesting subjects, and in as few words as can make them to be understood. Should we collect things of the same nature together, without regard to the places in which they happen, we should lose the historical form which the Gazette exacts of us. It is our method to introduce foreign intelligence by the nation acting immediately the most interesting part in foreign affairs, and so to pass off from the great action to less important occurrences. In our own country, we begin at the most southern state, and so travel homewards. We intend not needlessly to deviate from this practice."

But no adequate idea of these curious medleys can be formed without a specimen; and here is one, taken at random: —

Reports now are that the success of Russia has emboldened the Empress, after conferring distinguished honors upon her General, to promise a fleet and an army, to be at Jersey and Guernsey against France. This is in substance the tale of last spring, but it is not impossible that it may be realized. We have reason to suspect that Prussia will send her 20,000 troops to assist the Empire on their old station of the Rhine. A negotiation, it is said, has been checked between the English and the Royalists of La Vendee, by the Pacific measures of the French. And we are told that the Constitution of 1791 is read freely by the French nation. The English are represented to be suspicious and severe in their measures with the Italian States since their own failures in the Mediterranean. Robertspierre's fears respecting fanaticism, it is said, have been justified by some appearances near Lyons, and the books of moral instruction are found to be wanting, which have been promised by the Convention. We are told they begin to complain in France in want of raw materials for their manufactures. At HOME. The Lands proposed to be disposed of by the State of Georgia, were to have been granted to four companies. To the Georgia company for 250,000 dollars. The Georgia Mississippi company for 155,000 dollars. To the Upper Mississippi company for 35,000, and to the Tennessee company for 60,000 dollars. The State was to retain out of the first grant 620,000 acres, out of the 2d 138,000, out of the 3d 138,000, out of the 4th 248,000, and 50,000 besides out of the last grant for the Commissioners. A small shock of an Earthquake has been felt in Virginia. As the third Congress has closed, we shall have the laws and proceedings in full detail in the Gazette. We are happy to find that Congress have remembered the great services of Count de Grasse in their generous attention to his children, whom we are happy to find in this town, and know to be deserving of this public gratitude. Mr. Gallatin in a long and labored speech has endeavored to prove from facts that the elections in the Western Counties were valid, because those counties could not be proved to have been in a state of insurrection during the late commotions in those parts. The Tobacconists have presented a memorial to Congress, in which they complain of the Excise, and propose Taxes on real and personal estates as to be preferred by Government. A Bill has passed in the Assembly of New-York for a new Census of that State. Perhaps our information respecting the Democratic Society in Vermont was not just. Our General Court has adjourned. The principal Acts have been, to introduce the dollar and its parts as money of accounts; to appropriate 12,000*l.* for the payment of interest on the debt of the Commonwealth; to direct the payment of Costs in Criminal prosecutions; to establish a Nantucket bank; to assist Creditors in the recovery of their just demands; to explain the Militia Law; to bind apprentices and minors; to erect guideposts on public roads; and to incorporate the proprietors of Middlesex Canal. Last week was published in this town by the Rev. Dr. Barnard, a pertinent and excellent discourse delivered in the North Congregation on the last Thanksgiving. In the discourse, the Doctor has idolized no political theory, but has justly applauded our own federal Government, and intimately associated public happiness with public virtue. We subjoin the substance of his observations at the close. . . . *Salem Gazette, March* 10, 1795.

In June, 1796, the Gazette was published as a semi-weekly paper, on Tuesday and Friday. It is introduced by a pretty long address, which bears internal evidence that it proceeded from the pen of Mr. Bentley. The following is the closing part of it: —

We have not seen without great concern the abuses which have attended the liberty of diffusing useful knowledge by Gazettes. The privilege is inestimable, but it may become dangerous by faction. Nations have had just cause to apprehend, instead of the support of liberty, the destruction of all subordination from this engine of party. Instead of the friend of truth and knowledge, it has often been the vile slave of falsehood, of slander, and guilt. It has not enlightened but deceived mankind. It has taught men to hate their friends, and has betrayed them to their worst enemies. While we should behold with horror any attempts against the liberty of the Press, we cannot refuse to view with sincere complacency all attempts to prevent its abuses. By the wise precautions of the English nation, it has saved itself from destruction. The French are now involved in the evils they were too willing to see prevailing among their national enemies. They complain that their enemies publish the slanders which endanger the blessings of their revolution. But a licentious press is always an enemy in the bosom of any nation, and every nation can supply base passions enough to arm so powerful an enemy against its tranquility. We trust, then, we shall feel no incentives to abuse the public confidence, and we trust that our correspondents will not be so disingenuous as to urge us to any insults to men or measures. Moral papers may often find a place in a Gazette, but they more properly belong to publications of a different nature. Few men having leisure or inclination to write for such papers in this rising country, little success has attended the several attempts to imitate the European publications of this character. Some new experiments are now to be determined, but all the Editors complain that they have not the encouragement promised to them. We have seen essays in our Gazettes for moral purposes. Many of them have been rather whimsical than interesting. Nothing inconsistent with the chastity of the Spectator will in the end be beneficial to the public morals. Men cannot be incited, by a laugh, to practice duties, which belong only to a sober education, and to long and careful habits. We shall be careful to avoid religious papers. They tend to degrade the most important subject which can employ the thoughts of men. Devout thoughts belong to different hours from those we assign to the Gazette and to business. And as to religious controversy, few men understand it, and very few can manage it with calmness. And they, who have ability to think coolly, have better opportunities of communicating their thoughts to the world. We shall keep ourselves in our proper character. We shall reverence religion and the laws; we shall blot out no man's good services by obloquy; and we shall communicate every thing to the public, which has, in our judgment, truth, happiness, usefulness, or good government as its object. We shall be greatly obliged to all our commercial friends for the best foreign news, and shall rejoice in the public testimony, that we are impartial and useful, entertaining and innocent.

The Gazette of September 27, was nearly filled with President Washington's Farewell Address to the People of the United States. The summary of the next paper closed as follows: — "We cannot refuse to notice the Address of our worthy President, on account of which we relinquished this part of our Gazette in our last publication. With flowing tears we attentively examine an Address, which demands our admiration, while it seals our affections. His sentiments will be written on our hearts, and live with our prosperity, from which they will ever be inseparable. His services will be engraven on our memories, and Time will report them for the gratitude of the most distant ages. The virtuous lament that the wise are not immortal. There is a struggle between our duty to resign and our inclination to retain the Man, who is our richest blessing. May his future days be in peace, and his reward from his God.

'Time, to thy wing, and bring us, if you can,
'Midst all thy dead and living store,
'To such another man.'"

To this notice of the retiring President may properly be added that, which introduced the first message of Mr. Adams, at the commencement of an extra session of Congress, soon after he was inaugurated as President, in May, 1799. Perhaps no official document was ever more truly described in the same number of lines, than was this by Mr. Bentley: — "We can offer to the public the Address of President Adams at the opening of Congress. There is a manly freedom in it; while there is a precision, which is admirable. He has combined very noble sentiments. He awakens a sense of national honor, while he establishes the most deliberate wisdom. He feels every indignity offered to these States, while he permits no resentment, unfriendly to peace. He calls for defence, while he employs negotiation. He demands a policy, which has our own prosperity, and not the prejudice of foreign nations, as its object. In this critical conjuncture, when all eyes are turned towards him, he has conciliated the affections, and possessed the confidence of the United States. Long live the President."

The Gazette was conducted by Carleton, till the 25th of July, 1797. In the paper of that day, is the following notice: —

☞ The Customers of the Salem Gazette are respectfully informed that its publication is resumed by THO'S. C. CUSHING.

No reason is assigned for either of the changes, — that from Cushing to Carleton, in 1794, or that from Carleton to Cushing, in 1797. After the last-mentioned change, the Gazette had none of Mr. Bentley's Summaries. It may be supposed that politics had something to do with this last change. From that time, the Gazette had more of a partisan character, and that character was decidedly *federal*. It had previously been *neutral*. It appears, from advertisements in the Gazette, that Cushing & Carleton were partners in a book-selling establishment, while the Gazette was published by Carleton.

In the autumn of 1802, a severe political conflict agitated the county of Essex, and produced in the town of Salem a deplorable state of feeling. The occasion of it was the election of representatives to Congress.

For that district, the republican party nominated Jacob Crowninshield, an eminent merchant of Salem; the federal party nominated Timothy Pickering, who had been Secretary of state during a part of Mr. Adams's administration. Both parties grew angry, and each assailed the candidate of the other in rather intemperate language.

In the Gazette of November 12, is an address to the public, signed by the editor, which illustrates the angry temper, with which this electioneering campaign was carried on. Mr. Cushing states that on the Saturday evening previous, two gentlemen by the name of Crowninshield and Mr. Joseph Story, called at his house and requested a private interview. Having been seated, he was informed by the gentlemen that they had come on an unpleasant business, namely, certain publications in his paper, abusive of them and their friends. Mr. Story complained that he had been placed before the public in an injurious point of view — that he was a young man, come into the town to gain a livelihood in an honorable way — that he ought to receive countenance and protection from the community — that his expressing his political sentiments with freedom was perfectly justifiable — that he had no objection to his arguments being fairly combated, but that he would not submit to be arraigned before the public in the manner he had been. Capt. B. Crowninshield labored to show that many pieces published in the Gazette, had been highly injurious, and that the editor had been in the practice of making personal reflections against him and his family. He represented the danger to which he (Cushing) exposed himself by these means. After alluding to sundry circumstances of a threatening character, he concluded by saying that if he (Cushing) continued to publish such things as they had complained of, he would shoot him in the dark if he could not do it in the day time. Cushing states that his reply was of the following tenor: —

That it was my desire, and had been my uniform endeavor to keep my paper free from undue personalities — that I considered public characters and public conduct as proper subjects of animadversion — that such was the present state of parties, and irritation of the public mind, that possibly (for I would not be my own judge) I might have admitted expressions not strictly within the bounds prescribed to myself — that I could not say how I should conduct my paper in future, but should still be governed by the same regard to decency, and endeavor to give no just cause of offence — that threats, however, would have no effect upon me in that respect, but if they meant to address my reason and sense of propriety, on that ground I was willing to hear them. With respect to the asperity of language used in my paper, I observed, if there had been such, it was excited by that of the opposite paper — that the candidates for office in my paper against Capt. Jacob Crowninshield had been treated with a degree of indelicacy and abuse in the Register, which had not been exercised in return against him. I told them that it had been impossible for me, from appearances, not to view them in connection with the paper in which these things appeared. Here they disavowed all connection with the Register, otherwise than that of being its customers, except that Mr. Story acknowledged himself to be one of its writers. They observed at length, that, as to what was past, they had no more to say; their only object was, that I should refrain in future from personalities towards them and their friends. They left it to me to divulge the meeting or not, as I pleased; it would not be done by them. I informed them that I felt a disposition not to make it known.

The earnestness and loudness with which the conversation was begun, and the kind of language made use of, alarmed the females of Cushing's family, and they immediately called in some of the young men who were in his employ; so that there were assembled in an adjoining room, without his knowledge, quite a number of young men and lads. This was the means of the meeting being almost instantly known abroad, and the most prominent parts of the conversation, particularly the threat to shoot him, were immediately reported. A day or two after, many pressing requests were made to Cushing, that he should lay an account of the affair and a report of the conversation before the people, who considered the threats, as they had been rumored, not merely as personal to himself, but seriously concerning the whole community.

Other political topics were discussed in the Gazette with great freedom. One of these topics, was the invitation given by President Jefferson to Thomas Paine, to revisit the United States, and his offer of a national vessel to convey that somewhat celebrated personage to our shores. Paine accepted the invitation, and while the guest of the President, wrote a series of letters to the people, which were published in the National Intelligencer. The comments on these matters in the federal papers were numerous and severe, and the Gazette was not behind its cotemporaries, either in the number or severity of its remarks. Those remarks were highly seasoned with sarcasm, ridicule, and sober invective.

In the latter part of December of this year, the editor begged leave to inform his customers, that the disadvantages, under which he had, for a long time supported it, had, at length, reduced it to a point of depression, which made it necessary for him either to renounce it entirely and turn his attention wholly to more promising pursuits, or to make some new arrangements for prolonging its existence. He said he should attempt the latter, and he proposed certain alterations in the terms of advertising, the subscription price of the paper, &c. The attempt is presumed to have been successful, for the publication was continued, and, no doubt, with profit to the proprietor as it was with advantage to the public.

The two great causes of public agitation, and personal anger and resentment, which marked the early years of the present century, — the Embargo of 1807 and the War of 1812, — operated with more violence in Salem than in any other town in New-England. It was said, — and, probably, with truth, — that some of the fiercest politicians went about the streets, armed, either to commit or to repel personal assault. The Salem Gazette took a high and fearless stand against the measures of the administration, and the Essex Register was no less resolute in defending them. It would be difficult to find a newspaper war conducted with so much ferocity as that, which was carried on for several years between these two papers. A few extracts, taken almost at random, and from one or two volumes only of the Gazette, will illustrate the style and temper of the editor and his correspondents during this period: —

The accounts from Washington are daily more and more alarming. Our fears and dangers are not from foreign powers — them we could resist — but from the madness of our own government, who seem determined to go on hand in hand with Bonaparte, and bring this continent into the same state to which he has reduced that of Europe. The Non-Intercourse is to be renewed, and enforced if necessary with land and sea forces, and the Bank of the United States to be annihilated. All importers, whose goods shall arrive, will not only suffer the forfeiture of their property, but heavy fines in addition. These measures combined will nearly put an end to commerce, and ruin all the mercantile class, except those whose wealth secures them from their effects. Beggary and misery will spread through our towns — the spirit of the people will be broken down — and their necks bent to any yoke that is prepared for them. They submitted to the embargo and all its horrors; they will as tamely submit to their renewal. And for what purpose is all this evil to be accumulated upon us? Can any other reason be given for it, than that it is the will and order of Bonaparte? *January* 25, 1811.

The Toasts of the Southern Democrats are very amusing both for the matter and manner. A friend of Col. Duane, gave the following:—

"WILLIAM DUANE—The sheet anchor of democracy—as able as he is incorruptible, and as true to principle as the needle to the *Pole*."

Now we think this allusion to the "Pole" must hurt the "worthy man Duane's" *honorable* feelings, as it is said that once on a time when he lived at Calcutta, he was for none of his *good deeds* sentenced to be carried astride on a *Pole;* whence he has long been known by the appellation of *Straddlepolitan.* It must be admitted that he is a man of *extensive views*, for he has been able to see from *Pole* to *Pole.*

July 19, 1811.

The Governor and Council have separated and returned home with malignant hearts and bloody hands. Unrelenting intolerance is not yet fated, and shameless usurpation has not yet had its perfect work. After a long and agonizing struggle, the Jacobinic conspirators against the principles of pure republicanism have vanquished the conscience of the Governor, and he now ranks, not as the Chief of a Republic, but as the Rolando of a ferocious gang. What being is more deserving of heart-felt commiseration, than a man wedded and chained to iniquity, and at the same time sufficiently sensible to perceive the gnawings of the worm of conscience! It is said that even Caligula trembled when it thundered; and the ghastly visages of his Excellency and his Honor testify that their souls are as unquiet as that of Herod. *October* 25, 1811.

HERCULEAN TASK. By recent intelligence from Washington it appears that the new Speaker has laudably undertaken to preserve order in Congress Hall, and to keep the members all *awake.* Vain attempt! It is equal to the labor of Hercules in cutting off the fifty heads of the Hydra. If he succeeds in keeping a hundred democratic members *awake*, he will richly merit the appellation of a *rousing Speaker.* For ten years the majority in Congress has been *asleep* to the honor and interest of their country, and their measures have been like the troubled *dreams* of a sick man. Many of the members are sleepwalkers, and others are sleeptalkers, such as Father SMILIE, and RHEA of Tennessee, commonly called the Spinningwheel, who will whisper like a grove, and purr a lullaby, that like a powerful anodyne will lock in the arms of slumber more of the *watchful* guardians of the public weal, than the Speaker and Sergeant at Arms, when they wish to count the *eyes* and *noses* upon a question, can *awaken* in an hour. While MACON and VARNUM were Speakers, the Hall of Congress was a most tranquil and quiet dormitory; sometimes, indeed, RANDOLPH, QUINCY and GARDINIER alarmed the slumberers, and *broke them of their rest.* The sleepers always admired VARNUM, because he is a *sleepy looking* man, the very image of Morpheus; those who wished to enjoy a nap or *siesta*, would *look to him*, and in five minutes their eyelids would fall like trap doors, and in ten minutes they would snore. Sometimes the variety of nasal twangs produced a concert as entertaining as that of the Panharmonican. On such occasions the members to a cursory observer appeared most *wise* and cogitating, so that a stranger would have thought that the Bird of Wisdom ought to have been emblazoned behind the Speaker's chair as the national arms, instead of the royal Eagle "that bolts its cloudless thunder" on the heads of our foes. On some important occasions, when the majority has been determined to carry a favorite and contested point, they have appeared in the Congress Hall equipped for a night session, with a night cap, blanket and pillow, resolved to *sleep away* the eloquence and arguments of the friends of their country. During the debate, and until the question is called, they slumber upon the floor; and hence it is said that the honorable Mr. Such-a-one kept *possession of the floor* for a number of hours. A bird's eye view of the assembled sleeping sages of this happy land reminds the spectator of the lines of the poet:—

In eldest time, ere mortals writ or read,
Ere Pallas issu'd from the Thunderer's head,
Dulness o'er all possess'd her ancient right,
Daughter of Chaos and eternal Night.

It is a remarkable fact, that the most odious measures of democracy in Congress, such as the Forcing Act, Non-importation Act, &c. have been prepared at midnight, with no other light than the glare of a taper. Light is emblematical of purity and innocence, and is naturally repugnant to vice: hence profligates and bravoes, who harbor dark souls and foul thoughts, shun the light of the sun, and seek the broad mantle of darkness as a cover for their shameless enormities. The most hardened assassin, who in the silence of night commits deeds the most heinous with a firm and unerring hand, will blink and hang his head on the appearance of odious light:—

'Tis now the very witching time of night,
When church yards yawn, and hell itself breathes out
Contagion to this world:—
Now could I drink hot blood, and do such bitter deeds
As the *day would blush to look upon.*

If a stranger should by chance view our democratic Congress, holding the orgies of a nocturnal debate, and arrayed in the habiliments of the bed, he would fear that the troubled Spirits of our Fathers had started from their tombs to reproach and rebuke their degenerate sons for the disgrace and disasters which have been brought upon their ill fated country.

The astonished beholder, affrighted and petrified by the strange sight of such portentous spectres, would naturally exclaim,

> Angels and ministers of grace, defend us!
> Art thou a spirit of health, or goblin damn'd!
> Bring'st with thee airs from heaven, or blasts from hell!

November 29, 1811.

Signior Abramo Alberto Gallitini, it is now ascertained, is appointed Ambassador to negotiate a Peace. This gentleman is of *foreign* extraction, — came to our shores about 30 years ago, — taught our citizens the *French* tongue, and the *French* doctrines of the "holy right of insurrection," — was pardoned by Gen. Washington, — has had the care of the surpluses of the Revenue, which Jefferson thought ought not to be unproductive in the public vaults, exciting the cupidity of nations, — and has accumulated a princely fortune from his liberal salary and by other thrifty means in which foreigners generally excel. The jealous Potentates of Europe place around their persons a corps of foreign mercenary troops on whose subserviency and fidelity they may confidently rely; — Bonaparte has his Mamelukes, and the Grand Sultan his Janizaries; so our democratic Presidents have had their Swiss and Walloon Guards — trusty and secret men who never flinch like native citizens; — they can coolly talk of "Confiscation" and handle Hemp "as familiar as their garter;" *Col. Binns* the Irishman can deride New England as "the land of Codfish and Onions," — *Col. Duane* scoffs our merchants "as the worthless part of the community," — and Gales, Baptiste Irvine, Anthony Campbell, Pechin, Colonel Gray, Colonel De Lacroix and others are the soldiers of fortune, and patriotic Volunteers who are to defend Government from the people, and compel native citizens to feel how great a misfortune it was to be born in their native land.

Since it is a fact, that native born citizens are excluded from office and honor, and this War is a Foreign War on account of Foreigners only, no man certainly can be so well qualified to treat about these foreign affairs as Mons. Gallitini. *April* 10, 1813.

The "Three Alternatives," — *Embargo, Submission and War!* The American people are now afflicted and scourged with a complication of all the calamities and miseries within the power of their rulers to inflict. The morrow's sun will complete the period of SIX long and miserable years, since the evil minds of our oppressors doomed this nation to be plunged from the height of prosperity and peace into the bottomless pit of "Restrictive Energies, — into Embargoes — Non-Intercourse, and the Continental System! Six gloomy years have elapsed since we enjoyed liberty and the rights of Freemen. — We have been imprisoned within our own territory, and our rulers have been our prison-keepers. Oppression has followed oppression; still hope sustained our sinking hearts; but hope has failed, and we have nothing left but despair!

When our rulers formerly talked of the "alternatives" of Embargo, Submission or War, we did hope the nation would not be compelled to groan under the miseries of more than one of these burthens at a time. Experience, however, teaches us the absurdity of their measures, as well as the solecism of their language. Embargo, Submission and War are the only three signs in the political zodiac of our present rulers; and in one of these signs the nation has constantly been compelled to revolve; till at length, to fill up the measure of our sufferings, the cabinet has forced us — all at the same time — into WAR with England — SUBMISSION to France — and now, as we fear, EMBARGO with all the world! Thus, in consummation of all the projects of our democratic rulers, the nation is prostrate on its back, like the fabled giant Tityus, whose huge body covering nine acres of ground was chained to the earth, while vultures rested on his breast and mangled and feasted and revelled on his ever-growing vitals, — so is this nation chained by Embargoes, and devoured by the vulture, War.

December 21, 1813.

At the close of the year 1822, Mr. Cushing took leave of his friends and the public as an editor in the following notice: —

The subscriber having relinquished the establishment of the Salem Gazette to Messrs. Caleb Cushing and Ferdinand Andrews, he takes this opportunity of bidding adieu to his respected customers and patrons, as its editor. In the long course of years, in which he has stood before them in that capacity, he has experienced from them a constant stream of kindness, a coöperation and support, that have animated and encouraged him in his labors, which he hopes and trusts have been in some degree useful; while their candor and charity have covered a multitude of defects, of which he is deeply sensible. In turning over the list of his subscribers, he perceives many respectable names, which have stood there from his commencement in 1787 to the present time. It is not easy for him to express the gratitude he feels for favor so steady and persevering, and for a thousand distinct and various obligations from individuals, which he could specify, were it proper: he begs his friends to give him credit for all that he ought to say on this parting occasion; and to accept of his best wishes, that the opening year may smile upon them, and redouble upon their own heads the blessings they have communicated to others.

THOMAS C. CUSHING.

Mr. Cushing died on the 28th of September, 1824, at the age of sixty years. He was a native of Hingham, in the county of Plymouth, and began his profession, as an apprentice with Samuel Hall. Under the instruction of a master, whose sound judgement and liberal feelings had led him to espouse the American cause, and whose ability in his profession had given him a high rank among his brethren, Mr. Cushing, with talents of no ordinary cast, had imbibed those principles and laid the foundation of that rank, which he maintained both in his professional character and as an estimable member of society. Upon the expiration of his apprenticeship, he began a paper in Charlestown, under the title of the American Recorder, but soon after removed to Salem, and began the Mercury, in connection with John Dabney, as has been already stated. He continued to be the editor of the Salem Gazette, from the day that he resumed it in July, 1797, till about two years before his death, when infirm health obliged him to relinquish the publication. He conducted the paper with well known ability, and with a steadfast and conscientious adherence to the political principles inculcated by his master. The qualities of his heart were not less amiable than the faculties of his mind were respectable. His bosom was the seat of all the gentle virtues; his benevolence was unwearied; his friendship disinterested, ardent, and sincere; and his integrity steadfast, incorruptible, and unsuspected. In his domestic relations he was a bright example of conjugal attachment and parental tenderness. His death was a distressing calamity to his family and a severe affliction to a large circle of friends and acquaintance.*

Caleb, the son of Thomas C. Cushing, was connected with the Gazette only a few months. The paper was conducted by Ferdinand Andrews, till some time in 1827, when he sold his interest in it to Caleb Foote, and removed to Lancaster, in the county of Worcester, and published a paper there for several years. The Salem Gazette, now the oldest paper in Massachusetts, except the Massachusetts Spy, is still in the possession of Caleb Foote, editor and proprietor. It is a highly respectable and influential paper, and circulates extensively in the county of Essex. When Federalism went out of fashion, it naturally became Whig in its politics, and has held fast to the faith of its original editor and proprietor.

* See Salem Gazette, October 1, 1824.

THE NATIONAL GAZETTE.

In October, 1791, Philip Freneau, a clerk in the office of the Secretary of State, began, in Philadelphia, the publication of a paper called the National Gazette. Mr. Jefferson was then at the head of the State Department, and it was supposed, — probably not without reason, — that the paper received its political complexion from his influence and dictation. Certain it is that the paper was devoted to the dissemination and defence of his peculiar notions and wishes respecting the administration of public affairs. It is well known that Mr. Jefferson was strongly opposed to all the principles and measures of Mr. Hamilton, the Secretary of the treasury; and the National Gazette was the principal channel, through which all the opponents of the "funding system" poured forth their clamor and vituperation. John Adams, also, the Vice-President, had a share of the reproaches, that were liberally cast upon most of the principal Federalists who had any concern with the government. Nor did Washington himself entirely escape, though the attacks upon him were rather indirect. The Jacobin societies throughout the Union were upheld, and defended against the opposition of the Federalists, and all the proceedings of the French revolutionists were approved and commended. The leading Federalists were

12 *

charged with treason to liberty, adherence to England, affection for monarchical government, and for aristocratic distinctions of nobility. If evidence of this be required, take the following paragraph, published a few days after the election of President and Vice-President, in December, 1792:—

> The mask is at last torn from the monarchical party, who have, but with too much success, imposed themselves upon the public for the sincere friends of our republican constitution. Whatever may be the event of the competition for the Vice-Presidency, it has been the happy occasion of ascertaining the two following important truths:—first, that the name of Federalist has been assumed by men who approve the constitution merely as "a promising essay towards a well-ordered government;" that is to say, as a step towards a government of kings, lords, and commons. Secondly, that the spirit of the people continues firmly republican, and if the monarchical features of the party had been sooner held up to the public view, would have universally marked the division between two candidates (equally unassailed in their private characters) one of whom is as much attached to the equal principles of liberty entertained by the great mass of his fellow-citizens, as the other is devoted to the hereditary titles, orders, and balances, which they abhor as an insult to the rights and dignity of man.

The two candidates referred to were John Adams of Massachusetts, and George Clinton of New York.

The publication of a series of "Probationary Odes" was begun about the first of June, 1793, (and run to twelve or fifteen numbers) "by Jonathan Pindar, Esq., a cousin of Peter's, and candidate for the post of Poet-Laureat." They were probably written by Freneau, who, though he had no great poetical genius, was a fluent and rapid versifier. These Odes are chiefly lampoons on the principal officers of the administration and leading men in the government,— Adams, the Vice-President — Knox, Secretary of war — Hamilton, Secretary of the treasury, &c. The first is addressed "To all the Great Folks in a lump;" the second "To Atlas," meaning Mr. Hamilton; the third "To a Select Body of Great Men," meaning the Senate, &c. The fourth, which here follows, needs no explanation: —

TO A WOULD-BE GREAT MAN.

Jonathan defendeth the GREAT DEFENDER; magnifieth and exalteth *his works;* and confesseth his own littleness of understanding.

"*Certat tergeminis tollere honoribus.*" Hor.

Daddy Vice, Daddy Vice,
One may see in a trice
The drift of your fine publication;
As sure as a gun,
The thing was just done,
To secure you — a *pretty* HIGH station.

Defences you call
To knock down our wall,
And batter the STATES to the ground, sir;
So thick were your shot,
And so hellish fire-hot,
They 've scarce a whole bone to be found, sir —

When you tell us of *kings*,
And such pretty things,
Good mercy! how brilliant your page is!
So bright in each line
I vow now you 'll shine
Like — a glow-worm to all future ages.

When you handle your balance,
So vast are your talents,
Like Atlas your wonderful strength is;
You know every State
To a barley-corn weight,
For your steel-yard the continent length is.

On Davila's page
Your discourses so sage
Democratical numsculls bepuzzle,
With arguments tough
As white leather or buff,
The *republican* BULL-DOGS to *muzzle.*

'T is labor in vain,
Your senses to strain
Our brains any longer to muddle;
Like Colossus you stride
O'er our noddles so wide,
We look up like FROGS IN A PUDDLE.

The next Ode indicates a *wish* but a lack of *courage* to be severe on Washington: —

TO A TRULY GREAT MAN.

"*Justum et tenacem propositi virum.*" Hor.

George, on thy virtues often have I dwelt;
And still the theme is grateful to mine ear;
Thy gold let chemists ten times over melt,
From dross and base alloy they 'll find it clear.

Yet thou 'rt a man — although, perhaps, the first;
But man at best is but a being frail;
And since with error human nature 's curst,
I marvel not that thou shouldst sometimes fail.

That thou hast *long* and *nobly* served the state,
The nation *owns*, and *freely* gives thee thanks:
But Sir! — whatever speculators prate,
She gave thee not the power to establish BANKS.

No doubt thou thought 'st it was a phenix nest,
Which Congress were so busy to build up:
But there a crocodile had fixed his rest,
And snapped the *nations bowels* at a sup.

The greedy monster is not yet half cloyed,
Nor will be, whilst a leg or arm remains;
Those parts the last of all should be destroyed;
The next delicious morsel is *her brains.*

I trust thou 'st seen the monster by this time,
And hast prepared thy knife to cut his throat;
His scales are so damned hard, that in thy prime,
'Twould take thee twenty years to make it out.

God grant thee life to do it: — Fare thee well!
Another time examine well the nest;
Though of Arabia's spices it should smell,
It may produce some foul internal pest.

In April, 1793, the President issued his Proclamation, recommending the observation of strict neutrality towards all the belligerent powers of Europe. This was the signal of a powerful attack from all who espoused the cause of the French revolutionists. The Gazette was the principal channel, through which their vituperation reached the people. A number of writers assailed the President and his policy in terms of unmeasured invective. Some of these communications were written with ability, and were as ably replied to, in the Gazette, and other papers, which assumed the defence of the President, and undertook the task of refuting the arguments of his assailants. "Veritas" addressed "To the President of the United States" a series of letters, in which it was contended that the Proclamation was not consistent either with *duty* or *interest* — that *neutrality* was *ingratitude* to France — that it would provoke the French nation to hostilities — that it was issued in opposition to the general sentiment of the people and the will of the nation — and insinuated, pretty directly, that the President was under the influence of British emissaries. The following detached paragraphs exhibit some of the innuendoes, with which "Veritas" enriched his letters: —

I am aware, Sir, that some court satellites may have deceived you with respect to the sentiments of your fellow-citizens. The first magistrate of a country, whether he be called a king or a president, seldom knows the real state of the nation, particularly if he be so much buoyed up by official importance, as to think it beneath his dignity to mix occasionally with the people. Let me caution you, Sir, to beware that you do not view the state of the public mind, at this critical moment, through a fallacious medium. Let not the little buzz of the aristocratic few, and their contemptible minions, of speculators, tories, and British emissaries, be mistaken for the exalted and generous voice of the

American people. The spirit of 1776 is again aroused; and soon shall the mushroom lordlings of the day, the enemies of American as well as French liberty, be taught that American Whigs of 1776 will not suffer French Patriots of 1792 to be vilified with impunity by the common enemies of both.

* * * * *

It is to be hoped that our public councils have not been duped into any disgraceful negotiation, respecting the American ports now occupied by the British. If they have, let the infamous transaction be divulged. If they have not, let them publish the truth for the satisfaction of the public, and in vindication of their own conduct. Let government ever avoid that narrow policy, which involves in mystery the acts of public men, which ever creates distrust in the minds of the people, and is only fit to be practised by magistrates the most corrupt and worthless.

* * * * *

But notwithstanding all our endeavors to curry favor with Great-Britain, it is evident that she despises our professions and acts of neutrality. . . . . I conclude, Sir, by cautioning you not to take all upon your own shoulders at this critical juncture. Let the representatives of the people, who can alone express the national will, be speedily convened, and let all branches of the government unite their counsels and their efforts for the promotion of the public good.

* * * * *

Should the splendor and importance of great names continue to be held forth by court writers to deter individuals from a free investigation of public measures, I shall have no objection to resume my pen, and bring unquestionable arguments that elevated station is no proof of presidential or any other infallibility.

"A Friend to Peace" replied to "Veritas," first in the American Daily Advertiser, and afterwards in the National Gazette. These writers brought into the field another writer under the signature of "Philo-Veritas," who called the Proclamation a "consecrated bull," and pronounced it "improper, ill-timed, and illegal." The attacks on the President and all the members of his cabinet, except Mr. Jefferson, were continued with unabated bitterness for several months — sometimes with irony and sarcasm. As a specimen of the latter mode of attack, take the following parody on the Athanasian creed: —

A new Political Creed for the use of whom it may concern.

Whoever would live peaceably in Philadelphia, above all things it is necessary that he hold the Federal faith — and the Federal faith is this, that there are two governing powers in this country, both equal, and yet one superior: which faith except every one keep undefiledly, without doubt he shall be abused everlastingly.

The Briton is superior to the American, and the American is inferior to the Briton: and yet they are equal and the Briton shall govern the American.

The Briton, while here, is commanded to obey the American, and yet the American ought to obey the Briton.

And yet they ought not both to be obedient, but only one to be obedient. For there is one dominion nominal of the American, and another dominion real of the Briton.

And yet there are not two dominions, but only one dominion.

For like as we are compelled by the British constitution book to acknowledge that *subjects* must submit themselves to their monarchs, and be obedient to them in all things:

So we are forbid by our Federal executive to say that we are at all influenced by our treaty with France, or to pay regard to what it enforceth:

The American was created for the Briton, and the Briton for the American:

And yet the American shall be a slave to the Briton, and the Briton the tyrant of the American.

And Britons are of three denominations, and yet only of one soul, nature, and subsistency:

The Irishman of infinite impudence:

The Scotchman of cunning most inscrutable:

And the Englishman, of impertinence altogether insupportable:

The only true and honorable gentlemen of this our blessed country.

He, therefore, that would live in quiet, must thus think of the Briton and the American.

It is furthermore necessary that every *good* American should believe in the infallibility of the executive, when its proclamations are echoed by Britons:

For the true faith is, that we believe and confess that the government is fallible and infallible ·

Fallible in its republican nature, and infallible in its monarchical tendency, erring in its state of individuality, and unerring in its Federal complexity.

So that though it be both fallible and infallible, yet it is not twain, but one government only, as having consolidated all state dominion, in order to rule with sway uncontrolled.

This is the true Federal faith, which except a man believe and practise faithfully, beyond all doubt he shall be cursed perpetually.

Volumes might be filled with extracts from the political communications in the Gazette,—all censuring the acts of the government, and tending to create discontent among the people. The French government was uniformly upheld and defended in all its operations, and especially in its endeavors to involve our country in a war with Great-Britain. The French minister, Genet, who arrived in this country in 1793, and immediately began to arm and send out, from our ports, privateers to cruise against the British, was hailed and followed with hosannas, while Adams and Hamilton were assailed with unmitigated contumely and reproach. The extracts already offered are sufficient to fix the character of the paper. The papers of the 19th, 23d and 26th of October are printed on half sheets only, and the last contains the following notice:—

†‡† With the present number (208) concludes the second volume, and second year's publication of the National Gazette. Having just imported, on his own account, a considerable quantity of new and elegant printing types from Europe, it is the editor's intention to resume the publication of this paper in a short time, and previously to the meeting of Congress on the second day of December next. . . . . Printers of newspapers may omit sending their Gazettes in exchange, till further notified.

I am not aware that the publication was ever resumed.

In 1809, Freneau collected and published in two volumes, his poetical pieces, which had been printed in the newspapers from 1768 to 1795. Many of these originated from events in the Revolutionary war. "These poems (he says in a prefatory note,) were intended to expose to vice and treason their own hideous deformity; to depict virtue, honor, and patriotism in their native beauty." Many of these pieces were popular at the time of their publication, and are still recollected. Others were versifications of anecdotes and humorous stories. "Columbus to Ferdinand" and "The Indian Student" found a place in the school books of sixty years ago. I know not in what newspaper the annexed verses were first printed. They are worthy of a place in any specimens of poetry, although some of the lines may be pronounced prosaic. The last two stanzas present thoughts that are highly poetical; and the lines printed in Italics present an image supremely bold and beautiful: —

THE INDIAN BURYING GROUND.

In spite of all the learned have said,
I still my old opinion keep;
The *posture*, that *we* give the dead,
Points out the soul's eternal sleep.

Not so the ancients of these lands —
The Indian, when from life released,
Again is seated with his friends,
And shares again the joyous feast.*

His imaged birds, and painted bowl,
And venison, for a journey dressed,
Bespeak the nature of the soul,
ACTIVITY, that knows no rest.

His bow, for action ready bent,
And arrows, with a head of stone,

* The North American Indians bury their dead in a sitting posture, decorating the corpse with wampum, the images of birds, quadrupeds, &c.: And (if that of a warrior) with bows, arrows, tomahawks, and other military weapons.

Can only mean that life is spent,
And not the old ideas gone.

Thou, stranger, thou shalt come this way,
No fraud upon the dead commit—
Observe the swelling turf, and say
They do not *lie*, but here they *sit*.

Here still a lofty rock remains,
On which the curious eye may trace
(Now wasted half, by wearing rains,)
The fancies of a ruder race.

Here still an aged elm aspires,
Beneath whose far-projecting shade
(And which the shepherd still admires)
The children of the forest played!

There oft a restless Indian queen,
(Pale *Shebah*, with her braided hair,)
And many a barbarous form is seen
To chide the man that lingers there.

By midnight moons, o'er moistening dews,
In habit for the chase arrayed,
The hunter still the deer pursues,
The hunter and the deer, a shade!

And long shall timorous Fancy see
The painted chief, and pointed spear,
And Reason's self shall bow the knee
To shadows and delusions here.

THE AMERICAN APOLLO.

The publication of this paper begun with the year 1792. It was published weekly on Friday. I have not been able to find the first number. There is a volume in the Boston Athenæum, which opens with No. 40, and closes with No. 156, December 25, 1794, and this I presume to be the last publication, though it contains no notice of discontinuance. It was first printed by Belknap & Young; afterwards by Belknap & Hall; and from No. 131 to 156, by Joseph Belknap. This gentleman was a son of the Rev. Jeremy Belknap, and was educated to the trade of a printer. He was the editor of the Apollo; and probably received some aid from his father at the commencement of the enterprise.

The Apollo, at first, was well conducted, and maintained a respectable literary character. The editor's paragraphs discover a better knowledge of the English language and a more familiar acquaintance with composition, than those of some of the cotemporary Boston journals. The correspondents were numerous, and many of their contributions are of a character well adapted to amuse and improve the readers. The selections, in general, were judiciously made, and evince care and industry in collecting and condensing intelligence, and purity of taste in gathering sentiments, anecdotes, and historical fragments from popular authors. Its politics were of the Federal school, but neither ultra nor violent.

The Apollo appears to have pursued the tenor of its way without involving itself in any very serious conflict with other papers or their correspondents. On one occasion the editors congratulated "the *printers* of the Mercury on the rapid credit their paper was acquiring by the scurrility which occupied so large a portion of it from week to week." They lamented their own deficiency "of that *laudable gift*, which rendered the Apollo 'dull and sleepy' to the low and vulgar."

One of the correspondents of the Apollo had a little sparring with PHILENIA, (Mrs. Morton,) and MENANDER, (R. T. Paine.) In some "Stanzas to Mira," Philenia wrote, —

Since first Affliction's dreary form
Gloomed the bright summer of my days,
Ne'er has my *bankrupt bosom* known
A solace like *his* fearless praise.

On which "Truth," a correspondent of the Apollo, wrote the following: —

Thy "*bosom bankrupt!*" — ah! too true the thought:
A bankruptcy indeed that breast displays,
Which knows no joys but those from *flattery* caught,
Which knows no "solace" like Menander's praise.

By the next Centinel, MENANDER sent the following stanza to TRUTH: —

"Too true the thought!" Know, Truth, that "bankrupt breast"
A bank of *genius* and of *taste* contains;
While thy *lank muse*, of not a *sous* possest,
BEGS the *scant pittance* of ITS daily brains.

TRUTH rejoined, in the Apollo, —

A "BANK of *genius* and a BANK of *taste!*"
But few DISCOUNTS, Menander, there we find;
With all the charms of lofty nonsense graced
As well might WISDOM *issue* from *thy* mind:

A "BANK *of genius!*"—were it so, how blest!
There might *thy* "*bankrupt*" *Muse* a *credit* gain
WHICH, long by *hunger* and by *pride* oppressed,
"BEGS" not, but STEALS, to "ease ITS daily" pain.

A few other squibs of the like harmless character were exchanged, but these are sufficient to show the temper of the belligerents. A writer in the Apollo, addressed the following lines to TRUTH, which probably were an exponent of the public sentiment in regard to the controversy: —

Cannot Philenia's *harmless* lays
Draw from thy pen their *needed* praise?
Cannot the *puffing* of Menander
Make thee aside from Truth to wander?
Must thou for ever *rail* at such
Who please by *Flattery's* magic touch?
Canst not thou praise that *sappy* band,
Who, striving, grasp at Wisdom's wand?
Yet miss the blessing and the boon,
Like children crying for the moon.
Sure, friend, I think thee vastly wrong
To blast Philenia's *pretty* song,
And write against such *spicy* praise,
As makes the Boston people gaze;—
'T is waging war — and soon thou 'lt feel
Menander's strokes, like sharpened steel;
For such destruction 's in his quill,
As will ten thousand, like thee, kill—
He writes, and writes, then writes again;—
O Lord! such *squeezing* of the brain
Must needs convince all men of sense
That he 's to Wisdom's throne pretence,
Whilst Thou, meek Truth, must sit and sigh
To hear a herd of flatterers cry,—

Philenia 's great, Philenia 's wise,
Philenia, daughter of the skies!
Whose songs, whose music, and whose lyre
Charm each fond soul, and all inspire. IRONICUS.

A pleasant sort of correspondence was carried on in the Apollo, on celibacy, marriage, house-keeping, &c. by writers, who adopted the signatures of "A Bachelor," "Hymen," and "Ezekiel." The publication of an original novel, called "The Hapless Orphan," also caused a few angry communications between the *avowed* friends and the *alleged* enemies of American literature. The novel itself did not long outlive the controversy on its merits. Among the poetical contributions to the Apollo are a number signed "L. S." some of which are tolerable for newspaper poetry. The verses, which follow, are from a piece that fills nearly a column, entitled

CONSCIOUS GUILT.

Ye, who, o'erpowered by Satan, yield
To passion's cruel sway,
Ye know full well their torturing pain,
Who burning lust obey.

The Libyan sand or Greenland snow,
The hardy spirit bears;
But to endure the extremes of guilt
The bravest soul despairs.

The gnawing vulture ceaseless preys,
Yet still the soul remains,
Still keenly feels the tearing wound,
And lives to endless pains.

A correspondent requested the publication of an article, of which a part is annexed, said to be written by a person confined in the Boston work-house: —

THE CONTRAST, — SOLILOQUY IN SERVITUDE.

What revolutions oft take place
Among the busy human race!

Although with cautious steps we move,
Our best laid plans abortive prove;
When fairest prospects greet our eyes,
Adversity in ambush lies;
Thus are we all by Fortune cheated,
And our most sanguine hopes defeated.
To ward her strokes we strive in vain, —
The unconstant Deity will reign.

How changed my station and condition!
How unexpected the transition
From plenteous fare and various dishes,
All to the summit of my wishes,
To bull-head broth and shins decreed,
On which reluctantly I feed;
From generous punch and cheerful wine,
Of which I drank, when fixed to dine,
To simple water and small beer;
(Can these the languid spirits cheer?)
From China plate to wooden tray;
From silver can to mug of clay;
From feather bed to bed of straw;
('T is thus ordained by work-house law;)
From verdant meads and rising grounds,
Now circumscribed to narrow bounds;
From equal, friendly, social joys,
Cursed with obscenity and noise;
From easy business, my delight,
Now doomed to toil from morn to night;
From liberty, the gift of God,
Subjected to a tyrant's nod.

* * * * * *

With competence and ease once blest,
No cares intrusive marred my rest;
In rapturous dreams my conscious soul,
Unshackled, ranged from pole to pole;
Each cheerful day with pleasure crowned,
Complete felicity I found:
Now banished from the world, &c.

Governor Hancock, as is well known, was a violent opponent of theatrical exhibitions, and had, some time in the year 1792, ordered the Sheriff of Suffolk county to arrest the actors at the exhibition room in Board alley, for a violation of the law against stage-plays; in consequence of which Harper, the manager, was arrested and taken from the stage. The Governor was also a zealous advocate for the popular French doctrine of Liberty and Equality, and during the same year, had made himself a subject of raillery, by giving a ball to the colored people of Boston at his mansion-house. The Connecticut wit, who wrote the news-boy's Address to the Readers of the Hartford Courant, humorously touched upon these and some other topics, which had occupied some space in the Boston newspapers. The following extract from the Address was copied into the Apollo: —

And lo! where o'er the eastern shores,
Bostonia lifts her haughty towers,
What motley scenes salute our eyes!
What wonders upon wonders rise!
There each succeeding day still brings
A mixture strange of various things;
Small-pox, Physicians, State-Intriguers,
John Hancock's speeches, plays, and negroes.
Here Plays their *Heathen names* forsake,
And those of *Moral Lectures* take;
While, thus baptized, they hope to win
Indulgence for all future sin.
Now Hancock, fired with patriot rage,
Proscribes the Norvals of the stage;
Claps Harper under civil durance,
For having dared, with vile assurance,
By *Interludes* and *Plays* profane,
Pollute the glories of his reign:
Now, prompt to assert the *Rights of Man*,
On nature's most *extensive* plan,
Behold him, to his splendid hall,
The noble sons of Afric call;
While, as the sable bands advance,
With frolic mien in sportive dance,

Refreshing clouds of rich *perfume*
Are wafted o'er the spacious room.
There he, with keen delight surveys
Their graceful tricks, and winning ways;
Their tones enchanting, raptured hears,
Surpass the music of the spheres;
And, as he breathes the *fragrant air*,
He deems that Freedom's self dwells there!
While Cuffey near him takes his stand,
Hail fellow met, and grasps his hand;
With pleasure glistening in his eyes,
"Ah! Massa Gubbener," he cries, —
"Me glad to see you, for de people say,
You lub de Neegur better dan de play."

The *original* poetry of the Apollo was of an indifferent character, and is hardly worth quoting, for the exhibition of its quality. The most copious writer of this sort of verse, used the signature of "The Traveler;" and beside a number of smaller pieces, composed one of considerable length, which was continued through some five or six numbers of the paper, entitled "All the World 's a Stage."

THE MASSACHUSETTS MERCURY.

The first number of this paper was issued on the first day of January, 1793, by Alexander Young and Samuel Etheridge. It was a small half sheet, printed in four pages, quarto, and was published three times a week — on Monday, Wednesday, and Friday. After the publication of seventy-eight numbers, it was enlarged, printed on a whole demy sheet, with four folio pages, and issued only twice a week, — Tuesday and Friday.

In the first number of the enlarged edition, July 3, 1793, the editors say, — "The enlargement of the Mercury is contemplated as a duty, which they owe to their reputation, and the liberal share of the public countenance which they have received. They have had, frequently, occasion to regret that the limits of their former paper were so circumscribed, as to exclude many valuable and lengthy communications, whose insertion would have occupied so largely that other favors would have been repressed and variety rendered impracticable. . . . . But the inclination of the Editors is no longer shackled; and while they apologize for an apparent neglect to the more copious effusions of genius and speculation, they anticipate a continuance of literary favors, and of entertaining *packets* of every description, to replete and variegate the *Mail of the Mercury*." In this number of the paper, the word "Massachusetts" was struck from the title — for which no reason was assigned.

On the 6th of August following, the partnership of Young & Etheridge, as proprietors and editors of the Mercury, was dissolved; and, as may be concluded from the notice, that announces the dissolution, by the act of Young alone. In the next paper there was another advertisement concerning the affairs of the establishment, beginning thus — "Alexander Young, having dissolved the partnership under the firm of Young & Etheridge, in consequence of certain circumstances, ... he therefore begs leave to assure the public in general, and his friends in particular, that he shall continue to edit the Mercury in his own name, and upon its present plan." What these circumstances were does not appear, nor is it of much importance to know. Young continued sole editor and proprietor of the Mercury till the 8th of April, 1794, when he announced that he had "thought proper to receive into connection in the publication of this paper, Mr. Thomas Minns, whose abilities and sedulous attention to the duties of his profession will probably conduce to render this work more extensively useful and interesting." The accession of a new partner to the editorial department was the occasion of the following

ADDRESS TO THE PUBLIC.

That a "Free Press is the sure palladium and bulwark of the civil and religious liberties of every community," is a truth which Americans are taught to lisp from their cradle — to expatiate, therefore, on a position so universally allowed, appears unnecessary.

Conscious, however, that the low ribaldry and personal defamation, which frequently disgrace European publications, and sometimes contaminate the purer effusions of the American press, have a most certain tendency to depreciate its worth, obstruct its utility, and to sap the foundation of every thing dear and valuable to mankind, the Editors of the Mercury will ever strive, with the most cautious attention, to avoid the rocks, on which but too many of their cotemporaries have been shattered.

On the other hand, they aver, with the true independence of Americans, that no sinister views shall ever induce them to swerve from that strict impartiality — that ingenuous candor, and that scrutinizing vigilance, so necessary to the very existence of Republican Freedom: — Theirs shall be the task

"To drag the lurking villain into day,"

to expose the machinations of the vindictive, and to support real merit, though laboring under the oppression of obloquy and misfortune. Fearless of consequences, the decent, the modest essays and animadversions of the Theologian, the Moralist, and Politician, shall find a most ready insertion.

Public measures, of whatever nature or complexion, may be freely and liberally descanted upon in the pages of the Mercury; and while it will never be sullied by any attack on private characters, Gentlemen in public capacities, the Editors hope, will never fear a minute investigation of their conduct.

But while their particular attention is directed to the dearer concerns of their own country, the momentous affairs of Europe shall not be neglected — every event or occurrence — every species of intelligence, important or interesting, shall be equally sought after, and correctly detailed, with the same invariable adherence to truth, which, they trust, will ever be the leading characteristic of their conduct.

On these principles they venture to solicit a continuance of that patronage and support, which have hitherto been so liberally afforded to the Mercury, by the respectable and intelligent citizens of Massachusetts — and with the utmost fidelity subscribe themselves the Public's

Most devoted Servants,

YOUNG & MINNS.

From this date the prosperity of the Mercury was rapid in its progress. Its circulation extended, and the number of its advertising customers increased. The industry of the editors was indefatigable. One of them was constantly in the office, while the other was looking for the latest news at the insurance offices, on the exchange, or on the wharves, or attending to the indispensable out-door business of the concern. On the night before the publication day neither of them left the office till their form was ready for the press, which was seldom before twelve o'clock.

In June, 1796, Young & Minns were appointed Printers to the Legislature of Massachusetts — an appointment, which added to their responsibility and their income. In giving notice of it to the public, they say, —

As young men, they feel they shall give opportunity for the exercise of candor in the prosecution of a paper, which will now be considered of more importance, perhaps, than formerly. Their political sentiments have ever been strictly Republican; and their grand object, in the promulgation of intelligence, the dissemination of Truth. While, on the one hand, they have never parasitically flattered the wishes of the People, by representing occurrences *falsely* favorable to the French; on the other, they have never willfully omitted an instance of the misfortune and degradation of the COALITION against LIBERTY, of which *England* is a branch: THEY HAVE AIMED TO BE JUST.

Nor has Justice been studied, exclusively, in stating Foreign Intelligence. In the Domestic Department, it has been rigorously adhered to; they have never bitterly and maliciously abused the Rulers of our country; nor bestowed absurd and undeserved panegyric upon them. They have "Nothing extenuated, nor set down aught in malice."

A double assiduity will now be required to publish, to the acceptation of an extended and diversified patronage, the MASSACHUSETTS MERCURY. At the moment the Editors declare, with confidence, they never shall wreck on the rocks which have injured their predecessors — they promise cautiously to avoid the sands of an opposite extreme; and to be immutably IMPARTIAL.

At the beginning of the next year, January 3, 1797, the Mercury was again enlarged, and the word "Massachusetts" was restored to the title.

In the course of the next year the public feeling was considerably agitated by certain publications in Europe, by the Abbé Barruel and Professor Robison of Edinburgh, concerning the organization and influence of certain secret societies, called *Illuminati.* Professor Robison's work was entitled, "Proofs of a Conspiracy against all the Religions and Governments of Europe, carried on in the secret meetings of Free Masons, Illuminati, and Reading Societies; by John Robison, A. M. Professor of Natural Philosophy, and Secretary to the Royal Society of Edinburgh." The Rev. Dr. Morse, of Charlestown, in a Fast-Day Sermon, adverted to the subject of secret societies, and after giving a summary account of the principles and plan of the Illuminati, and the probable evidence of their having commenced their demoralizing work in this country, said — "Let any who doubt the truth and fairness of the foregoing representation, read for themselves. The book, which is my authority, ought to be read by every American. It throws more light upon the causes which have brought the world into its present disorganized state (I speak for myself) than any, I had almost said, than all other books beside."

Dr. Morse's Sermon was printed, with some explanatory notes, and an appendix, containing extracts from

Professor Robison's "Proofs." An interesting controversy followed, and the Mercury was the channel, through which the most respectable of the adverse parties held their communications with the public. Some of the Free Masons were exceedingly angry with Dr. Morse, and attacked him with virulence. He wrote a justification of himself, and of the character of Professor Robison, which was published in the Mercury, and extended to seven or eight numbers, or to thrice that number of columns. Doctor Josiah Bartlett, of Charlestown, then Grand Master of the Grand Lodge of Massachusetts, undertook the defence of the Free Masons against any injurious imputations that might be cast upon them in consequence of the writings of Dr. Morse. He even went so far as to say that the notes accompanying the Sermon were sufficient to explain the author's sentiments in regard to Free Masonry in this country; and added that he had "too high an opinion of his [Dr. Morse's] independence and consistency of conduct, to suppose that he would have assisted in his professional character at a late public solemnity, if he was really unfriendly to the institution." * The chief attempts to invalidate the credit of Professor Robison's "Proofs," which appeared in the Mercury, were made by the Rev. Dr. Bentley of Salem, and an anonymous writer under the signature of "Censor." Some other writers occasionally touched upon the subject, just forcibly enough to keep it before the public, but without adding any interest to the controversy. An abridgement of Barruel's "Memoirs of

* The *Corinthian Lodge* was publicly constituted, and its officers installed, at Concord, two months after the publication of the Fast Day Sermon, on which occasion Dr. Morse delivered, at their request, a very acceptable discourse, before the officers of the Grand Lodge and a large assembly of the Fraternity.

Jacobinism," originally written for a Hartford paper, was published in the Mercury, in 1799, after which the correspondents of the paper seemed disposed to let the subject rest.

The commencement of the present century, January, 1801, may be remembered as a new era in the history of this paper. WARREN DUTTON, a gentleman of fine talents, and a scholar of high reputation, from New-Haven, became its editor, and was aided by the contributions of many good writers. It was generally understood that this arrangement was effected through the agency of Dr. Morse. The mechanical execution of the paper was much improved, and the pages enlarged. The title also, underwent a change, and now appeared as

NEW-ENGLAND PALLADIUM.

The style of the new editor, as well as the moral and political principles, which the Palladium was intended to inculcate and enforce, are illustrated in the following elegantly-written article, with which he began his career: —

ADDRESS TO THE PUBLIC.

At the close of a century, it is natural and useful to pause for a moment, and review the years which have past; to examine the moral and political condition of mankind, and calculate their progress in wisdom, knowledge, and happiness. The idea of a perpetual and irresistible advancement towards a better and more perfect state of society is so grateful and alluring, that we are apt to lose sight of the real character of men, and invest them with ideal degrees of perfection; to overlook all the lessons of experience and corrected reason; to neglect the means of happiness, which lie within our reach, and gaze upon the visions of distant good. It is not strange, therefore, that men of warm hearts have been fascinated with the delusive appearance of great, and hitherto unknown blessings, so soon to be realized; that they have given up the acquisitions of past ages, and, for a while, forgotten that they were men. Happily for mankind, they have awaked from this dream of moral and political perfection to a serious consideration of the character and condition of man; to examine the rectitude and perfection of his reason, its nature, extent and province,—and to reflect upon those new maxims in morals and policy, which have been hidden from the wisdom of ages. They have been led to observe their influence upon the conduct, character, and happiness of individuals and nations, and beheld their secret, renovating progress. Their reflections upon the great changes, in the modes of thinking and acting, in governments and religion, have terminated in a settled belief, that modern liberty and equality, the emancipation and regeneration of the world, the perfectibility of reason, and all the farrago of political creed-mongers, are founded in the vanity, pride, and wickedness of the human heart; and that they are calculated to call into action all its restless and licentious propensities, to chill its virtues, and corrupt its best affections. The efforts of political philosophists were primarily designed to effect a revolution in the moral state of man; to weaken his sense of obligation, by placing him in an insulated state; to darken the limits of moral good and evil, by sophistry and scepticism, and, by the corruption of his moral taste and sentiments, to prepare his mind for the reception of Atheism. The causes, which have produced this singular state of depravity among the civilized nations of the world, may be traced in their operation through the greatest part of the last century. The spirit of free-thinking, prevalent in Europe, at an early period, has been gradually diminishing the reverence for religious institutions, exalting reason with its weaknesses and imperfections, above all, which is called God, till at length, uniting with the spirit of modern liberty and revolution, it has gone forth the terror and the destroyer of nations. Yet the revolutions, which have marked the close of the last century, with every circumstance of cruelty and dumb dismay, have been represented as the necessary regimen for a new and more perfect state. The cries of poverty and wretchedness, of despair and death, have been silenced with the lullaby of liberty. Human victims have been the viands at the carnival of freedom, and its rites have been celebrated with the orgies of demons.

14 *

The reason of man, acting and concluding through the medium of vanity, of pride, of prejudice, and of every vicious propensity, has developed and sanctioned all the maxims and principles in the new code of morals and policy; converted his rights into a vast "magazine of offensive weapons," and wielded them for the purposes of invasion and destruction. After all this noise, turmoil, and devastation, what good has resulted to the world? What new principles have been devised and adopted, which experience has proved useful and salutary? What new grounds have been found for the security of civil or religious rights? or, in what manner has the cause of sound and useful science been promoted?

It is well known, that the people, who first settled this country, brought with them the true principles of liberty, and that their literary, civil, and religious establishments have been, from that time to this, its only solid support. The spirit, which grew out of these institutions, while nourished and supported by them, has been their vigilant guardian and protector. While it inculcated submission to all lawful and righteous authority, it stood ready to meet aggression and invasion, in every form. It carried this country through a long, disastrous war, and secured to its inhabitants a government, suited to its social, literary, and moral condition. If, therefore, the foundations of this government are not supported, the superstructure must fall. Whenever the manners and habits of the people, in this country, become licentious and corrupt, the government must of course become the object of calumny and abuse; and if this corruption cannot be checked, or controled, a system of government, better suited to their habits and state of society, will be found absolutely necessary. How far this moral and political corruption has spread, the spirit of abuse and misrepresentation, of slander and insurrection, so fully manifested in this country, must declare.

For ourselves, we consider the line of duty as limited and defined. We know that the great body of the New-England people are of one mind; that they still reverence, cherish, and support the institutions of their venerable forefathers; and that, for the maintenance of these, in their purity and simplicity, no price will be thought too high, no sacrifice too great. Whatever changes, therefore, may take place in the political condition of this country, the principles, which we espouse, will forever remain the same. They are not the doctrines and opinions of a day; they do not vary with every turn of circumstance, nor suit themselves to every change of civil administration; but they are founded upon the unchanging laws of truth and justice, sanctioned by long experience, and defended by weapons tempered from the " armory of God." For the defence of these invaluable blessings, we stand prepared, on the one hand, to meet and repel the industrious malevolence of bad men, in every form, and, on the other, to preserve the good manners and habits of New-England. And, while we are desirous, and zealous to diffuse a correct taste in literature, to encourage useful science, and to maintain the principles of well-regulated society, we shall not be inattentive to the open or disguised attacks of the enemies of our peace. In every lawful and authorized way, we are pledged, by our situation, to unravel the designs and expose the practices of factious and unprincipled men, and to exhibit, for the habitual consideration of our countrymen, those theoretic ideas of liberty, which always terminate in practical slavery.

Resting, therefore, in the justice and goodness of our cause, we heartily join in the determination of the New-England farmer, merchant, and man of letters, to "quit themselves like men, and, having done all, to stand."

Immediately following this address is an extract from a Poem (filling more than three columns) entitled "THE RETROSPECT. Scene — *Summit of the Alps*," introduced by a note to the Editor, stating that it was written in the year 1796, with an intention to have it published, the following January, — that, at the close of 1797, it received some additions, relating to the principal events of that year, — but that it had never been published. It has considerable poetical merit, and the sentiments were such as pervaded all productions written by those, who saw every thing that was bad and could discover nothing that was good in the progress of the French war against the other powers of Europe. The Poet supposes himself on the summit of the Alps, and addressed by an imaginary genius, in numbers describing the scenes surveyed from that position. A few lines are sufficient to afford a specimen of the style: —

Where soft Italia's summer hills arise,
Where the fields purple in Elysian skies,
Where amorous Ocean bids his vernal gale
Scent the glad lawn, and wanton o'er the vale,

Where Love, with zone unbound, on pleasure's wing,
Laughs round the year, and hails eternal spring,
How changed the scene! The native now no more
With veins of milk, and soul of harmless lore,
Seeks the still walk, the smiling garden hails,
Bedews his greens, and breathes dissolving gales;
No more, while Philomel forgets to sing,
Tunes the soft voice, or strikes the silver string;
No more enraptured, joins the morning throng,
The slow procession, and the solemn song;
To the proud temple bends his silent way,
Kneels to the passing Host, and seems to pray.
From sleep and death he wakes to life unknown,
And glows with thoughts and wishes, not his own;
Through his roused nerves he feels the clarion thrill,
His bosom throbs, his veins with horror chill,
With sparkling flames his frenzied eye-balls roll,
And Freedom's mania rages through his soul.
Aghast he sees a new-born Cæsar rise,
And grasp at all beneath Italian skies;
Aghast he sees the crimson ensigns play,
Fire sweep the fields, and ruin cloud the day.

Some of the best writers in New-England then enriched the columns of the Palladium with their productions, and these together with the spicy and pungent paragraphs of the Editor, soon elevated the character of the paper, as a political and literary journal, to an equality with the highest in the country. Among the political contributors, was Fisher Ames, a man highly distinguished among the eminent statesmen and patriots, who procured the ratification of the Federal Constitution in Massachusetts, and who had been a conspicuous and influential member of the House of Representatives of the United States during the eight years of Washington's administration. Owing to ill health, he had retired from public life, but did not withdraw his mind from politics. His essays in the Palladium, for some years, were numerous. Soon after his death, which happened on the fourth of July, 1808, they were published, in a volume with several contributions to other papers and some of his public speeches, by a number of his friends.

A series of numbers under the title of *The Projector*, and another series, entitled *Morpheus*, were written chiefly in an ironical style, and directed against the writings of William Godwin and intended to overthrow the principles of the Godwinian school of politics and morals. Other political essays, earnestly and eloquently illustrating and enforcing the doctrines of Federalism, and exposing in the deepest tones of invective the principles of the Jacobin party, may be found in the Palladium under the titles of *The Political Whip-Top*, *British Influence*, *Americanus*, *Aristomanes*, *Novanglus*, *Laicus*, *Quintilian*, *Equality*, and others. *The Observer* treated chiefly of the moral and social condition of society. *The Restorator*, which extended to about thirty numbers, was confined to literary topics. Seven numbers were devoted to a discussion of the style of *Junius*, and his merits as a political writer. One or two numbers animadverted, in terms not remarkably respectful, on the character and works of Noah Webster, who was then about publishing the first edition of his Columbian Dictionary. Webster replied in a style rather acrimonious, but made a satisfactory defence — satisfactory to those, at least, who contend for American rights in literature as well as in government, commerce, and manufactures.

The editorials of Mr. Dutton were written with much earnestness and energy, and in a style greatly superior to what the public had been accustomed to see in the

Boston newspapers. As his name never appeared in the paper, as that of its editor, the precise time when he withdrew from it is not known.

His retirement, and the discontinuance of the contributions of some of the popular correspondents, caused a retiring ebb in the tide of its prosperity. But though its political influence began to diminish, it continued to be a favorite with the mercantile community, as a vehicle of commercial and shipping intelligence. For many years, its marine department was the fullest and most accurate of any that was published. The patronage of the state was retained many years by Young & Minns, and its character as the official paper of the state government, gave it currency among men of business, with whom politics was a matter of but little concern in comparison with their private and professional concerns. Minns, who acted as principal editor, seldom wrote an article of any length ; but he had a peculiar practice of condensing *items* of news to a paragraph of two or three lines, — superadding, perhaps, a remark of his own, of about the same length.

The original poetry, which appeared from time to time in the Palladium, was not much above the ordinary level of the newspaper standard. The lampoon, that follows, is one of the best of the poetical squibs of the day. It is necessary to say, in the way of explanation, that the admirers of Mr. Jefferson, living in the town of Cheshire, Berkshire county, manufactured an immensely large cheese, and sent it to him as a token of their respect and affection. The cheese was conveyed to the city of Washington and presented to Mr. Jefferson by Elder John Leland, the pastor of a Baptist church in Cheshire : —

THE MAMMOTH CHEESE.

AN EPICO-LYRICO BALLAD.

From meadows, rich with clover red,
  A thousand heifers come;
The tinkling bells the tidings spread,
The milk-maid muffles up her head,
  And wakes the village hum.

In shining pans the snowy flood
  Through whitened canvas pours;
The dying pots of otter good,
And rennet, tinged with madder blood,
  Are sought among their stores.

The quivering curd, in panniers stowed,
  Is loaded on the jade,
The stumbling beast supports the load,
While trickling whey bedews the road,
  Along the dusty glade.

As Cairo's slaves, to bondage bred,
  The arid deserts roam,
Through trackless sands undaunted tread,
With skins of water on their head,
  To cheer their masters' home,—

So here, full many a sturdy swain
  His precious luggage bore:
Old misers too forgot their gain,
And bed-rid cripples, free from pain,
  Now took the road before.

The widow, with her dripping mite,
  Upon her saddle borne,
Rode up in haste to see the sight,
And aid a charity so right,
  A *pauper* so forlorn.

The circling throng an opening drew
  Upon the verdant grass,
To let the vast procession through,
To spread their rich repast in view,
  And Elder J. L. pass.

Then Elder J. with lifted eyes,
  In musing posture stood,
Invoked a blessing from the skies,

To save from vermin, mites, and flies,
  And keep the bounty good.

Now mellow strokes the yielding pile
  From polished steel receives,
And shining nymphs stand still awhile,
Or mix the mass with salt and oil,
  With sage and savory leaves.

Then, sexton-like, the patriot troop,
  With naked arms and crown,
Embraced, with hardy hands, the scoop,
And filled the vast expanded hoop,
  While beetles smashed it down.

Next girding screws, the ponderous beam,
  With heft immense, drew down;
The gushing whey, from every seam,
Flowed through the streets, a rapid stream,
  And shad came up to town.

Soon after the passage of the Embargo act in 1807, several pieces of doggerel appeared in the Palladium, ridiculing that unpopular measure. The annexed verses are extracted from one of them, entitled "New Hobbies," a parody on a well known song: —

Ever since the great flood, and perhaps, long before,
Men have all had their hobbies — some one, and some more:
But, whether we ride upon one, two, or three,
Hobby-horseical riding has always been free.
All on hobbies.

The Embargo's the hobby, which Democrats ride,
It is Jefferson's glory and Madison's pride;
May all swear to support it, whatever it cost,
From Tommy the Great, down to ——— *
Curse such hobbies.

* * * * * *

If we cross the Atlantic, in Europe we find
Kings, emperors, and subjects to riding inclined;
The whim 's universal, let this proof content us,
There is no place discovered where "*non est inventus.*"
All on hobbies.

* Ichabod Frost, a somewhat noted broker, at that time, in State-street.

John Bull has his hobby — his "overgrown navy,"
Which thousands of Frenchmen has sent to old Davy:
'T is the strength of his nation, the scourge of proud France;
'T is his shield and his helmet, his buckler and lance.
Powerful hobby.

Napoleon the despot his hobby bestrides;
Not content with one empire, on kingdoms he rides;
But in mounting poor Spain, and while seizing the reins
She kicked till poor Bona. got flung for his pains.
Curb your hobby.

Let 's beware, lest America next be his aim;
If it should, as Spain served him, we 'll serve him the same;
True Yankees will never submit to his straddle,
But will kick hard enough to kick him from his saddle.
Spur your hobbies.

The marine department of the Palladium was managed for many years, entirely, by HENRY INGRAHAM BLAKE, — a journeyman printer, whose ambition to acquire the reputation of the best ship-news reporter, set all competition at defiance. When he entered upon this employment, the incidents of navigation were but imperfectly given in the newspapers. He may be almost said to have *invented* the present *universal* mode of reporting clearances, arrivals, disasters, and the various incidents connected with the shipping interest of the country. There was a time when this individual, — familiarly known among printers, merchants, and seamen, by the name of Harry Blake, — might command any salary he might choose to ask from any newspaper establishment in Boston. He knew the name, the owner, the captain's name, and the number of his crew, of every thing that sailed from the harbor of Boston, from the smallest craft that had sail and rudder to the most magnificent specimen of naval architecture; and he was able to tell the position of almost every vessel, and the time when she would arrive at her port of destination, if not prevented by unforeseen and improbable accident. He was faithful to his employers, and proud of his employment. He would visit the wharves at midnight, to obtain an item for the morning's paper; and has frequently gone out alone in a boat to meet a ship that was coming into the harbor, in darkness, storm, and tempest, to secure information wherewith to enrich his journal. The intelligence he thus obtained he carried in his memory to the printing-office, put it in type, and, if the paper had been partially worked off, he would stop the press to insert it. Whenever he made a memorandum of the information he gathered in his walks among the shipping in the harbor, or at the boarding-houses of the captain's clerks, or mates, it was written with a pencil, in characters, which no mortal but himself could read or understand, on a bit of paper no bigger than his hand, and some times on the margin of any old newspaper he might have in his pocket. After establishing the reputation of the Palladium Marine Journal, above that of all its cotemporaries, and enjoying his triumph as king of ship-news collectors, for some cause unknown he sought for a *change*, not of employment but of employer, and enlisted in the service of the Boston Courier, in which he continued many years. This course of life was, to Harry Blake, no labor, but recreation; but it was, nevertheless, an employment that must, inevitably, diminish the capability of performing it. Exposure to cold and wet, to the scorching heats of July, and the tempestuous snows and hail of January, was too much for a human constitution. Of itself it was enough to destroy a man, though his muscles were made of steel and his bones of oak. But Harry Blake suffered domestic troubles to lead him to indulgences not justified by strict requirements of temperance. Seldom, too, when he found or made acquaintances on ship-board, was he allowed to depart without partaking of a social cup. At length he sank under the pressure of intellectual and physical disorders, which benevolent friends had sought to alleviate, but which it was beyond the power of kindness to avert. His death happened some years ago, but there are many of his cotemporaries, who remember him with affectionate regret. Like Yorick's, his ghost may still have the consolation of hearing, in some of the printing-offices, a reminiscent sigh, accompanied with the exclamation, *Alas ! poor Harry Blake.*

On the first of September, 1828, the publication of the Palladium was transferred to other hands, and the change was thus announced —

TO THE PUBLIC.

After nearly forty years' duty in the Editorial field, we now make our valedictory obeisance, and respectfully withdraw, that the young and energetic may come forward to serve their cotemporaries and others. The Palladium will hereafter be published by Mr. G. V. H. Forbes, for some time advantageously known as the Editor of a very respectable and useful paper in this city.*

We cannot neglect this opportunity to offer our most grateful acknowledgements to those whose encouragement has sustained us, and particularly the individuals who extended the hand of generous friendship to our inexperienced and untried youth, and continued warm to the last. Among our first patrons were numbered the sires and grandsires of many of the generation now in active business.

We tender sincere thanks to our Professional Brethren for the good feelings they have always manifested towards us, and for contributing their full share to the uninterrupted harmony that has existed, which no variance in religion, politics, or interests, has ever, in the least, disturbed; and we most cordially reciprocate the kind wishes which have been recently expressed. * * * * *

* "Zion's Herald" — a Methodist paper.

Having been honored with the good will of the public, we know its value, as constituting an indispensable part of the basis of happiness, and hope to retain it to the end of our pilgrimage. With aspirations for blessings on our country we add, with the interesting associations which belong to the word, our professional ADIEU.

Boston, September 1, 1828. YOUNG & MINNS.

This was a deadly blow to a flourishing and profitable business. Whatever might have been the talents of the new editor, as the conductor of a religious publication, it soon appeared that he was not equal to the task he had undertaken. He abandoned it in November, 1829. The Palladium then became the property of E. Kingman, a gentleman, who had, for several years, been the Washington correspondent of editors, in sundry places. He was an excellent writer of letters; but the event proved that he could succeed much better as a reporter at the capital in Washington, than in the editorial department of a business paper in Boston. The next year, the whole establishment was disposed of to Adams & Hudson, then proprietors of the Columbian Centinel, who continued the publication of the Palladium on Tuesday and Friday, the two papers being made up chiefly of the same matter. In 1840, the subscription lists of both these papers, together with that of the Boston Gazette, were purchased by the proprietors of the Boston Daily Advertiser.

ALEXANDER YOUNG, the original projector, and owner of the Mercury and the Palladium, was a native of Boston, and the son of Alexander Young, whose ancestors were also inhabitants of that town. He used frequently to speak of working as a printer at Plymouth, and at the office of Isaiah Thomas in Worcester, — but whether as an apprentiee or journeyman at either place is not recollected. He died in Boston, March 24, 1834, aged sixty-six.

Thomas Minns was also a native of Boston. I have heard that he served his apprenticeship at Plymouth, with Nathaniel Coverly; but there are reasons for doubt as to that point. He also died in Boston, in 1834.

There have been very few partnerships in business, that have continued so long uninterrupted as that of Young & Minns. Whatever differences of temper and sentiment might have existed between them, there were other attributes, which they held in common, — industry, economy, integrity, perseverance, generosity; and this was the whole secret, though it was no secret to their friends and acquaintance, which kept them in harmonious union, for near forty years, in a business, which, of all others, is most trying to human patience and good nature. Every one, who has had the management of a newspaper in a place of any importance, can understand this. Their habits of industry and personal attention to their business were proverbial, and continued as long as they were publishers of the paper. Each of them accumulated what may be called a *handsome* property; but such untiring labor, and judicious economy in any mercantile pursuit, would have insured the possession of a million.

When Young & Minns retired from the publication of the Palladium, the printers and editors of Boston invited them to a social festival, as a token of respect and affection, to which they were justly entitled.

THE FARMER'S WEEKLY MUSEUM.

THE paper, which was long known by this title, and which, for a time, enjoyed a degree of popularity then unprecedented in the case of any one published in a country village, was begun in April, 1793, at Walpole, New-Hampshire, by Isaiah Thomas and David Carlisle. Carlisle was a native of Walpole, and had served an apprenticeship with Thomas, at Worcester, which was then just completed. Thomas furnished the printing-office with its types and press, and a bookstore with a handsome assortment of books, and the whole business of printing and bookselling was carried on under the firm of Thomas & Carlisle.

The paper was first published with the title of the New-Hampshire Journal.

It soon gained a respectable circulation in New-Hampshire, and was liberally patronized in Vermont, particularly in the towns lying opposite to Walpole, on Connecticut river. The business intercourse between the two states was constant, and a similarity of taste and habits existed among the inhabitants of both. The New-Hampshire Journal was found, by the people of Vermont, to be a convenient paper for advertising, and two or three post-routes were established on that side of the river. There seemed to be a propriety in giving to the paper a title expressive of the locality of those to whose accommodation it was, in some measure adapted, and, at the commencement of the second year, it was called The New-Hampshire and Vermont Journal, or, Farmer's Weekly Museum. Carlisle was then the sole editor of the paper; but he received aid from several correspondents, one of whom was the Rev. William Fessenden, the minister of Walpole. He wrote a long series of articles under the title of the Religionist.

In 1795, Joseph Dennie, took up his residence in Walpole, and began to write for the Museum that series of papers, — which did more to extend his reputation than all his other literary efforts, — entitled "The Lay Preacher." These *lay sermons* were republished in nearly all the newspapers in the nation. They found a place in the columns of the city journals, sometimes to the exclusion of advertisements, and, wherever a newspaper was printed in a rural district, they were welcomed by both editors and readers as a kind of "God-send." It is believed that these contributions were, at first, voluntary and entirely gratuitous; but, in the spring of 1796, — Carlisle having become, nominally, the sole proprietor of the paper, — an arrangement was made with Dennie, by which the entire control of it, — except the selection of news and the advertising department, — was transferred to him.

When the new arrangement with respect to the property was made, at the commencement of the fourth volume, the public were informed of it, in the following Address, which, if not wholly written by Dennie, underwent his revision and improvements: —

TO THE PUBLIC.

Three years have elapsed, since the present publisher of this paper commenced the Farmer's Weekly Museum, in connection with Mr. Isaiah Thomas. That gentleman, from the multiplicity of his Massachusetts business, has thought proper to retire from the Press at Walpole; and his late partner has to regret the loss of a valuable assistant, and that he is no longer sheltered by his extensive reputation.

But, though he now finds himself floating *alone* on the stream of life, he is confident that his PATRONS will not suffer him to sink without a struggle. The generous encouragement of three years represses the sigh of anxiety; and, though the influential name of Thomas be taken from the Museum, it will still be perused, if meritorious by the industry of its editor, or the genius of its writers.

Notwithstanding the usual enterprize of youth, the publisher acknowledges that in the infancy of the paper, he doubted whether it would reach maturity in a corner of a *young* state, in a corner where a Printing-Press was scarcely known. But agreeable experience has convinced him that, not without reason, have the sons of New Hampshire been praised for their love of letters, and liberal patronage of the Press has dissipated each doubt of its good fortune.

Addresses of this nature are commonly pregnant with promises, which are rarely realized. Beginning with flame, and ending with smoke, most of the periodical works of our country have dwindled from the first number. To guard against a circumstance so disgraceful shall be the peculiar care of the publisher. He is convinced that the industry of Franklin is a better auxiliary to an editor, than even that philosopher's abilities. Unremitting industry he pledges himself to manifest; and, by the frequent arrivals of the mails, by a weekly post from Boston, and the aid of several men of letters in the vicinity, it will be in his power to announce early intelligence, and to decorate his pages with useful and elegant literature.

The publisher is making arrangements to establish an extensive correspondence with political and literary characters, in various parts of the United States. He will make it his care to procure the best written pamphlets on "the transient topic of the times," European magazines and reviews, and, in general, such books as will furnish him with extracts curious and novel. Every thing, *that will promote the substantial interests of the yeomanry*, every thing, that will amuse the imagination, enrich the head, or improve the heart, shall ever hold a front place in the Farmer's Museum.

The political creed of this paper has already been so clearly manifested, that perhaps it is superfluous for the publisher to avow the firmness of his Federalism. Happy to imitate the loyal spirit of the country that cherishes him, he will ever support the constituted authorities of America. Implicitly believing that "our officers are peace and our exactors righteousness," he is willing to swear that he will defend the admirable constitution of the United States, and expose the nefarious schemes of the disorganizer and the Jacobin. Rejoicing under the mild but dignified administration of WASHINGTON, he rests satisfied with the *genuine* and *rational* liberty of this country, and will not make a voyage of enthusiasm to France, in quest of a fairer goddess or a more perfect freedom.

Ardently grateful for the past, and hopeful of the future, he thanks his numerous customers for former smiles, and deems himself entitled to a continuance of favor, if he persevere in attempts to deserve it. As he has received manifold obligations from the citizens of Vermont, who have manifested most liberal regard for the Press, by fostering a paper not published within their own territory, it would be the extreme of ingratitude to be careless of their interest. He shall therefore view it as a matter of moment to adapt his paper, as far as possible, to their meridian. A condensed statement of their politics, abstracts of the acts of their Legislature, and every thing relevant to the sale or the taxation of their lands, claim, and shall receive, a place in his Vermont Journal.

The publisher having thus manifested his gratitude, to his partner and his patrons, explained his politics, and described his resources, now invites those, who *cultivate* and *adorn* the beautiful banks of the Connecticut, to *come*, *see*, and subscribe. His object is not to exhibit a mere gazette of dry detail or doleful narrative of bloody murder, but a *Literary*, no less than a political vehicle. The Walpole Post shall sometimes knock at the door of his customers,

"News from all nations lumbering at his back,"

and sometimes he shall be freighted with only a *light load* of *Literature;* the short sermons of the LAY PREACHER, the fantastic FARRAGO, and *small parcels* of the fancy goods of Messrs. COLON & SPONDEE.

DAVID CARLISLE, JUN.

During this year, the Lay Preacher was pretty constant in the weekly production of his labors; and he was aided in his task as an editor, by Royal Tyler, (then a lawyer in Guilford, Vermont,) who furnished all those agreeable and humorous articles, purporting to be "From the Shop of Messrs. Colon & Spondee."

Thomas Green Fessenden,—who graduated at Dartmouth College, in August, was the author of sundry pieces of humorous political doggerel. The motto of the Museum was,—"Ho, every one, that thirsteth for novelty—come!"

At the beginning of the fifth volume, April, 1797, the titles of the paper were transposed, so as to read,—"The Farmer's Weekly Museum: New-Hampshire and Vermont Journal;" and the last year's motto gave place to the following lines from John Bunyan:—

. . . . . . Wouldst thou remember
From New-Year's day to the last of December,
Then read . . . . . .

Sundry improvements were made in the typography and size of the paper, and in the arrangement of the contents, as proposed in the following notice

TO PATRONS.

The Editor, flattered, animated by patronage, hastens to display more than verbal gratitude. He presents this number of the Museum on paper of royal size; and has the pleasure to announce to his subscribers a weekly miscellany, as ample as the city papers. The different articles are shown in a new, and, he hopes, neat array. Those speculations, strictly pertinent to the Belles Lettres, he has arranged, as distinctly as possible, in the last page, under the title of "The DESSERT." A simple device, emblematical of wine, fruit, and flowers, explained by a very concise Latin, and a poetical English motto, sufficiently indicates the general design. *Politics*, *Biography*, *Economics*, *Morals*, and *Daily Detail*, will be restrained to the first pages. Under the local head of the paper, the reader will regularly find a compressed statement of foreign and domestic occurrences, by the title of "Incidents abroad" and "Incidents at Home." Paragraphs, with appropriate heads, are to succeed next, containing the intelligence, or the jest, of the hour.

The Editor hopes that the varied matter, and cheapness of the Museum, will induce some to compose and some to subscribe for a paper, whose object is sedulously to improve, and harmlessly to amuse.

As a literary periodical, the Museum had now no rival. Its circulation extended from Maine to Georgia, and large packages, filled, weekly, an extra mail-bag, to supply the subscribers in New-York, Philadelphia, Charleston, and intervening cities.

For three years succeeding this arrangement, the Museum was more richly supplied with original communications of a literary character than any other paper, that had then, or has since, been published in the United States. "Colon & Spondee" came out, almost every week, with new varieties of their small wares; — T. G. Fessenden produced his political lampoons, under the signature of "Simon Spunkey;" — Isaac Story, opened a shop with the sign of "Peter Quince," and endeavored to rival Peter Pindar in his humorous style of versification; "Common Sense in Dishabille" was furnished by David Everett; — and beside these, "The Meddler," "The Hermit," "The Rural Wanderer," "Peter Pencil," "Beri Hesdin," and numerous other writers, whose contributions I am not able to assign to the authors *by name,* enriched the Museum, and gave to it an unprecedented popularity. Dennie, however, was not merely the responsible editor, but was the enlivening spirit, around which the others congregated, and to which they made their obeisance as the sheaves of Jacob's sons, of old, did to the sheaf of Joseph. The selected articles were of his choosing. He gathered the exotics, and his criticism stamped them as genuine products of the garden of genius. The weekly summary of "Incidents Abroad" and "Incidents at Home," which was not the least attractive feature of the Museum, was prepared by him; and though this feature of the Museum has had many imitators, I know of none, which can claim any near relationship or striking resemblance. The notes "To Readers and Correspondents," make, of themselves, an amusing department. These were also the sole composition of Dennie, and were frequently written in the printing-office, and extended or contracted in length, so as precisely to fit the space, in which the last column of the form might be deficient of matter.

In less than a year from the time when the Museum put on this new and promising aspect, Carlisle became involved in embarrassments, and the property fell back into the possession of Thomas. In noticing this change, the Editor said, — "Hence it may be easily concluded that its establishment is liberal and permanent, and that no effort of enterprize will be wanting to render it worthy of general favor. The Editor will still attempt, by variegated Literature and pure Politics, to interest the numerous readers, by whose patronage he is honored. But he must be permitted to remark, that a paper so cheap, so closely printed, and so free from advertisements, must, to support its present reputation, attach not only copious subscriptions, but *punctual payment*. Semi-annual anticipation of the dues of this paper, an augmentation of its subscribers, prompt and generous settlements, will animate and retain the conductor in his course. Like every other industrious workman, he has a right to *bread*, and sometimes, to write "all cheerily," he ought to have *wine*. The incumbrance of excessive wealth is scarcely to be dreaded by an author, but for the decent recompense of literary labor he has an importunate claim. If the public will merely *compensate* that labor, the task shall be fulfilled by the Editor, with his best possible exertions."

From this it may be concluded, that the *paying patronage* of the paper was not equal to the desires of the editor; and that his expectations of better support were not realized in their fullest extent, is evident from the incidents and changes, which soon after followed. Alexander Thomas, a relative of Isaiah Thomas, had been taken into the partnership in the Bookstore connected with the Printing-Office, and about the first of June, 1798, took upon himself the charge of conducting the paper, while Dennie took a recess from his labors as Lay Preacher, though he continued to write summaries, criticisms, and "paragraphs with appropriate heads." On his return from a visit to Boston, which had been extended somewhat beyond the proposed term of absence, he saluted his readers in a sprightly Lay Sermon, in which are the following paragraphs: —

"*Here am I, for* THOU DIDST CALL ME."

With a voice, O Public, so finely modulated, so gratefully soothing to the ear of an ambitious author, that he hearkens to the summons, and is actually inditing a sermon, apologetical for laziness and neglect of his flock.

But who is there among the sons of men, of such self-denying humor, that will not, sometimes, flee from confinement and his cottage to breathe a little fresh air, and ramble, yea, run, a moment, from the drudgery of methodized life?

The Clergyman, fatigued with Flavel, and panting under the unusual load of heavy sermons, asks from the parish a respite; and, as he cheerily urges his pacer, plodding and slow, like his owner, sings, instead of David's Psalms, a hymn to the goddess of leisure.

The Lawyer, choked with the dust of courts, and deafened by the gibberish of the laws, canters from the circuit; and, placid at his desk, suffers not a plea in bar to obstruct the current of his yawning humor.

The Doctor, too, and the Merchant, in gaping hours, scorn the recipe and the invoice, and idly dream of subjects more pleasant than subjects consumptive, or subjects commercial.

Many circumstances may, at any stage of his course, command a Lay Preacher to rest from his labors. Like a Bishop Watson, or Porteus, he is not invested with holy lawn, to inspire awe in the vulgar; nor is he, like them, brilliant and learned, to excite the admiration of the wise. Reflecting, in sober hours, on the obscurity of his station, and the simplicity of his lessons, he has perceived that many object to a sermon from the woods, and that many exclaim, "a wooden sermon!" Moreover, in that narrow circle, which may justly be denominated my listening parishioners, *Who hath believed our report?* Neither by smiles nor by frowns, neither by grand precepts, nor merry allusion, has the Lay Preacher driven the rake from his mistress, nor the reveler from his wine. Men persevere in tracing the path, which passion has chosen, or habit has worn smooth; and the monitory sermon, if read, is soon forgotten.

To those, who, from the intimacy or the partiality of friendship, are anxious that my weekly advice should again be given, and to the public, who have condescended once or twice to ask for me, I will narrate the private motives, which have persuaded me to be silent for a year.

In the first place, I honestly declare, with wonted frankness, that many *evil* spirits have domineered over my mind, and that Laziness, Spleen, and Ill-humor have been too frequently suffered to lock up my quills, and to overset my ink-horn.

Like a venerable predecessor, I have been, during the above period, "in journeyings often, in weariness and painfulness, and in watchings;" all which are unfriendly to preaching; nor do I believe the Archbishop of Canterbury himself could indite a pastoral letter, or make a visitation charge, successfully, under such unfavorable circumstances.

He, who resolves to speculate, flies, in conformity to the suggestion of Horace, to the grove, and, in a lonely situation, converses with few besides his books and himself. But, if an author keep no other company, he will not be long qualified to give interest and novelty to his researches. Every line will savor of the lamp, and every page will be mouldy, by the damp air of a monkish cell. Hence, to write what the world will gaily read, it is necessary, sometimes, for a man of letters to obey the advice of the poet, Green, and make

"Trips to the TOWN, life to amuse,
To purchase books, and hear the news,
To see old friends, brush off the clown,
And quicken taste."

Unless he occasionally go to the great city, and forsake his closet for a saunter in "vanity fair," how could a Lay Preacher correctly describe or justly censure fashionable follies, and the blameful luxury of a capital? To ridicule, with point and effect, the fantastic foppery of dress, one must actually look down the street, or through the coffee-house, and mark the peacock beau, sporting his "Joseph's coat," or jockey pantaloons. To laugh at gowns without a waist, or the brick-dust hue of coquelicot riband, the writer should at least drink tea in the Tontine buildings, and go, one morning, with giggling girls to that great box of millinery, the shop of Mrs. Milliquet.

Now, it scarcely, from these premises, need be inferred, that, to gather materials is the work of one day, and to put them into form is reserved to the next. It is unreasonable to expect that an essayist should be seen constantly with a pen in his hand. His effusions would become wretchedly trite, if he were not permitted to go abroad, searching for some new object, or some new face, to serve as fresh topics for speculation. While I was mingling in the crowd on 'change, lounging in booksellers' shops, arguing in a coffee-house, or chatting with sensible women round a supper-table, I was, in fact, composing Lay Preachers. The process, though invisible, still continued. I entered hints in my note-book, though I did not expand them in the Museum; and kept, for future use, the fruit of my observations, as my prudent and tender mother used to store for me autumnal russetings to bless my infant palate in the scarce and the spring time.

But though for a year the Lay Preacher's desk has been shut, yet his books have been open and his thoughts awake. Having seen some novel objects, and read many curious tomes in the course of his vacation, perhaps he is qualified to resume his labors with some degree of spirit. He has meditated not merely the works of the *fathers*, but the lighter productions of the *sons;* and perused, laboriously, many a heavy book, with a view, by studious chemistry to extract some essence to relieve the spirits of his readers. At any rate, to continue, to the end of this sermon, the same egotism, with which it began, he is determined, as this mode of writing is approved by those, whom it is his ardent wish to please, to lay aside every weight of interest, which might bias him to more gainful occupations; to lay aside that sin of indolence, which doth so easily beset an invalid and an author, and to run with patience the race, that is set before him.

For three or four weeks succeeding the appearance of this apology, the Lay Preacher performed the promised service, and then again became silent. In the beginning of November, in one of his notes to "Readers and Correspondents," he said, —

The Lay Preacher has not locked up his pulpit door. Absorbed in the perusal of church history, and the holy life of Hilarion, the Hermit, he has, with the absence of an author, forgotten to write with periodical regularity. He will soon open his Notes, and then

—— —— "Hear him but reason in divinity,
And, all admiring, with an inward wish,
You would desire that he were made a prelate."

Business is rather dull at "the Shop of Colon and Spondee." Customers are few, and Mr. Weiser, the old tenant, rings his bason about their ears. He tosses about his powder with such an air of gracefulness, and brandishes his keen razor with such dexterity, that the partners think seriously of quitting the premises.

The Editor implores his correspondents to afford him some literary and political aid. He is timorous, lest his readers should be nauseated with similar dishes, cooked by the same hand. Associates will, in the language of recruiting, meet with kind treatment.

Wanted, a bale of American Biography; a quantity of Quips and Cranks; a load of Wit, and a few bundles from the Parnassian Shrubbery; pointed Darts of Criticism; and above all, during the dreary dullness of November, two or three genial sunshine days of American Patronage.

A month passed away and a note to the reader said, —"Next week, if the source of all mental exertion give the invalid and sluggish author leave, the Lay Preacher will take up the neglected thread of his speculations." "Next week," (December 10,) he fulfilled this conditional promise, and published a sermon from the text, — "*She maketh herself coverings of tapestry; her clothing is silk and purple.*" The whole article, — two columns and a half, — was a critique on the romances of Mrs. Radcliffe." Nothing more is seen of the Lay Preacher till the first of April, 1799. But, in the mean time (February 11,) a still more importunate address to the public, indicates discontent and solicitude, and a persevering ambition in his favorite pursuit. It is entitled to a place here, as an exhibition of the discouraging reminiscences and flattering hopes, which alternately affect the minds of many other editors, as they did the aspiring spirit of Dennie: —

TO THE PUBLIC.

The well wishers to literary exertion are once more warned, that such is the care, expense and fatigue, in conducting a Gazette upon the plan of the FARMER'S MUSEUM, that to preserve its spirit, and ensure its continuance, frequent communications must be made, new subscriptions must be added, and the charges of the paper punctually paid. If men of letters fail to coöperate with the Editor, one of these consequences must ensue. Either, from the limited faculties of the human mind; from lassitude; from that hypochondria, which generally infests the sedentary studious; or from real indisposition, the little that an unassisted and imperfect individual can produce, will be weak and stale; or if, in a laborious hour, he produce much, and cover his columns with his own effusions, an intolerable sameness appears; and his miscellany is defrauded of its very essentials, Novelty, Variety and Use. If men fail to encourage the circulation of this paper, or tardily, or grudgingly, or *never* pay the small sum, for which it is sold, such are the various expenses attached to the establishment, it is impossible it should be permanent. From an experience of four laborious years, in this department, the Editor is convinced that without a very flowing subscription, without *assiduous* patronage, without the *countenance* of the *first* characters in the country, without *much* original literary matter, and without a *generous premium*, *periodically* paid, no really useful and diversified paper can be supported in America. The Farmer's Museum, which is in fact a Magazine in a minor form, is composed of many originals, procured by pecuniary compensation, and of selections from English Journals, Reviews and Magazines, purchased in large numbers, at an *expensive rate*. The Post Office tax for many of the essays, communications, and letters, pertinent and *essential* to the paper, is frequent, and often heavy. The expenses of paper, and other rude materials in the hands of the printer, exceed twenty dollars per week; and the folding and directing of the papers, for distant subscribers, demand considerable time and *cash*, for which the Proprietors of this paper, make no additional charge to their customers; though in other offices, particularly at the southward, a sum, *equal to two thirds of the whole price of the Museum* is required for this subaltern service alone. From these statements it must appear evident, to the considerate and the generous, among the readers of this paper, that if it acquire not many friends, and if its price be not paid with a merchant's punctuality, "confusion and every evil work," among our types, "must ensue." With much watching, and with continued exertion, the Conductor of this paper has, for a period, not brief in continuance, and certainly not trivial in value, as it respects an important stage of human life, endeavored to disseminate among his countrymen literary articles, in a cheap and familiar form. Notwithstanding the respectable assistance he has received, the expense incurred, the pains employed, and enthusiasm exercised, in this behalf, he is sorry to declare that two of his earlier attempts in this line, far from being *remunerated, or even smiled upon*, involved him in debt, and that for the present undertaking of a large, and he may add *useful* paper, at a *lower* price than any other of the size and quality of letter press in the United States, he is so moderately, not to say penuriously, requited, that, were it not for an aversion to relinquish literature, however neglected, he should instantly engage in some of the coarser vocations of life, and interdict himself from pen and ink forever. Public encouragement will rouse him from lethargy, will dispel despondence, will incite the Preacher to sermonize, the Poet to versify, and Literary Labor to "work willingly with her hands." Failure of patronage and payment will close the Museum, and crush the fondly fostered hopes of an anxious Editor.

From this period to the first of April much originality shall be exhibited to our readers. A number of periodical effusions, of a sprightly cast, will appear; a bird's eye view of *Foreign* literature may be pretty generally found, under the local head of the paper; and curious Biography and Anecdote will continue to diversify its columns.

Provided the Editor can meet a recompense barely sufficient to alleviate the labor, and equal the expense, he proposes to make improvements in the Museum on the first of April, at which time a new volume of this paper commences. By an economy of the press, the quantity of matter shall be increased, some new types shall be employed, certain decorations attempted, new writers engaged, and more originality produced. The title of the paper will be changed to the FARMER'S MUSEUM and LAY PREACHER'S GAZETTE; and from that time the lectures and sermons of that writer will frequently appear. A series of Critical Speculations, principally upon American works, will be procured, and an article, under the head of "Federal Biography," containing authentic anecdotes of the principal personages in the United States, will be occasionally introduced. This last article, if well executed, will, from its utility and interest, be worth treble the price of the paper. To realize this plan, which, if accomplished, will render the Museum as valuable as is possible for a work in such a fugitive form, *Patronage and subscribers must increase.* The Editor has a *right* to declare, that a Gazette, embracing the useful and amusing objects above indicated, is entitled to copious subscription, general currency, and a liberal reward. If the public will cherish these efforts, the Editor *pledges* himself for the satisfactory discharge of his duties. On the contrary, in proportion to popular neglect and parsimony, the spirit of the paper will evaporate, the columns will grow dull, and gradually merit the shameful title of the most stupid production in the United States.

How truly may it be said of Dennie, —

> The bounding pulse, the languid limb,
> The changing spirit's rise and fall, —
> We know that these were felt by him,
> For they are felt by all, —

all editors, at least, who have a proper feeling of their responsibilities, and a proper ambition to carry out the honorable destiny of their profession. In looking over a file of the Museum, after a lapse of near fifty years, and revivifying my personal recollections of Dennie, it would not be possible to suppress a token of admiration of his assiduity and perseverance, and a sigh of regret that his susceptible nature was so often compelled to suffer mortification and disappointment, where he expected sympathy and encouragement. A few weeks before the time appointed to present the proposed improvements in the mechanical appearance of the Museum, Dennie said, — "Among other important improvements, an American Biography will occasionally appear. The 'Shop of Colon and Spondee' will not be shut up: The partners have obtained a tolerable credit with the house of Apollo & Co. and both the stock in trade, and the demand on the literary market, indicate nothing like bankruptcy. The Lay Preacher will sometimes officiate, and continue to sow the seed of good doctrine, though, as usual, it should fall by the way-side, or be choked with thorns. To ensure success to these honest and earnest efforts to please the reading part of the community, information and assistance from men of learning and taste, is, with *persevering importunity*, required. Memorials of American personages of note, *original* poetry, scientific researches, notices of new books and pamphlets, and witty anecdotes, are sought for *as for hidden treasures*. All, or any of these articles will be, to the Editor, *the pearl of great price*. The Editor sanguinely hopes that inattention to these particulars will not compel him to exclaim, with the neglected Milton, —

> Alas! what boots it, with incessant care,
> To tend the homely, slighted *Author's* trade?
> Were it not better done, as others use,
> To sport with Amaryllis in the shade,
> Or with the tangles of Nerea's hair?"

At length the first of April came, and with it, the "Farmer's Museum, or Lay Preacher's Gazette," in a new and promising dress. The Lay Preacher himself honored the occasion and the day with one of his best sermons, and which is too sensible a piece of admonition not to be admitted among the specimens of his genius: —

"*Oh foolish Gallatians, who hath bewitched you?*"

Horace, in a facetious satire, alluding to a common custom among the Romans, who, during the Saturnalia, or Christmas holidays of old time, permitted every slave to be sovereign and saucy, bids his servant, Davus, to recollect the good natured law in mitigation of servitude, and to avail himself of the licentiousness of December. The poet, though apprized of the consequences of such indulgence, which would infallibly produce either scurrilous language, harsh reproof, or unpleasant instruction, satisfies himself by simply stating the sanction of antiquity. It was the will of his ancestors; it was an old usage; and, therefore, Davus had a title to be insolent and could plead prescription in favor of the Rights of slaves.

Customs, equally whimsical, have prevailed in every age. If the Romans had their Saturnalia, the chimney-sweepers of England consider May-day as their own; and the first of April is a festal season to the whole body corporate of Fools.

As by a curious coincidence of circumstances, the renewal of my lay labors occurs on All Fools' day, as it is merrily styled in the Almanac, it will not be impertinent to say, in my concise manner, a word or two, concerning this singular festival.

It is well known, that I am a most laborious examiner of books, new and old; but, in the whole course of a long life, devoted to study, I never could discover the origin of the custom of elaborately making a fool, only in the spring of the year. My love of investigation, and my zeal for the honor and dignity of human nature, have induced me to inquire, most anxiously, why this thing was so. The shades of many departed candles, three worn out lamps, and a bookseller's bill, both long and unpaid, can attest the time I have consumed, and the musty folios I have read, in the progress of this laudable inquisitiveness. Four times I peeped into the magical volumes of Cornelius Agrippa; twice I have consulted that prying author, who wrote of arts lost and found; I have looked for the first April fool day, by the obscure light of Jacob Behmen's "Aurora;" I have "read Alexander Ross over;" and, many times, when at college, did I raise the devil to satisfy my curiosity in this behalf. All this watching and toil, like much of my labor of life, has proved ineffectual; and the day of fools still wants its successful antiquarian, though it has at length found its preacher.

Relinquishing, therefore, all ideas of discovering the origin of this carnival time for fools, I must satisfy myself, and attempt to satisfy my readers, with a view of its rites and ceremonies; or a sarcasm upon these vernal worshipers of that simple being, exalted, by Erasmus, into a goddess, and styled, in his elegant latinity, "Moria," or the deity of weak ones.

On the first of every April, there appears to be a general combination to expose the common weakness of humanity. The philosopher and the idiot; the high and the low; the bond man and free, are all equally exposed to the juggling tricks of the priesthood of Folly. All the "idly busy" stand at the door and the lattice, and, like the wisdom of Solomon, cry "whoso is simple, let him turn in hither." From the many passages, interspersed through the writings of this prince, on the subject of folly, I am persuaded that he knew more of the first of April, than, in his pride of learning, he chose to acknowledge. Indeed, in the course of my Biblical researches, I once conjectured that the day, the amorous monarch enrolled in his list of pleasures three hundred wives and seven hundred concubines, was the earliest epoch of All Fools' day; and that his noted aphorism, of "the mouth of fools feedeth on foolishness," was dictated on the first of April.

One cannot help smiling at the levity or absurdity of man, in consecrating a day to the ludicrous purpose of striving to metamorphose into an idiot every neighbor, however stored with wisdom, or pregnant with wit. At other seasons, we discern no formal process for exposing the general weakness; on every other holiday, each one is allowed to possess his mental stock in quietness, and the fool and the philosopher are marked with characters as distinct as those of the ass and zebra. But on the earliest day of the second genial month, the greatest pains are employed to confound the distinctions of nature, and to compel even the wary and the sagacious to make a pilgrimage to the shrine of St. Folly.

It may be asked, in a tone less growling than that of Johnson, and less misanthropical than that of Swift, why mankind are so anxious to form fools, when the business appears to be fully done, on the largest scale, and we find them in shoals already made? I can see no reason for this superfluous care. Whether the foolish are sought for in the vernal or autumnal months; on whatever day of the year, weakness and imperfection are wanted, it is but opening the eyes, and the inquirer is gratified. Folly is not a rare, exotic bird, or far-fetched wild beast, kept carefully in museums, and to be seen only for a fee. She is at our doors; she stands at our elbows; she meets us each moment in the street. Her bubble is as frequent as "the idle wind;" and her face is common as Doll Tearsheet's in the bagnio, and notorious as the perfidy of the French.

It is time for injured April to assert his rights, and no longer to suffer such an idle profanation of his day. Surely the first of a month, the immediate harbinger of the fairest portion of the year, ought not to be distinguished only in the rubric of folly. April may be commenced with much more propriety, than by acting like fools ourselves, or striving to surprize others into fatuity. This day should be, indeed, a festal one, but not dedicated to "idiot laughter," and the petty tricks of childhood. It should be a kind of vernal thanksgiving. The goddess Flora, rather than Folly, should have our vows. We should rejoice, that "the mandrakes give a smell," and that "at our gates are all manner of pleasant flowers." Our sports should be sylvan. We should exult that the gloomy shadows of Winter are fled away; that the south wind is come, and blows upon our gardens; and the vines, with the tender grape, give a good smell. Instead of tampering with the credulity of our neighbor or friend, we should, in the forcible words of Milton, "go out, and see the riches of Nature, and partake in her rejoicing with heaven and earth." Joy, excited by the lapse of Winter, and its horrors, and Hope, animated by the prospect of "the flowery prime," will not ask for an All Fools' day to enlarge the delights of Spring. Even to him, who has but low pretensions to philosophy, all nature, gay and revived, will be a much finer sight, than all men foolish, or exposed to the taunts of Folly. Let us, therefore, be more solicitous to enjoy and improve the season; to crown ourselves with the chaplets of the field, and with "rose buds, before they be withered," than to invest the silly with their cap and bells.

At this new epoch in the history of the Museum, the old motto from Bunyan was discarded with the old and worn-out types, and the following, from Goldsmith, adopted: —

Hither, each week, the peasant shall repair,
To sweet oblivion of his daily care;
Again the farmer's news — the barber's tale,
Again the woodman's ballad shall prevail.

The essays of the Lay Preacher were continued, with tolerable though not constant punctuality till the beginning of September, when they were again suspended, and never again revived, as contributions to the Museum. Dennie was invited to Philadelphia, to a different employment, and the editorial management of the paper was given to Alexander Thomas, who conducted it with good taste and discretion, — aided by many of the correspondents that had given it popularity during the administration of Dennie. In consequence of the departure of Dennie and the entire suspension of his labors, the title "Lay Preacher's Gazette" was expunged and that of Literary Gazette took its place. This was in February, 1800. Thenceforward there was sensible decadence in the contents of the paper.

The weekly summaries, which had frequently filled two or three columns, dwindled down to less than half a column, and had none of the raciness and agreeable humor, that had formerly made them attractive.

In October, 1801, the proprietors, Thomas & Thomas, published an advertisement, stating that they had made a temporary disposal of the establishment to DAVID NEWHALL, whom they recommended to the patrons of the paper, for industry and ability. Newhall published an Address, in which he wisely refrained from promising too much, as "addresses of this kind are generally pregnant with promises, which are rarely realized." The dimensions of the paper were reduced, and the spirit evaporated.

In 1803, the publication was resumed by Thomas & Thomas. The next year the paper was again enlarged, and the second title was dropped. On this occasion the publishers said, — "Though the state of the country is such as to render most interesting the political department, and the arts and falsehoods circulating by reams over the state, render it necessary to pay prime attention to correct political information, yet our columns will be occasionally varied with the insertion of brief essays on religion and morality. The interest of the Farmer shall claim our notice in the publication of useful agricultural hints, inventions, and improvements. The Sentimentalist and the Wit will occasionally find a repast at our Dessert, and we trust that the variety we shall offer will be palatable to the tastes of all."

From this time to October, 1806, the Museum was respectably conducted, but had no remarkable excellence to distinguish it from many other newspapers in the country towns of New-England. It then dwindled down to its former contracted size.

In March, 1807, the publication was suspended. In stating their reasons for this suspension the publishers said, after alluding to the smallness of the income and the difficulties of collecting it, — "Were it deemed practicable or probable that a longer continuance of our efforts in favor of the former wise, prudent, and patriotic administration, would be the means of restoring them, we should cheerfully maintain the post we have occupied. But where failure is conceived to be the certain consequence of exertion, a person may be excused for withdrawing his forces." They concluded with a recommendation of the New-Hampshire Sentinel, published at Keene, by John Prentiss, on principles similar to their own, to the favor of their subscribers.

What encouragement they had for reviving the publication does not appear; but it *was* revived in October, 1808, and published by Thomas & Thomas and Cheever Felch. In July, 1809, the names of Thomas & Thomas disappeared from the imprint, and that of Cheever Felch remained as the sole publisher and editor.

Alexander Thomas had long suffered from declining health, and made a visit to the Saratoga Springs, hoping thereby to obtain relief; but he died the day after his arrival, July 2, 1809, aged thirty-five.

At the close of the year following the revival of the publication, Felch expressed his gratitude for the encouragement he had received, and, as new arrangements for business had been made, he should continue his endeavor to merit the patronage of the public. But notwithstanding all these flattering assurances, the Farmer's Museum rapidly approached its end. In October, 1810, the publication was again suspended, and was never again revived. In his farewell address to the public, the editor declared that the subscription would by no means remunerate the trouble of conducting the paper in a proper manner, and that a multiplicity of other business prevented his paying that attention to it, which it demanded. The following is a part of his valedictory: —

The public is assured, that I entertain a grateful sense of its liberal patronage, as well as for the confidence it has placed in me. And it is a pleasing reflection, that, in no instance, have I intentionally misled that confidence. In the course of my editorial labors, I have deemed it necessary to take decided and bold ground, which has exposed me to the bitter invectives of opposing partisans. But this ground was taken from a full conviction of its rectitude. I have always thought that the man, who conducted a public paper, and dared not publish the truth, for fear of giving offence, was not only a coward, but a villain, and, in matters of consequence, a traitor to his country. Believing this, I have pursued a different course. When I have found the truth, I have not feared to publish it. In my articles upon individual characters, I have been guided by the strictest adherence to facts. And, in many cases, for fear of over-stepping the truth, I have omitted publishing some of the most glaring things. No man has any cause of complaint against me; and whatever bluster some individuals may have made, they have not dared the attempt of clearing themselves from the charges. If it were attempted, they well knew it was in my power to affix on them others of a deeper cast.

Quitting the editorial cares, I also quitted the bickerings of party politics. 'Tis in vain to attempt to stand against the current of the times. An infatuation has seized the public mind; and as people are more ready to believe falsehood than truth, so the party, which is the most corrupt, and will resort to the most base methods, and dress up the most plausible falsehoods, will, of course, generally carry its points. We are treading the steps of former republics, and we shall most certainly share their fate. The man, who does most for his country, and opposes the most strenuously our career to destruction, shall fare the worst. Let us then go down with the current, and a few years shall find us the groveling slaves of a foreign despot, an upstart tyrant — of our own.

Felch continued some time in Walpole, in the business of bookselling. He took orders in the Episcopal church, and, in 1814, was a chaplain in the navy.

It remains to take some further notice of Dennie and his literary associates.

When Dennie left Walpole for Philadelphia in September, 1799, it was understood to be in consequence of an invitation from the editor of the United States Gazette, with whom he was to share the responsibility of editing that paper. He entered upon that service, but his connection with it was of short continuance. Before the end of the year 1800, in company with Asbury Dickens, a bookseller of Philadelphia, he began the publication of the "Port Folio," — a weekly paper, "combining in the manner of the Tattler, politics, with essays and disquisitions on topics, scientific, moral, humorous, and literary." In his prospectus, he enumerated his literary offspring, and declared that he was not weary in well-doing. "The Tablet, a favorite child, (he said) after buffeting the billows of adverse fortune, for thirteen short weeks, sickened and died; and so it had fared with other similar productions of his pen." He conducted the Port Folio, wholly or in part, till January, 1812, when he died — a premature victim to social indulgence. If his epitaph were to be written by one of his convivial companions, the writer might be prompted to offer something like the following: —

Farewell! may the turf, where thy cold relics rest,
Bear herbs — odoriferous herbs! o'er thy breast,
May their heads thyme, and sage, and pot marjoram wave,
And fat be the gander, that feeds on thy grave.

I have a vivid recollection of Dennie's personal appearance, in 1796, when I began my apprenticeship in the printing-office of David Carlisle. In person, he was rather below than above the middling height, and was of a slender frame. He was particularly attentive to his dress, which, when he appeared in the street, on a pleasant day, approached the highest notch of the fashion. I remember, one delightful morning in May, he came into the office, dressed in a pea-green coat, white vest, nankin small-clothes, white silk stockings, and shoes, or *pumps*, fastened with silver buckles, which covered at least half the foot from the instep to the toe. His small-clothes were tied at the knees, with riband of the same color, in double bows, the ends reaching down to the ancles. He had just emerged from the barber's shop. His hair, *in front*, was well loaded with pomatum, frizzled, or *craped*, and powdered; the *ear-locks* had undergone the same process; *behind*, his natural hair was augmented by the addition of a large *queue*, (called, vulgarly, the *false tail*,) which, enrolled in some yards of black ribband, reached half way down his back. Thus *accommodated*, the Lay Preacher stands before my *mind's eye*, as life-like and sprightly as if it were but yesterday that I saw the reality.

Among his familiar acquaintance, and in the company of literary men, Dennie must have been a delightful and fascinating companion. In the printing-office, his conversation with the apprentices was pleasant and instructive. His deportment towards them was marked with great urbanity and gentleness. Being the youngest apprentice, — in vulgar phrase, the *printer's devil*, — it was my lot to call upon him for copy, and carry the proof to him. Thus, for seven or eight months, my intercourse with him was almost daily, and was as familiar as propriety would sanction between an editor and an apprentice. I never saw him otherwise than in good humor.

Dennie wrote with great rapidity, and generally postponed his task till he was called upon for *copy*. It was frequently necessary to go to his office, and it was not uncommon to find him in bed at a late hour in the morning. His *copy* was often given out in small portions, a paragraph or two at a time; sometimes it was written in the printing-office, while the compositor was waiting to put it in type. One of the best of his Lay sermons was written at the village tavern, directly opposite to the office, in a chamber where he and his friends were amusing themselves with cards. It was delivered to me by piece-meal, at four or five different times. If he happened to be engaged in a game, when I applied for copy, he would ask some one to *play his hand for him, while he could give the devil his due*. When I called for the closing paragraph of the sermon, he said, *call again in five minutes*. "No," — said Tyler — "I 'll write the improvement for you." He accordingly wrote a concluding paragraph, and Dennie never saw it till it was in print.

For some unaccountable cause, (unaccountable by me,) Dennie hated, or despised, the faculty of Harvard College, and he never neglected an opportunity to lampoon the individuals, of which it was composed, and would often step a little out of his way to level his arrows at the professors and tutors, and exult in the belief that he had hit the mark.

It has been frequently remarked that Dennie left no

work, that will sustain the reputation he enjoyed as a writer. The Lay Preacher, the most elaborate of all his literary compositions, is now unknown to the great mass of the reading public, and is almost forgotten by those who read and admired it, as it came fresh from the press. It is true, that there are some things in this series of essays, that have not the attributes that will insure immortality; but it is also true, that they contain much, which bears the stamp of genius, and which ought not to sink into oblivion. He was a professed admirer of the style of Addison and Sterne, and was not unwilling to have his Lay Preacher compared with the Spectator and the "Sermons by Mr. Yorick."

I have never met with any Biography of Dennie, though I have been told that a volume bearing that title was published at Philadelphia. The materials for such a work doubtless existed; though, if not published, they may now be difficult of access. There must have been many letters of his among his literary friends, which, if they partake of the spirit and sprightliness of his conversation, would exhibit his character in very attractive colors. Whatever deficiences there might have been in his character, they died with him, as they should. His virtues ought to be remembered by those, who beheld the manifestations of his genius in its brightest period, and *they* should present to the public his literary, intellectual, and moral portrait.

It has been asserted that Dennie practised law with reputation and success; but the fact, I apprehend, was otherwise. The contrary assertion, — that he never appeared in court but once, *as an advocate*, I have no doubt, is much nearer the truth. The following account of his first and last attempt to address a court was written by his friend Tyler, for the New-England Galaxy and published in that paper, July 24, 1818. It was doubtless *embellished* by the writer, but the main facts were often mentioned when Dennie was editor of the Museum, were understood to be accurately narrated, and I have reason to believe that they were never denied or controverted : —

I well recollect that soon after he had terminated his noviciate, was admitted to the oath of an attorney and had opened an office, *I was present at his debut as an advocate at the bar.* No young lawyer ever entered on practice with more favorable auspices. The senior members of the bar augured success, and he numbered all who were valuable among the juniors as particular friends. As it was generally known when he was to deliver "his maiden speech," by a kind of tacit agreement the gentlemen of the bar resolved to afford him the most favorable arena for the display of his eloquence. The opposing counsel had engaged to suspend all interference, although his statements deviated ever so far from fact.

Mr. Dennie had been engaged on behalf of the defendant to support a motion for an imparlance or continuance in an action brought by certain plaintiffs for the recovery of the contents of a promissory note. The execution of the note could not be contested, it was given for a valuable consideration, and was justly due. A very liberal indulgence had already been extended to the defendant by several previous imparlances, and nothing remained for the most adroit advocate to press upon the court but the untoward effects a judgement and consequent writ of execution would have upon the fortunes of his client.

The court opened, and, as if by previous concert, all other business was suspended, and our young advocate, after bowing gracefully, assumed the attitude of an orator, and addressed the court.

I wish I could transcribe this address, as the lawyers say, "in hæc verba," but I can give only a mere sketch. Twenty years have elapsed, and I remember it as I do an original picture of Claude Loraine; to do justice to the original I should possess the talents of the matchless artist.

He began with a luminous history of compulsory payments; he showed clearly that as knowledge was diffused humanity prevailed even from the savage era, when the debtor, his wife and children, were sold into slavery to satisfy the demands of the creditor, and the corpse of the insolvent was denied the rites of sepulture, through the iron age of our English ancestors, when the debtor was incarcerated in "salva et areta custodia," down to the present day, when by the amelioration of the laws, the statutes of bankruptcy and gaol delivery had humanely liberated the body of the unfortunate debtor from prison, upon the surrender of his estate. He observed, that in the progress of knowledge, the municipal courts had, by interposing the "law's delay" between the vindictive avarice of the creditor, and the ruin of the debtor, always to the honor of the judiciary department, preceded the Legislative in the merciful march of humanity. That the time was not far distant when the Legislative would repeal those statutes which provided for imprisonment for debt, and punished a virtuous man as a criminal merely because he was poor.

But aside of these general considerations, he begged leave to lay the defendant's unhappy case before the court; he would "a round unvarnished tale deliver." His client was an husbandman, a husband, and the father of a large family, who depended *solely* on the labor of his hands for bread — he had seen better days — but his patrimonial farm had been sold for Continental money, and the whole lost by depreciation, whilst others had been getting gain. A deep scar in his side, occasioned by the thrust of a British bayonet at the battle of Bunker-Hill, was all he had to remunerate him for his services as a soldier during the revolutionary war. Here the "poet's eye began to roll in a fine frenzy." We saw the hapless husbandman "plodding his weary way" through the chill blast of a winter's storm, and seeking through the drifting snow his log cottage, beneath the craggy side of an abrupt precipice; "the taper's solitary ray" appears — vanishes — and again lights up hope in his heart — the door opens — his children run "to lisp their sire's return and climb his knees the envied kiss to share" — "the busy housewife" prepares the frugal repast, the wicker chair is drawn before the capacious hearth, "and the crackling fagot flies;" the labors of the day are forgotten and all is serenity and domestic bliss — the family bible is opened — the psalm is sung, and the father of the family rises in the midst of his offspring and invokes a blessing upon his country and his government, and fervently prays that its freedom and independence may last as long as the sun and moon shall endure — acknowledges his own trespasses, and pours out his heart in gratitude, that in the midst of judgement God had remembered mercy — that though despoiled of wealth, the wife of his youth was continued unto him — that his children were blessed with health, that they had a roof to cover them from the wintry storm, and that under his Divine protection they might sleep in peace, with none to disturb them or make them afraid. But scarcely does the incense of prayer ascend from that golden censer, a good man's heart, when an appalling knock is heard; the wooden latch is broken, the door is widely thrown open — Enter the bailiff, "down whose hard unmeaning face ne'er stole the pitying tear," with the writ of execution, issued in this cause; he arrests the hapless father, and amidst the swoonings of the wife, the sobbings and imbecile opposition of his children, he is dragged "through the pelting of the pitiless storm" to a loathsome prison.

Was not this a case to be distinguished from the common herd of parties, which cumbered the court's docket? — Was not some considerations to be had for a brave man, who had bled for that independence, without which their honors would not now dignify the bench as the magistrates of a free people? — Was rigid justice untempered with mercy to be alone found in the Judicial Courts of a people renowned for their humanity? and shall "human laws, which should be made only to check the arm of wickedness," be changed into instruments of oppression and cruelty?

The orator ceased — mute attention accompanied the delivery, and at the close all were charmed, and all silent; even the opposing counsel sat hesitating betwixt his fees and his feelings, and forbore to reply. This silence, which our young advocate seemed to notice with peculiar complacency, was broken from the bench. The Judge, an unlettered farmer, who, by the prevalence of party, had obtained the summit of yeoman ambition, a seat on the bench of an Inferior Court, who knew only the technical jargon of the court, and to whom the language and pathos of Dennie were alike unintelligible, sat, during the delivery of the address, rolling a pair of "lack lustre eyes" with a vacant stare, sometime at the orator and then at the bar, as if seeking most curiously for meaning, and who was perhaps restrained only by the respectful attention of the latter from interrupting the speaker. The Judge broke silence.

Judge. I confess I am in rather a kind of a quandary; I profess I am somewhat dubus; I can't say that I know for sartin *what the young gentleman would be at.*

Counsellor V. My brother Dennie, may it please your honor, has been enforcing his motion for an Imparlance on the part of the Defendant, in the cause of Patrick McGripinclaw *et alii*, Plaintiffs, *vs.* Noadiah Chubber.

Judge. Oh! Ay! now I believe I understand — the young man wants the cause *to be hung up for the next term, duz he?*

Counsellor V. Yes, may it please the court.

Judge. Well, well, if that 's all he wants, why couldn't he say so in a few words, pat to the purpose, without all this *larry cum lurry?*

Our advocate took his hat and gloves from the table, cast a look of ineffable contempt upon the Bæotian magistrate, and stalked out of the court house.

Although Mr. Dennie affected to view his unlucky debut in its proper light, and would frequently tell the story of his discomfiture with great humor, yet his friends perceived he was deeply wounded — disgusted with the profession. To entice him to a second essay, some months afterwards, I observed to him, "That I was engaged as counsel in an action for seduction. An unfortunate girl, the daughter of a poor but respectable widow, had been ruined by the promises of a base but wealthy man; that the facts would be well substantiated, and the whole effort of her counsel directed to the enhancement of damages: this depending principally upon the eloquence of her counsel, presented a fine opportunity for the display of his peculiar talents. That I would introduce him into the cause, and he might open it before a presiding Judge who possessed a taste for fine speaking, and would justly appreciate the force and classical purity of his rhetoric.

His reply convinced me that he had taken *a final leave* of the "noisy bar."

D. "It may do for you, my friend, to pursue this sordid business — you can address the ignoble vulgar in their own Alsatia dialect. I remember the Bæotian Judge, and it is the last time I will ever attempt to batter down a mud wall with roses."

Dennie's most intimate friend and associate in his literary enterprizes was Royal Tyler. This gentleman was a native of Boston. He graduated at Harvard College in 1776; and studied law, — it has been said, — in the office of John Adams. For a short time, he was connected with the army, and was an aid to General Lincoln. He also acted in the same capacity, when that officer commanded the military force of Massachusetts, called out to suppress the rebellion of Daniel Shays. He was also deputed by Governor Bowdoin to the government of New-York, to make arrangements for the delivery of Shays and his adherents to the authorities of Massachusetts, should they escape to that state. While conducting this agency, in the city of New-

York, he offered to the manager of the theatre a comedy, entitled "The Contrast," which he had written at intervals of military service. The comedy was performed, and received with a good degree of applause. In 1797, he wrote a three-act comedy, called "The Georgia Spec, or Land in the Moon," which was performed several times at the Boston theatre. It censured the wickedness of the speculators in what was called the Yazoo purchase, and laughed at the folly of those, who were their victims.

Tyler's contributions to the Farmer's Museum were numerous; and, if collected, would fill several volumes. He wrote rapidly, and could vary his style "from grave to gay, from lively to severe," as easily as he could draw on his glove. Most of the articles, purporting to be "from the Shop of Messrs. Colon & Spondee," were written by him; the poetical pieces, I believe, are all of his composition. These he generally threw off with a dash of the pen, seldom taking any pains to revise them. They are noted for inaccuracy of rhymes, — a defect, which he thought hardly worthy of his attention; but they are remarkable for sprightliness of thought and expression, and an easy flow of language. They embraced topics of all sorts, local and general, temporary and permanent, and were well charged with wit and humor. The complexion of the political articles was purely *federal.* The original idea of this fictitious Shop of Colon & Spondee, was the offspring of Tyler's prolific brain; and the first public manifestation of it was made in the Eagle, a paper published at Hanover, N. H., in the following style: —

VARIETY STORE.

To the Literati. Messrs. Colon & Spondee, wholesale dealers in *Verse*, *Prose* and *Music*, beg leave to inform the public and the learned in particular, that—previous to the ensuing Commencement—they purpose to open a fresh assortment of *Lexicographic*, *Burgersdician*, and *Parnassian Goods*, suitable for the season, at the room on the Plain,* lately occupied by Mr. Frederic Wiser, Tonsor,—if it can be procured—where they will expose to sale Salutatory and Valedictory Orations, Syllogistic and Forensic Disputations and Dialogues, among the living and the dead—Theses and Masters' Questions, Latin, Greek, Hebrew, Syriac, Arabic and the ancient Coptic, neatly modified into Dialogues, Orations, &c. on the shortest notice—with Dissertations on the Targum and Talmud and Collations after the manner of Kennicott—Hebrew roots and other simples—Dead Languages for living Drones—Oriental Languages with or without points, prefixes, or suffixes—Attic, Doric, Ionic, and Æolic Dialects, with the Wabash, Onondaga, and Mohawk Gutterals—Synalœphas, Elisions, and Ellipses of the newest *cut*—v's added and dove-tailed to their vowels, with a small assortment of the genuine Peloponnesian Nasal Twangs—Classic Compliments adapted to all dignities, with superlatives in *o*, and gerunds in *di*, *gratis*—Monologues, Dialogues, Trialogues, Tetralogues, and so on from *one* to *twenty*-logues.

Anagrams, Acrostics, Anacreontics; Chronograms, Epigrams, Hudibrastics and Panegyrics; Rebuses, Charades, Puns and Conundrums, by the *gross*, or *single dozen.* Sonnets, Elegies, Epithalamiums; Bucolics, Georgics, Pastorals: Epic Poems, Dedications, and Adulatory Prefaces, in *verse* and *prose.*

Ether, Mist, Sleet, Rain, Snow, Lightning, and Thunder, prepared and personified, after the manner of Della Crusca, with a quantity of *Brown Horror* and *Blue Fear*, from the same Manufactory; with a pleasing variety of high-colored *Compound* Epithets, well assorted—Farragoes, and other Brunonian Opiates—Anti-Institutes, or the new and concise patent mode of applying *forty letters* to the spelling of a monosyllable—Love Letters by the Ream—Summary Arguments, both *Merry* and *Serious*—Sermons, moral, occasional, or polemical—Sermons for Texts, and Texts for Sermons—Old Orations scoured, Forensics furbished, Blunt Epigrams newly pointed, and Cold Conferences hashed; with *Extemporaneous* Prayers *corrected* and *amended*—Alliterations artfully allied—and periods polished to perfection.

* At Hanover. Before the Farmer's Museum became the repository of these articles, a few were published in the Federal Orrery, and in the Tablet.

Airs, Canons, Catches, and Cantatas — Fuges, Overtures, and Symphonies for any number of Instruments —— Serenades for Nocturnal Lovers — with *Rose Trees* full blown, and *Black* Jokes *of all colors* —— Amens and Hallelujahs, trilled, quavered and slurred —— with Couplets, Syncopations, Minims, and Crotchet Rests, for female voices —— and *Solos*, with *three* parts, for hand organs.

Classic College Bows, clear starched, lately imported from Cambridge, and now used by all the topping scientific connoisseurs, in hair and wigs, in this country.

Adventures, Paragraphs, Letters from Correspondents, Country Seats for Rural Members of Congress, provided for Editors of Newspapers — with Accidental Deaths, Battles, Bloody Murders, Premature News, Tempests, Thunder and Lightning, and Hail-Stones, of all dimensions, adapted to the Season.

Circles squared, Mathematical points divided into quarters, and half shares; and jointed Asymptotes, which will meet at any given distance.

Syllogisms in Bocardo, and Baralipton; and other coarse Wrapping-Paper, *gratis*, to those who buy the smallest article.

☞ *On hand a few Tierces of Attic Salt —— Also, Cash, and the highest price, given for* RAW WIT, *for the use of the Manufactory, or taken in exchange for the above Articles.*

Tyler was extremely fond of amusing himself and others with specimens of his skill in alliteration. One of these, a sort of love epistle, "From Fond Frederic to Fanny False Fair," has the following stanzas: —

The sweetest seraph's softest smile,
The gorgeous gems of gentle grace,
The slippery serpent's scathful stile,
Frequent false Fanny's flattering face.

Headstrong with hazy halcyon hope,
I follow, fond, the fickle fair;
Nor shun the sudden, stunning stroke,
Which drives me deep in dank despair.

* * * * *

Nor systems, suns, nor sparkling stars,
In confused Chaos countervolved,
Could ape the ambling of her airs,
When random ruin she resolved.

Fair Fanny's fame shall flourish far,
Till teaz-ed Time shall, toiling, tire;
And Daphne, Delia, Dorcas, dear,
Shall fail to fan fierce Fanny's fire.

To these there was given an answer, alphabetically arranged, beginning —

Artful ape of amorous airs,
Baneful bait thy ballad bears;
Coaxing coxcomb, curb thy course, &c.

The following verses are in a different style, and, it must be admitted that they have an air of unstudied ease and elegance, which are seldom seen in the productions of those, who write for newspapers: —

SPONDEE'S MISTRESSES.

I.

Let Cowley soft in amorous verse,
The rovings of his love rehearse,
  With passion most unruly,
Boast how he woo'd sweet Amoret,
The sobbing Jane, and sprightly Bet,
The lily fair and smart brunette,
  In sweet succession truly.

II.

But list, ye lovers, and you 'll swear,
I roved with him beyond compare,
  And was far more unlucky;
For never yet in Yankee coast
Were found such girls, who so could boast,
An honest lover's heart to roast,
  From Casco to Kentucky.

III.

When first the girls nicknamed me beau,
And I was all for dress and show,
  I set me out a courting.
A romping Miss, with heedless art,
First caught, then almost broke, my heart,
Miss Conduct named; we soon did part;
  I did not like such sporting.

IV.

The next coquet, who raised a flame,
Was far more grave, and somewhat lame,
  She in my heart did rankle;
She conquered with a sudden glance;
The spiteful slut was called Miss Chance;
I took the gipsy out to dance;
  She almost broke my ankle.

V.

A thoughtless girl, just in her teens,
Was the next fair, whom Love it seems
  Had made me prize most highly:
I thought to court a lovely mate,
But, how it made my heart to ache, —
It was that jade, the vile Miss Take;
  In troth, Love did it slily.

VI.

And last, Miss Fortune, whimpering, came,
Cured me of Love's tormenting flame,
  And all my beau pretences;
In Widow's weeds, the prude appears;
See now — she drowns me with her tears,
With bony fist, now slaps my ears,
  And brings me to my senses.

In 1799, Tyler wrote an Ode for the celebration of the fourth of July at Windsor, Vermont, highly charged with federal politics and patriotism. It consists of eighty-four lines; and though it might be here introduced as a good specimen of the author's poetry, I prefer appropriating the space it might occupy to the following Convivial Song, which he wrote for the same occasion, and which was sung at a select meeting in the evening: —

Tune — "Here's to our noble selves, Boys."

I.

Come, fill each brimming glass, boys,
  Red or white has equal joys,
Come fill each brimming glass, boys,
    And toast your country's glory;

Does any here to fear incline,
And o'er Columbia's danger whine,
Why let him quaff this gen'rous wine,
He 'll tell another story.

II.

Here 's Washington, the brave, boys,
Source of all Columbia's joys,
Here 's Washington the brave, boys,
Come rise and toast him standing:
For he 's the hero firm and brave,
Who all our country's glory gave,
And once again he shall us save,
Our armies bold commanding.

III.

Here 's to the gallant Tar, boys,
Whose cannon's roar our foe annoys,
Here 's to the gallant Tar, boys,
His country's cause defending;
For warlike Truxton's noble name,
Like Nelson's shall extend his fame,
And loud through all the earth proclaim
His glory, never ending.

IV.

Here 's to our native land, boys,
Land of liberty and joys,
Here 's to our native land, boys,
Your glasses raise for drinking;
And he that will not drink this toast,
May he in France of freedom boast,
There dangling on a lantern post,
Or in the Rhone be sinking.

V.

Here 's to our Vermont Fair, boys,
Pledges bright of Federal joys,
Here 's to our Vermont Fair, boys,
Fill high to Love and Beauty;
For while we toast their glowing charms,
Their virtue every bosom warms,
We 'll die to guard them safe from harms;
It is a Federal duty.

VI.

Here 's to Vermont state, boys,
  And all her manly rustic joys,
Here 's to Vermont state, boys,
    Columbia's brave defender;
For while our pines ascend on high,
And while our mountains mock the sky,
Our Independence, Liberty,
    We never will surrender.

VII.

Here 's to the Sage of Quincy, boys,
  Legal head of all our joys,
Here 's to the Sage of Quincy, boys,
    Who guards us while we 're drinking;
For while we quaff the boozy wine,
And sense and tipsy mirth combine,
With temperate head he sits sublime,
    And for our good is thinking.

VIII.

Now come join hand in hand, boys,
  Mystic type of Federal joys,
Now come join hand in hand, boys,
    Like brother, brother greeting;
For while our union we pursue,
'Tis I and he, and you and you,
Our pleasure all may yet renew,
    At our next Federal meeting.

In 1799, Tyler published, in two volumes, a novel, entitled "The Algerine Captive: or the Life and Adventures of Captain Updike Underhill, six years a prisoner among the Algerines." It was popular, in its day, and sold rapidly, but is now entirely *out of the market.* About the year 1800, he was elected by the Legislature of Vermont, Chief Justice of the Superior Court, — an office, which he held by annual reëlection, for a number of years. While he held this important place, his literary taste was in constant exercise. He wrote many articles for the Port Folio, and some for other papers. At a later period he communicated many pieces for the New-England Galaxy, written in his own peculiarly humorous style. He died at Brattleboro', in 1826. For several years before his death, he suffered much from a cancer in the face, which compelled him to withdraw himself from all society, except that of his family and most intimate friends. No collection of his writings has ever been published.

The articles, entitled "Common Sense in Dishabille," were written by DAVID EVERETT, at that time a lawyer in Boston. This gentleman was left an orphan at a very early age, and was indebted for support to some of his relatives living in the county of Norfolk, Mass. He had an overpowering ambition for a better education than could be obtained at the common schools in the country, and by industry and perseverance, he fitted himself for college. He graduated at Dartmouth about the year 1796; afterwards studied law in Boston; and, while pursuing that study, was an usher in one of the public schools. In due time, he was admitted to the bar and commenced the practice of law in Boston. He was a fluent and ready writer, and the columns of Russell's Boston Gazette, and some other newspapers, from 1796 to 1802, bear testimony to his talent and industry. He was contributor to a small literary paper called "The Nightingale," in 1796, and, about the same time wrote a tragedy in blank verse, called "Daranzel, or the Persian Patriot." In 1802, he removed to Amherst, N. H. but returned to Boston in the course of six or seven years. In 1809, in connection with Munroe & French, he established the Boston Patriot, which he edited for two or three years, and left it for the purpose of editing "The Pilot," a paper, that was got up in 1812, to aid the election of Dewitt Clinton to the office of President of the United States. While editor of the Patriot he wrote a series of essays, explanatory of the Apocalypse, which were afterwards published in a pamphlet. The Pilot was a short-lived paper, and existed only during the political campaign of 1812. Not long after this, Mr. Everett left Boston for Ohio, and died in that state in 1817. The numbers of "Common Sense in Dishabille" were re-published in many of the newspapers, and were afterwards collected and printed in a small volume. The following is the first number: —

COMMON SENSE IN DISHABILLE.

No. I.

"Refined sense and exalted sense, are not half so good as common sense," says one author; "common sense is the best sense in the world," says another. Follow its dictates, says my pen. It will serve better to keep you out of fire and water, and I may add, out of gaol, too, than the philosophy of a Newton, the genius of a Dryden, or the metaphysics of an Edwards. Its seeds are sown in thy mental garden, good reader! cultivate them by observation, reflection, and reading such authors as have brought them to the greatest perfection. I do not intend by this to recommend the writings of Thomas Pain and his deistical colleagues: I had rather see spiders' webs hanging on the shelves of thy library. Common sense is of a peaceable, contented temper, and would be the very last to declare war with Heaven. Its counsels will assist thee in thy domestic economy and every honest employment of life; but they will differ from the advice of the professions of counselors in two respects; they will always be to thy advantage, and will cost thee nothing. It will seldom address thee in Greek or Latin, but in plain English.

Quit your pillow; and go about your business, if you have any, is its first injunction; if not, seek some. Let the sun's first beams shine on your heads in the morning, and you shall not want a good hat to defend your head against its scorching rays at noon. Earn your breakfast before you eat it, and the sheriff shall not deprive you of your supper. Pursue your calling with diligence, and your creditor shall not interrupt you. Be temperate, and the physician shall look in vain for your name on his day-book. If you have a small farm, or a trade, that will support your family and add a hundred dollars a year to your capital, be contented, and never go to Boston, or Hartford, or New-York, to buy land in Georgia, that is to be made on the eighth day of the creation.

Isaac Story, the writer of the articles "From the Shop of Peter Quince," graduated at Harvard College, in 1793.

Except that, which follows, all his contributions were imitations of the odes of Peter Pindar, alluding to incidents that have now but little interest: —

A PATRIOTIC SONG.

Tune — President's March.

I.

"Lo! I quit my native skies —
To arms! my patriot sons arise.
Guard your *freedom*, *rights* and *fame;*
Guard your *freedom*, *rights* and *fame;*
Preserve the clime, your fathers gave;
Heaven's sacred boon from *villains* save —
Lest such daring, impious foes,
Your grandeur in oblivion close —
Your virtue, wisdom, worth decline,
And gasp, convulsed, at *freedom's* shrine.
Rise! my sons, to arms arise!
Guard your heaven descended prize;
Prove to France, the *world*, and me —
Columbia's sons are brave and free."

II.

We hear, blest shade, your warning voice;
Approve your call — pursue your choice —
With hearts united, firm and free,
With hearts united, firm and free.
The sacred boon your valor won,
Shall wake to arms each patriot son;
And glowing with the glorious cause,
Of *freedom*, *country*, *rights* and *laws* —
The storm of worlds our arms will brave,
Or sink with freedom to the grave.

Peaceful, seek your native skies —
Lo! to arms your sons arise;
Firm and fixed our foes to brave,
Till heaven's trump shall burst the grave.

III.

" Worthy sons of glorious sires!
Behold, the warning shade retires;
Pleased your martial fame to spread —
Pleased your martial fame to spread —
Where immortal patriots stand,
Watching freedom's favorite land;
Charmed to hear such deeds of fame,
In holy choir they 'll breathe your name,
Till ancient heroes catch the sound,
And thus the heavens with joy rebound —
Happy nation! brave and free;
Friends to man and liberty —
Long enjoy the sacred boon,
Which immortal valor won."

IV.

Illustrious shade, to thee we swear,
To freedom's altar we 'll repair;
And, like a band of Spartans, brave,
And, like a band of Spartans, brave,
To Pluto's realm each foe convey —
O'er lawless tyrants bear the sway —
Till freedom's banner is unfurled,
And waves around the darkened world;
Till from the centre to each pole,
In rapturous sounds shall constant roll —
Hail! sweet freedom, gift divine —
Lo! we bend before thy shrine,
Firmly fixed on this decree —
To FOLLOW DEATH, OR LIBERTY.

THOMAS G. FESSENDEN, son of the Rev. William Fessenden, the minister of Walpole, graduated at Dartmouth College, in 1796. While in college, he had gained notoriety by writing poetical trifles, and particularly by a Yankee ballad, called "Jonathan's Courtship," which had been published in a pamphlet and secured for its author an uncommon share of popularity among the rural population. The most important of his contributions to the Museum were signed "Simon Spunkey," and were written in the Hudibrastic style, satirizing French and democratic politics. His Ode for the New Year, 1798, filled a whole page of the Museum, and thus it began:—

Old Time, a persevering codger,
Like debtor dunned, a nimble dodger,
Who, having scampered one inch by you,
Will never afterwards come nigh you;—
Whose foretop one might hide a cat in,
But bald behind as school-boy's Latin;—
Who never yet, by saint or sinner,
Was bribed to stay till after dinner;—
Who never bates his usual jog,
Nor stops his steed for oats or grog,
But Jehu-like, drives all the world round,
As swift as top by truant twirled round;—
Who lowers at love-sick poetaster,
But puffs productions of a master;—
Before whom grandeur's gorgeous palaces
Melt, like a dream's fantastic fallacies;—
Now jogs the band with shag-bark elbow,
And aims with lifted scythe a fell blow
To level Simon's reputation,
Unless the poet scrawl narration,
A kind of Hudibrastic summary,
Of politics and other flummery,
Of matters tragical and queer,
Which mark the annals of last year;—
And, with a congee, low and pleasant,
Wish people happy through the present.
Now, gentle reader, take the trouble
To mount my nag,—he carries double,—
I mean my Pegasus so antic,
And bid him canter 'cross the Atlantic,
While we, as close as bride and groom, stick,
And ride, like witches on a broom-stick.

The poet proceeds to review the principal events that had happened in Europe during the preceding year, and then

From Europe turns his bounding Pegasus
Where fighting fellows make a plaguy fuss,
To blithe Columbia's peaceful shores,
Where no rude din of battle roars,
Where Plenty fills her wicker basket,
And Wealth unlocks his golden casket;
Health strings the nerves of every farmer,
And tints the cheek of ruddy charmer;
Where once was nought but desert howling,
With swamps, scarce fit to pasture owl in;
Where meagre famine often drilled us,
Where Indians tomahawked and killed us,
We quaff the bumper, smoke cigar,
Nor dread the howl of Indian war;
Where lately stood but two or three men,
Are many hardy bands of freemen,
&c. &c. &c.

Some severe touches at the printers and editors of Jacobin papers, at members of Congress, and other politicians, and various topics of public interest, fill up the poem. It was in that year, that the frigate Constitution was built in Boston. On the day appointed for the launch, an immense crowd assembled to witness the passage of the ship into the water; but from defect in the preparatory steps, the workmen were unable to get it from the stocks, and, of course, there was no launch, until several days afterwards. This circumstance is thus referred to: —

But man is under contribution,
To sing the frigate Constitution,
Lest this, our pithy Ode, be lost on
Commercial wits and tars of Boston.
Bostonians built a stately frigate,
And undertook to man and rig it,

Which set Sedition's sons a-scowling,
And maddened Jacobins to howling.
The foresaid frigate, on a day,
Appointed was to glide away,
To hoary Ocean's oozy bed,
With Neptune then and there to wed.
The wished-for day arrived, when lo!
Miss Constitution would not go.
How Jacobinic sinners scoff,
Because she fails to travel off!
They swore she was prophetic wench,
And foresaw trouble from the French,
If she to federal folly kept tune,
And sought the arms of Master Neptune.
At length, in merry mood she went in,
And floats her natural element in,
And may she ever triumph there,
The watery god's peculiar care.

After a compliment to the printer and the writers of the Museum, he concludes in this strain: —

Now, Courteous Reader, since a while
To sing, in Della Cruscan style,
By frolic Fancy borne along,
We stemmed the cataract of song!
'Tis time, I think, with aching heart,
For Muse and you and I to part;
Still cherishing the hope, however,
That we three gentlefolks so clever,
When eke another season passes,
May meet on summit of Parnassus;
Like crazy Sybil, who did mutter once,
As sage Apollo gave her utterance,
To trill a new-year's ode sublimer
Than ever flowed from lips of rhymer.

Fessenden had the common-place book of Yankee comparisons always at the nib of his pen. Here is one of his pieces, — not political, — ludicrously rich in these sportive metaphors: —

PETER PERIWINKLE, TO TABITHA TOWZER.

A MOST DELICATE LOVE SONG.

My TABITHA TOWZER is fair,
  No guinea pig ever was neater,
Like a hackmatak slender and spare,
  And sweet as a musk-rat, or sweeter!

My TABITHA TOWZER is sleek,
  When dressed in her pretty new tucker,
Like an otter that paddles the creek,
  In quest of a pout, or a sucker!

Her forehead is smooth as a tray,
  Nay smoother than that, on my soul,
And turned, as a body may say,
  Like a delicate, neat wooden bowl.

To what shall I liken her hair,
  So pretty, so flowing and fine?
For similes sure must be rare,
  When we speak of a nymph so divine.

Not the head of a Nazarite seer,
  That never was shaven nor shorn;
Nought equals the locks of my dear,
  But the silk of an ear of green corn.

My dearest has two pretty eyes,
  Glass buttons shone never so bright,
Their lustre pellucid outvies
  The bug that oft twinkles by night.

My dear has a beautiful nose,
  With a sled-runner crook in the middle,
Which one would be led to suppose,
  Was meant for the head of a fiddle.

The lips of my charmer are sweet,
  As a hogshead of maple molasses,
The ruby red tint of her cheek,
  The gill of a salmon surpasses.

Description must fail in her chin,
  At least till our language is richer,
'Tis fairer than dipper of tin,
  Or beautiful china cream pitcher.

So pretty a neck, I 'll be bound,
  Never joined head and body together,
Like a crooked necked squash on the ground,
  Long whitened by winter-like weather.

Should I mention her gait, or her air,
  You might think I intended to banter;
She moves with more grace you would swear,
  Than a foundered horse forced to a canter!

Should I speak of the rest of her charms,
  I might, by some phrase that 's improper,
Give modesty's bosom alarms,
  Which I would not do for a copper.

I felt t' other day very droll,
  As by her I chanced to be marching,
My heart waxed hot as a coal,
  And hopped like a pea, that is parching!

I 'll trudge away one of these nights,
  To see my delectable creature,
I 'll tell her 'tis hard if she slights
  Her pining, poetical Peter.

But then I 'll be surly and sad,
  Should she cruelly send me a jogging,
Like a bully, when some spunky lad,
  Gives the quarrelsome devil a flogging!

I 'll tell her, "t' wont answer for me,
  To be whining about you so idle,
Should you give me the bag, d' ye see,
  I 'll hang my 'nown self,' with a bridle!"

The expenses of his education at Dartmouth College, Fessenden defrayed chiefly by his own exertions. During the vacations, he added to his slender means by instructing a village school, and occasionally procured some further addition to his finances by teaching psalmody several evenings in the week, after finishing his daily task as a schoolmaster. In the autumn of 1796, he commenced the study of the law at Rutland, Vermont.

After completing his preparatory studies, he formed a partnership, as a practitioner, with Nathaniel Chipman, — a gentleman then eminent for legal, literary, and scientific attainments, and afterwards a judge of the superior court.

In 1801, he was employed as an agent for a company formed in Vermont, for the purpose of securing, in London, a patent for a newly-invented hydraulic machine. He spent some time in London, and while there, wrote one of his principal poems, namely, "The Modern Philosopher, or Terrible Tractoration! By Christopher Caustick, M. D., A. S. S." &c. which ran through two or three editions in England, and three in the United States. After his return, he published another poem, entitled "Democracy unveiled; or Tyranny stripped of the Garb of Patriotism." The first of these is a satire on medical quackery; the second, a scourge for the democratic politicians. Both these poems are written in the Hudibrastic verse, and, though now seldom read, and but little known, will always be valued by those, who take pleasure in reviewing the vagaries and caprices of scientific men, and the wrangling of politicians.

In 1803, Fessenden was the editor of a weekly political paper in New-York, the title of which, if my memory serves me, was "The Investigator." It was printed in the octavo form. Its existence was brief and unprofitable. About this time, he revised his two poems, — mentioned above, — and made considerable additions to both. The notes are copious and entertaining.

Tired of writing upon politics, Fessenden retired to the vicinity of his native place, and gave his attention to less exciting but more useful discussions. He was, for a time, the editor of a paper printed at Bellows Falls, in Vermont, which he made a useful vehicle of rural and agricultural amusement and instruction; and compiled a small volume of recipes and maxims, adapted to the use of farmers and mechanics.

In 1822, a paper called the "New-England Farmer" was established in Boston, and Mr. Fessenden was regularly installed as its editor, — a place which he filled till his death. In conducting this paper he displayed untiring industry in collecting all sorts of information, that could be serviceable to agriculturists and gardeners in their domestic operations; and though he had but little *practical* knowledge of agriculture, he managed by the aid of others, and by constantly consulting the best authors, to make the Farmer an interesting and highly useful paper. Among his correspondents and advisers were those scientific agriculturists, the late John Lowell, John Prince, and Peter C. Brooks, and John Welles and Josiah Quincy, who are still living. While engaged in editing this paper, he compiled and published several volumes, for the purpose of assisting the rural population in farming and gardening.

Mr. Fessenden, after two days illness, died on the 10th of November, 1837, aged sixty-five. He was buried at Mount Auburn. Over his remains, his friends erected a monument, which bears the following inscription: —

THOMAS GREEN FESSENDEN,
died Nov. 11, 1837:
aged 65.

This monument is erected by the Massachusetts Society for promoting agriculture — by the Horticultural Society of Massachusetts, and individuals, as a testimony of respect for the talents and acquirements of the deceased, and his labors in promoting the objects of the above institutions.

THE FEDERAL ORRERY.

The publication of the Federal Orrery was begun October 20, 1794. It was edited by Thomas Paine, and printed by Weld & Greenough, at No. 42 Cornhill, — now Washington-street, — Boston. It was published semi-weekly, on Monday and Thursday, at the price of two dollars and a half a year. Mr. Paine was the projector, and, probably, the sole proprietor of the paper. He had graduated at Harvard College in 1792, with a reputation for scholarship and literary talent, much above the ordinary rank, and his proposals for publishing the Orrery were received by the public with extraordinary favor.

The subscription to the paper, even before the appearance of the first number, was exceedingly liberal — surpassing that, which had been given beforehand, to any other Boston paper. The following is his opening address

TO THE PUBLIC.

Confiding in the smiles of an indulgent and generous public, the editor of the Orrery is enabled to anticipate the earliest period, which his most sanguine hopes had contemplated, as the commencement of his publication. Under auspices so flattering, were he to procrastinate, but for a day, the active execution of his office, he would be guilty of ingratitude to that republican liberality, which has so *universally* countenanced, and that literary friendship, which has so splendidly supported, his proposals.

To the sons and daughters of science and taste, he returns his most respectful thanks for the reception of many elegant favors; — to the merchants of this metropolis, he feels a deep obligation for the extensive circulation, to which they have so greatly contributed; — and to every description of his numerous friends, he presents the warm tribute of grateful acknowledgement.

In the prosecution of a work, whose birth has been propitiated by an unprecedented patronage, the editor will most rigidly adhere to those principles of impartiality, which he professed in his proposals. Speculations, whether moral or political, will find a ready insertion; and any strictures, in answer, will be equally acceptable. The Orrery will be the *agent* of all parties, but the *slave* of none. As subjects of discussion, it will never be the *trumpeter* or the *denouncer*, of public men or national measures: — Republicans have the eye of an eagle, and can penetrate their *spots*, while they admire their *splendor*. The administrators of a free government should expect the scrutiny of their political creators; — but the demon of private slander shall never conduct the orbit of the smallest satellite, that twinkles in the horizon of the Orrery.

The promises held out in the prospectus, and the high literary reputation of the editor, led to anticipations, which, it is unpleasant to say, were but partially realized. Public expectation was not satisfied. The editor devoted much of his time to other pursuits, and entrusted the care of his subscription list and the accounts of his advertising customers, to those, who were unfaithful or incompetent. That constancy of attention, which is the imperative duty of an editor and publisher, became irksome, and, of course was too often neglected. After publishing three volumes, of fifty-two numbers each, Paine abandoned the establishment, and it was sold to Benjamin Sweetser, in whose hands it expired.

The Orrery took a decided stand in favor of the federal party; and, notwithstanding the complacent tone of the prospectus, was not remarkable for urbanity in its intercourse with political antagonists. Toward the Jacobin clubs, and especially in reference to the Chronicle and its correspondents, it was fierce in its opposition, merciless in ridicule, and implacable in resentment.

A number of writers contributed to fill the columns of the Orrery — chiefly on politics; but the most remarkable portion of the political matter was a series of papers, entitled "Remarks on the Jacobiniad," and these contributed largely to its notoriety and circulation. They were introduced by a note, signed X. Z. and dated at Worcester. The writer says — "I am requested, by a critical friend, to send you the following remarks on a poem, that deserves, I think, to be better known. He informs me, that there were but few copies of the poem struck off for some particular friends, and that the author's name is a secret." It will be understood that no such poem had been printed or written; but that the writer chose this mode of satirizing and caricaturing the most prominent persons in the Jacobin club of Boston. The "Remarks" are interspersed with extracts from the imaginary Poem, — almost every couplet of which was a sharp-edged satire or galling lampoon. The portraits, thus hung up to public ridicule, were too like the original, not to be readily recognized. They were sometimes designated by the real names of the persons they were intended to expose, and, at others, by letters corresponding to the number of syllables. The persons thus attacked were stung to madness. In one instance, a personal assault on the editor of the Orrery, in one of the most public places in State-street, was the consequence of one of the "Remarks." I refrain from making extracts from these papers, for the reason, that very few readers would understand their application, without the accompaniment of notes, *biographical and historical,* which it is not in my power to prepare; and the preparation of which would be thought by some an ungracious act. The political asperities, which tormented society at that period, have been softened by the all-subduing hand of time; the clamor of the old party hostilities long ago subsided; the slumber of years has crept over the fires, which then heated the blood and flamed in the bosoms of Federalists and Jacobins; and it might be unkind to rake from the ashes a single spark, to awaken individual sensibilities from the oblivion of nearly half a century.

The authorship of the "Remarks on the Jacobiniad" was attributed to the Rev. John S. J. Gardiner, then assistant rector of Trinity church, Boston; and he was bitterly and ferociously assailed in Edes's Boston Gazette and in the Chronicle, on the presumption that he was the author. I am not aware that the imputation was either admitted or denied. Soon after their appearance in the Orrery, the numbers were published in a duodecimo volume, *embellished* with caricature likenesses of many of those, against whom the unmerciful satire of the author was directed. The book is not now to be found, but in the libraries of the book-worm and the antiquarian.

When the Orrery first appeared it was expected that Mrs. Morton, — a lady, who had delighted the public with some of her poetical effusions, — would be a liberal contributor to its columns. A poetical correspondence, between her and Paine, under the signatures of "Philenia" and "Menander," had been previously carried on in the Massachusetts Magazine and in some of the newspapers. Mrs. Morton had also published a poem, entitled "Beacon Hill," — a production of much merit, but now almost forgotten. Her poetry was then read with avidity, and generally admired, and the expectation of seeing many of her productions in the Orrery, aided it in its claim to popularity. But there is very little of her writing to be found in it, and that little, is of an uninteresting character. Her contributions were discontinued before the close of the first volume.

The oblivion, which has fallen upon the literary reputation of Mrs. Morton, affords a melancholy lesson to the poets of the present generation, who are crowding the avenues to public favor. Fifty years ago, — one little half century, — the Poems of Philenia were *as* popular as those of the *most* popular of the magazine poets, of the year 1850. About twenty-five years ago, they were published in an imposing octavo, by one of the Boston booksellers; and the question was then often asked, who is Philenia? Who is Mrs. Morton? But that octavo, it is presumed, is not now to be found, except in some public library, or in those repositories of "antique books," kept in Cornhill by Messrs. Drake & Burnham. Yet which of the ladies, who write for the Magazines, the Souvenirs, and the Forget-me-nots, have produced any thing sweeter and purer, than the following Hymn, written by Mrs. Morton for the anniversary celebration of the Humane Society?

REANIMATION.

Who, from the shades of gloomy night,
When the last tear of hope is shed,
Can bid the soul return to light,
And break the slumber of the dead?

No human skill that heart can warm,
Which the cold blast of nature froze;
Recall to life the perished form;
The secret of the grave disclose.

But thou, our saving God, we know,
Canst arm the mortal hand with power
To bid the stagnant pulses flow,
The animating heart restore.

Thy will, ere nature's tutored hand
Could with young life these limbs unfold;
Did the imprisoned brain expand,
And all its countless fibres told.

As from the dust, thy forming breath
Could the unconscious being raise;
So can the silent voice of death
Wake at thy call in songs of praise.

Since *twice* to die is ours alone,
And *twice* the birth of life to see;
O let us, suppliant at thy throne,
Devote our *second* life to thee.

The concluding stanza was intended to be sung by persons who had been reanimated after having been drowned.

The articles in the Orrery purporting to come from "the Shop of Messrs. Colon & Spondee," were written by Royal Tyler of Guilford, Vermont, and Joseph Dennie — gentlemen much better known a few years afterwards in connection with the Farmer's Museum. Their first communication was introduced by the following advertisement: —

MESSRS. COLON & SPONDEE request their brother haberdasher, T. P. to open an account current with their *shop* at the foot of the Green

Mountain; and as their junior partner served the concluding year of his apprenticeship in the same *warehouse* of Apollo, clipped the *tape* of rhetoric with the same *scissors*, and handled the *yardstick* of sentiment behind the same *counter*, they doubt not of his ready compliance with the *credit* they require.

These contributions were not very numerous, nor remarkable for any merit that requires republication.

A series of articles appeared in the Orrery, under the head of "Omnium Gatherum," which were written by the late William Biglow, and are full of the quiet and gentle humor, for which that gentleman was, all his life, celebrated. In the first number, he sketches his own life and character, as follows: —

I was born in a small country village, of reputable, industrious parents, at a time when they were as poor as poverty herself. Nothing remarkable was at that time observed in me, except that I was, in the phrase of the hamlet, "a desperate cross body." This, however, must have been owing to some indisposition of body; for I naturally possess a very peaceable temper.

At a proper age I was sent to school — five weeks, in winter, to a master, who could read; and as long, in summer, to an old maid, who could knit. Possessing a strong attachment to books, I soon passed from my primer to my psalter, and thence in a short time to my Bible, which were the only books we used. At this early period of life, I perused all the neighboring libraries, which contained "Pilgrim's Progress," "Day of Doom," and many other compositions equally elegant and entertaining.

Among my schoolfellows, I was so peaceful and condescending, that I was generally denominated a coward. But that, which was attributed to pusillanimity, was rather the effect of good nature. However violently enraged, one smile from my adversary would instantaneously assuage my anger, and determine me to become his faithful friend.

Though this complaisance led my schoolmates to practise many impositions upon me, yet I esteemed this inconvenience sufficiently compensated, as it caused me to become a great favorite of my old grandmother. So great was her esteem for me, that she took me, at a very early age, to wait on her, and my venerable old grandfather. In this situation I passed several years; and, as constantly as Saturday night came round, I very piously said my catechism, and supped on hasty-pudding; and, with equal devotion, rode to meeting on Sunday, and carried my aunt behind me on a pillion.

There began my poetical career, by composing "*a ballad, containing a true and surprising account of how the Deacon's son went a courting, lost his saddle, and found it again,*" which had a great run in the village. This circumstance added to my former fame at school; and my great aversion to every species of manual labor determined my father to give me a public education. I was accordingly sent to our parson's, where I attended closely and entirely to my studies, and, in a short time, became a member of the university.

When I came to college, I was, like most great authors, awkward and bashful; and my classmates immediately concluded that I was either a *fool* or a *genius.* My instructers, however, were decidedly of the former opinion. I was by no means an idle fellow; but I paid very little attention to the stated exercises of the college, choosing rather to follow my own inclinations, than those of my governors. I studiously avoided cultivating an acquaintance with any, except a few selected classmates, and this seclusion continued me an unpolished country fellow. At length I have found my way through, and have retired into a neat rural village, and taken a small school, resolving to hide myself from the noise, insults, and injuries of the world, behind my own insignificance. I here pass for a good soul; and, because I *cannot* be genteel, I do all in my power to make people believe that I *will not.*

Notwithstanding I have passed in the world, thus silent and unknown, I have, as far as my opportunities would permit, made very accurate observations upon men and manners. When your paper made its appearance among us, I concluded that some of my compositions might be of service to you, and determined to publish them periodically. * * * * After this explanation, you will readily perceive what kind of fare I shall be likely to serve up; and, if you will give this a place in your literary oglio, I will do my endeavor shortly to prepare a still more palatable morsel. CHARLES CHATTERBOX, ESQ.

The next number of "Omnium Gatherum" was the following, in which the "quaint airs of the laughter-loving muse" cannot fail to divert the imagination: —

A WILL:

Being the last words of CHARLES CHATTERBOX, Esq. late worthy and much lamented member of the Laughing Club of Harvard University, who departed college life, June 21, 1794, in the twenty-first year of his age.

I, CHARLEY CHATTER, sound of mind,
To making fun am much inclined;

So, having cause to apprehend
My college life is near its end,
All future quarrels to prevent,
I seal this will and testament.

My soul and body, while together,
I send the storms of life to weather;
To steer as safely as they can,
To honor God, and profit man.

Imprimis, then, my bed and bedding,
My only chattels, worth the sledding,
Consisting of a maple stead,
A counterpane, and coverlet,
Two cases with the pillows in,
A blanket, cord, a winch and pin,
Two sheets, a feather bed and hay-tick,
I order sledded up to *Natick;*
And that with care the sledder save them
For those kind parents, first who gave them.

Item. The Laughing Club, so blest,
Who think this life, what 'tis — a jest, —
Collect its flowers from every spray,
And laugh its goading thorns away;
From whom to-morrow I dissever,
Take one sweet grin, and leave forever;
My chest, and all that in it is,
I give and I bequeath them, viz.:
Westminster grammar, old and poor,
Another one, compiled by Moor;
A bunch of pamphlets pro and con,
The doctrine of salva—ti—on;
The college laws, I 'm freed from minding,
A Hebrew psalter, stripped from binding.
A Hebrew Bible, too, lies nigh it,
Unsold — because no one would buy it.

My manuscripts, in prose and verse,
They take for better and for worse;
Their minds enlighten with the best,
And pipes and candles with the rest;
Provided that from them they cull
My college exercises dull,

On threadbare theme, with mind unwilling,
Strained out thro' fear of fine one shilling,
To teachers paid t' avert an evil,
Like Indian worship to the devil.
The above-named manuscripts, I say,
To club aforesaid I convey,
Provided that said themes, so given,
Full proofs that *genius won't be driven*,
To our physicians be presented,
As the best opiates yet invented.

Item. The government of college,
Those liberal *helluos* of knowledge,
Who, e'en in these degenerate days,
Deserve the world's unceasing praise;
Who, friends of science and of men,
Stand forth Gomorrah's righteous ten;
On them I nought, but thanks, bestow,
For, like my cash, my credit 's low;
So I can give nor clothes nor wines,
But bid them welcome to my fines.

Item. My study desk of pine,
That workbench, sacred to the nine,
Which oft hath groan'd beneath my metre,
I give to pay my debts to PETER.

Item. Two penknives with white handles,
A bunch of quills, and pound of candles,
A lexicon compiled by COLE,
A pewter spoon, and earthen bowl,
A hammer, and two homespun towels,
For which I yearn with tender bowels,
Since I no longer can control them,
I leave to those sly lads, who stole them.

Item. A gown much greased in Commons,
A hat between a man's and woman's,
A tattered coat of college blue,
A fustian waistcoat torn in two,
With all my rust, through college carried,
I give to classmate O——,* who 's *married*.

* Jesse Olds, a classmate, afterwards a clergyman in a country town.

Item. C—— P——s* has my knife,
During his natural college life;
That knife, which ugliness inherits,
And due to his superior merits,
And when from Harvard he shall steer,
I order him to leave it here,
That 't may from class to class descend,
Till time and ugliness shall end.

The said C—— P——s, humor's son,
Who long shall stay when I am gone,
The Muses' most successful suitor
I constitute my executor;
And for his trouble to requite him,
Member of Laughing Club I write him.

Myself on life's broad sea I throw,
Sail with its joy, or stem its wo,
No other friend to take my part,
Than careless head and honest heart.
My purse is drained, my debts are paid,
My glass is run, my will is made,
To beaüteous Cam. I bid adieu,
And with the world begin anew.

June 20th, 1794.

While Biglow was writing these articles for the Orrery, he was teaching a school, and pursuing studies preparatory to the profession of a clergyman. The following poem formed a part of No. III. and was written as a response to a question, whether he had chosen the profession best adapted to his disposition and talents: —

THE CHEERFUL PARSON.

Since bards are all wishing, pray why may not I?
Though but a poor rhymer, for once I will try.
The life, that I choose, would be pleasant to scarce one,
Yet the life, that I choose, is the life of a parson.

First on me, kind heaven, a fortune bestow,
Too high for contempt and for envy too low,

* Charles Prentiss, a member of the junior class, when this was written; afterwards editor of the Rural Repository.

On which I with prudence may hope to subsist,
Should I be for my damnable doctrine dismissed.

In a rich farming village, where P——s shall plead,
And D——r feel pulses, give physic, and bleed,
Where A——t the youths and the children shall teach,
There may I be called and there settled to preach.

Not damning a man for a different opinion,
I 'd mix with the Calvinist, Baptist, Arminian,
Treat each like a man, like a Christian and brother,
Preach love to our Maker, ourselves and each other.

On a snug, little farm, I 'd provide me a seat,
With buildings all simple, substantial and neat;
Some sheep and some cattle my pastures to graze,
And a middle prized pony, to draw my new chaise.

When I find it no longer "good being alone,"
May a mild, rural nymph "become bone of my bone;"
Not fixed, like a puppet, on fashion's stiff wires,
But who *can* be genteel, when occasion requires.

Whose wealth is not money, whose beauty 's not paint;
Not an infidel romp, nor a sour-hearted saint;
Whose religion 's not heat, and her virtue not coldness,
Nor her modesty fear, nor her wit manly boldness.

Thus settled, with care I 'd apportion my time
To my sermons, my garden, my wife, and my rhyme,
To teach the untaught, and to better the bad,
To laugh with the merry, and weep with the sad.

At the feast, where religion might be a spectator,
Where friendship presided, and mirth was a waiter,
I 'd fear not to join with the good-humored clan,
And prove that a parson may still be a man.

Thus blest, may my life be slid smoothly away,
And I still grow more grave, as my hair grows more gray;
With age may the hope of the Christian increase,
And strew life's descent with the blossoms of peace.

And when we leave this world, as leave it we must,
With rapture meet death, and sink into the dust,
With a tear in each eye may the parish all say,
"They were a kind pair, and did good in their day."

CHARLES CHATTERBOX, ESQ.

The next three numbers of "Omnium Gatherum" purport to be "Extracts from the Age of Freedom; being an Investigation of good and bad government; in imitation of Mr. Pain's Age of Reason, and intended for a second part of the same tune." These are intended to expose the sophistry of the Age of Reason, by adopting a similar form of argument, in reference to well known, and well established facts, — such as the discovery of America, the Revolution, and the birth and life of George Washington, — all of which, by this mode of reasoning, are showed to be fables, and entitled to no credit. The *imitation* is well maintained. The eighth number is a good-humored touch at one of the political follies of the day: —

ELECTIONEERING.

CHARLEY, *in a hypocondriac fit, complaineth of his condition; prayeth earnestly to be delivered; displayeth a great share of vanity; and threateneth destruction and devastation.*

From school returned, with heart depressed,
With aching head, and anxious breast,
With hand, grown weak by ferule holding,
And voice as trumpet hoarse with scolding,
Of A B C and ciphering sick,
And tired of one-pound-ten per week, —
I loll me down in easy chair,
And give my humble soul to prayer.

O Public! monster many-headed,
Courted by bards, by statesmen dreaded,
Who, with thy cords of firm contexture,
Doth Varnum raise and pull down Dexter,*
To thee, most humbly, I petition;
O pity my forlorn condition!

* Joseph B. Varnum and Samuel Dexter, rival candidates for a seat in the United States House of Representatives from the county of Middlesex, Mass. Gen. Varnum was elected for several terms in succession, and was Speaker of the House. Mr. Dexter was an eminent lawyer, and was Secretary of the Treasury during a part of the administration of the elder Adams.

To gain thy favor, long I 've hunted ;
My hostess and myself affronted ;
With all the meekness of a kitten
A history of my life have written,
Which, like most other histories,
Contains some truths and many lies ;
My verse exposed to critic sneers,
To pious pouts, and ribald leers,
And, of my wit and learning vain,
Even dared to laugh at Thomas Pain !

All this was to increase thy joy ;
Then grant, O grant some high employ,
In which thy humble suppliant may
Have little labor and great pay ;
Which will convince, when you bestow it,
That money will enrich a poet.

The President's great chair I shun ;
I cannot fight like Washington ;
For when our enemies combat us,
The careless boobies fly right at us,
Which frights this coward soul of mine ;
But then in Congress I could shine.

I there could take the strongest side, —
I 'm to no party yet allied,
No demo- nor aristo- crat,
Nought but a bard, and hardly that :
Yet I can sit, and look sedate,
Can sleep or hear a long debate,
Can vote the wrong side, or the right ;
And pray what more is requisite ?

But if your bar 'gainst cabin windows,
Your would-be captain's progress hinders.
Put me, if you will raise me fast,
In federal ships before the mast ;
Instead of some old wealthy dough-pate,
Make me a scribe, or judge of probate ;
Or, rather than be fretting here,
Make me a counselor one year.

O Public ! on thy bard take pity
And listen to his doleful ditty ;

Let not a flower of wit so full,
His fragrance waste in desert's school.
A dray-horse drone, who ploughed his way
Through craggy wilds of algebra,
In Euclid's ship knew every rope,
Learned Pike by heart, while I learned Pope,
Yet never sipped Parnassian wine,
Would keep as good a school as mine.

O Public! let me hear thee say,
"Charley, six dollars by the day;"
Or but "five dollars and a half,"
And your petitioner shall laugh.
But, if you keep me here becloistered
By power unknown, by wealth unfostered,
My ink I'll spill, my paper burn,
My table to a wash-bench turn,
My standish for old pewter vend,
My pen shall in a tooth-pick end,
I'll from my jews-harp break the tongue,
And you no more shall hear my song.

CHARLES CHATTERBOX, Esq.

Soon after this publication there appeared in the Orrery a column of poetry addressed to Mr. Chatterbox, giving an account of "the occupations of a Social Recluse," signed "Roger Roundelay." Judging from the style and versification one might suppose it to have been written by Mr. Biglow himself. The next paper brought out a response from Chatterbox, entitled "the Occupations of the Schoolmaster; inscribed 'to well-beloved Roger Roundelay, Esq.'" After a sketch of his employment in the morning, from sunrise till nine o'clock, he proceeds —

'Tis nine; I to the school-house go,
Sauntering with pensive steps and slow;
Thus pray for blessings to attend us, —

* * * * * *

"*Hiatus, maxime, deflendus.*"

At length, "world without end, Amen,"
Gives each one leave to teaze my brain;
Then, Jack, here, take your copy, quick—
Tom, here 's your pen,—sit down you, Dick.
Sir, Tim has pricked me,— Tim, you lout—
Sir, my nose bleeds—may 'n 't I go out?—
Sam, with his ruler, struck my ear;—
Sam, blockhead, bring your ruler here.

First class, prepare yourselves to read—
Jack, where 's your hat?—*'Tis on my head.*
Quick, take it off—read, the first class;—
After these things it came to pass,
That M, O, mo, S, E, S, ses, Moses—
Sir, John heaves paper at our noses.
Come here to me, you booby, John—
Mind there your writing—well—read on—
Who laughs?—*I, to see that hen run*—
Great A, little A, R, O, N, ron—
Aaron it spells;—Come hither, Abel,
And sit you down beneath my table.
Go—you have read enough for now—
The second class—Tom, where 's your bow?—

Thus vexed and mad, till noon I prate on;
O what a simpleton was Satan!
Had but poor Job met my disaster,
To be ordained a country master,
He had, at least, obeyed his bride
In one respect—he would have "*died.*"

* * * * * *

Now back to school I stalk, and soon
Ferule those boys that fought at noon;
To travelers who refused to bow;
Who apples stole, or stoned a cow;
Proceed along from class to class,
To act again the forenoon farce,
Till thousand dins my ears assail
While looks, and threats, and flattering fail,
While, nigh to go, with care and toil, hence,
With lifted broom, I sue for silence;
Then not one tongue can dare deplore,
And not one foot to scrape the floor.

When thus, from noise and riot free,
I drop this sad soliloquy! —
When the schoolmaster's year is done,
What profits him beneath the sun?
While lazy knaves their treasures hoard,
He labors hard to pay his board:
Cashless from Natick came I hither,
And cashless soon return I thither.

At last, my tour of duty done,
I finish school as I begun;
Dismiss my scholars and ill nature,
And hasten home, a happy creature;
See vices grow, and long to *lather* 'em,
So fall in haste to chopping *Gatherum;*
Gatherum, not seasoned to allure
"The literary epicure;"
But, in the opinion of its hasher,
'Twill serve the temperate for a *rasher*.

During the first year of the Orrery, several well-written political communications appeared in its columns, but altogether on the side of the Federalists. An election of members of Congress, occasioned a few smart electioneering pieces. On politics, Paine, himself, wrote generally short and desultory paragraphs, and squibs, aimed at the Chronicle and the heads of its party. Most of these, being of a local and temporary character, were soon forgotten, except by the individuals, who suffered from the smart; and few of them would now be of any interest, without a tedious explanation.

The riotous proceedings, which disturbed the quiet of Boston, soon after the publication of Jay's Treaty, were noticed by the editor, and reprobated in strong language. In the Orrery of September 14, there is an article addressed to Governor Adams, personally, saying, "However harmless and amusing you may view the '*water-melon frolics*,' — as you have been pleased to term them, they may be death to your fellow-citizens and constituents. Against your apparent connivance, let us not again remonstrate in vain. . . . The dwellings of our citizens have been attacked, and recourse for self-preservation, 'nature's first law!' has been had to a measure the most dangerous and fatal. If your supineness is not construed to an approbation of these riots, it is at least suspected to have proceeded from your enmity to the federal administration."

The same paper has the following: — "The EDITOR OF THE ORRERY feels the liveliest sense of gratitude for the *very great* and unexpected influx of patronage, which he has received from the most enlightened and respectable part of the community, since the publication of his last paper. So cordial a public countenance, for a single exertion in the cause of federal republicanism, he believes has been rarely experienced. To his *old* and *new* patrons he returns the sincerest thanks of a devoted heart; and assures them, that if an *inspirited* attention to utility and amusement — to the support of government and *ridicule* of *mobocracy* — will entitle him to the confidence of the *real* friends of his country, or promote the interest of federal republicanism — *the sin of* NEGLIGENCE *shall no longer be laid at his door.*"

It does not *distinctly* appear why there was any "unexpected influx of patronage," during the week preceding this publication; but it is supposed to have been caused by the publication of "The LYARS, a political eclogue — altered to the meridian of Boston." It was an imaginary dialogue between "Genet, Jarvis, and Austin," — an exceedingly coarse attack upon Dr. Jarvis and Benjamin Austin, jun. which occasioned an assault upon Paine by Samuel Jarvis, a brother of the Doctor.

The twenty-first of September, 1795, was the third anniversary of the institution of the French Republic. It was celebrated by a public procession, and a dinner in Fanueil Hall, got up by the Jacobin party. This gave to Paine an excellent opportunity to lampoon the leaders of the party, and to exercise his talent for ribaldry; — an opportunity, which he improved, by the composition of the following

SONG OF LIBERTY AND EQUALITY,

Which ought to have been sung in Fanueil Hall on the 21st *inst. the Birth-Day of the French Republic; and ought to be sung on the Birth-Day of all other Republics, whether male or female, that may hereafter be born.*

TUNE — "Black Sloven."

Ye sons of equality, freedom, and fun,
Come rouse at the sound of the gun — the gun;
Awake from your stupor, for feasting prepare,
With Sansculotte stomachs let every one meet,
Like bears o'er a carcase, to *fight* and to *eat* —
Freely we 'll share
Whate 'er stands before us,
While Freedom's the chorus — Huzza.

'Tis three years, *this moment*, since Freedom, by chance,
Was safely delivered of France — of France;
And the brat is well grown, for so tender an age;
Besure her *complexion* is hardly so good —
'Tis thought that her mother was longing for blood;
For, when in a rage,
She 's rather uncivil,
Cuts throats like a devil — Huzza.

But this is no matter, her votaries say,
Who *honestly* pocket her PAY — her PAY;
Republics may murder, as much as they will;
In this all the glory of freedom consists,
That each man may do whatever he lists,

Fight, ravish and kill,
Keep aristocrats under
By bloodshed and plunder — Huzza.

Now, bright in the east, see the morning appear,
Its rays will EQUALITY cheer — will cheer;
Call out *gaunt* SEDITION from cellar and shed;
At the sound of the bell see the *virtuous* throng,
Come squinting, and skulking, and sneaking along;
Thus the thief from his bed,
When the bailiff approaches,
Most manfully poaches — Huzza.

From the statehouse* in order the Sansculottes move,
Like cattle, or swine, in a drove — a drove;
Composed of all colors, and figures, and shapes;
Two and two, as the patriarch NOAH of old,
Drove into the Ark, the *unclean* of the fold,
Skunks, woodchucks and apes,
Toads, adders, and lizards,
And vultures and buzzards — Huzza.

Behold in the vanguard, three standards on high,
In majesty wave through the sky — the sky:
A charming collection of brotherly souls —
In union, *French*, *Dutch* and *American* drawn!
Like the *wolf* and the *cub* shaking hands with the FAWN;
Sing liberty poles,
With tag, rag, and bobtail,
Proceed on by wholesale — Huzza.

Now mixed with the rabble, six gem'men are seen,
Of various sizes, and mien — and mien;
Ashamed of their fellows, they seem to *be shy* —
There 's *Crafty* and *Crooked*, and *Little* and *Great*,
A genuine mixture of Sansculotte state;
While by-standers cry —
"Behold our Selectmen!
A parcel of picked men" — Huzza.

There moves an old *Baboon*,‡ in shape of a man,
The friend of fat beef, and the *Can* — the *Can!*

* The procession was formed on the lower floor of the Old State House, in State-street, and marched through Merchants-Row to Faneuil Hall.

‡ William Cooper, more than fifty years, the Town Clerk of Boston.

Determined to eat, e'en if liberty bleeds;
While just in his rear, bent by age like a bow,
A bedridden printer * enriches the show—
  Sing Baboon and EDES !
    A promising couple
    The jug to unstopple, —Huzza.

There marches, *great* SHUBAEL, † thy Jacobin whelp,
Whose business is only to *yelp* — to *yelp;*
And paragraphs write for the Boston Gazette;
While wriggling and scratching, like *Sawney M'Bear*
Strut those truth-loving partners, the *Chronicle* PAIR. ‡
  Poor freedom will sweat,
    While *Sammy* '*s* a barking
    With *Adams* and *Larkin*, — Huzza.

There moves great *Honestus's* § three corner'd hat,
A shelter for *wisdom* and *fat* — and *fat;*
In search of the DOCTOR, || his guardian and guide :
Alas, for the doctor he searches in vain,
Ashamed of the club, he is *tortured with pain* —
  Let blackguards deride,
    At HONEE for hunting,
    And DOCTOR for grunting — Huzza.

Now striving amain for a fortunate chance
To *taste* of the Freedom of France — of France;
Stealing softly through alleys, and winding through lanes
Our mob-loving g——r ¶ marches in haste,
His *eyes* up to *Heaven* — *his heart with the feast;*
  In anarchy's strains,

* Benjamin Edes, the printer and proprietor of the Boston Gazette.

† Shubael Hewes, who kept a shop in Washington (then Marlboro') street, opposite the westerly door of the Old South meeting-house. His son, Samuel Hews, to whom the offensive allusion is made in the song, was an ardent supporter of the principles of the French revolutionists, and an active member of the Jacobin Club. He was also a writer for the Chronicle.

‡ "The Chronicle Pair" — Adams and Larkin, printers and editors of that paper.

§ Benjamin Austin, jun., a distinguished political writer in the Chronicle, under the signature of *Honestus*.

|| Doctor Charles Jarvis, a celebrated orator at public meetings. He was one of the leading politicians of his day, and one of the best of extempore speakers. Many persons still living have a vivid recollection of his power in a popular assembly.

¶ Samuel Adams, then Governor of Massachusetts, and one of the distinguished patriots of the Revolution. He had identified himself with the anti-federal party,

Psalm-singing, and praying,
He smiles at man-slaying — Huzza.

Lo, down in yon corner — *afraid to be seen*,
PEREZ * pokes out the end of his chin — his chin;
All ready to join — *when the corner they turn ;*
O Perez, *thy case* might a hero abash,
Thou fearest thy neighbors — thou *lovest French cash* —
Sansculottes, with scorn,
Behold thy dissembling,
Thy blustering, and trembling — Huzza.

Now seated in order the table around,
Their toasts, and their tushes rebound — rebound;
Good eating and drinking make Sansculottes roar;
For Poverty first bid them take up their trade,
Her dictates more patriots, than Freedom's, have made.
Then freedom adore,
Who saves you from starving,
And sets you all laughing — Huzza.

Now citizen governor toasts a long prayer,
And Honee says all that he dare — he dare;
But citizen GOOSE † durst not give out his name,
While Mr. JUTAU ‡ brings the sick doctor up;
And remembers the CHIEF in the Jacobin cup —
Sing, O fie, for shame!
GOOSE, MALLET, and HONEE,
And BABOON the bony — Huzza.

Farewell, ye Sansculottes — I leave ye to dine,
With your hoofs in your dishes, like swine — like swine,

at the adoption of the Federal Constitution, and very naturally fell in with the views and feelings of those who sympathized most closely with the French revolutionists. He was a member of the Old South Church, and a participator in the prayer-meetings of the Calvinists.

* Perez Morton, a lawyer of good standing. He did not join the procession at the place whence it started, but awaited its arrival at the store of one of his political associates, near Faneuil Hall. He represented the town of Dorchester in the General Court; was several times Speaker of the House of Representatives; and held the office of Attorney-General for a number of years from 1809.

† John Kuhn, a respectable citizen, a tailor by profession. He was brother to Jacob Kuhn, whom every body recollects as the Sergeant-at-Arms in the Legislature.

‡ John Jutau, a French emigrant, and an auctioneer.

For once stuff your stomachs, as long as they 'll hold;
The Doctor will help you to purge it away,
And PEREZ and HONEE *attend you for pay;*
While SAMUEL the old,
On stool of repentance,
Will whine out a sentence — TO HEAVEN.

Sometime in March, 1796, an original comedy, called "The Traveler Returned," was brought out at the Boston theatre, of which Mr. Paine said — "As an American production, it met with a very favorable reception. The author, we think, possesses a dramatic talent, which is capable of improvement. But experience is necessary to theatrical effect; and, in producing it, art is equally as essential as genius. The *tedium* of uninteresting solemnity constitutes the principal defect in the Traveler Returned. That it has many good scenes cannot be denied. * * * But the author seems not to be aware, that novelty of incident, picturesque situation, and brilliancy of dialogue are cardinal requisites in genteel comedy. We hope that the public have not condemned him for substituting *broad humor* for *wit,* and *dullness* for *pathos.* Long and frequent soliloquies are, in comedy, highly unnatural; and on the social interviews of polished life, pedantry should never intrude." He then gives a sketch of the fable of the piece; and concludes his criticism as follows: — "Should the comedy be again represented, for the author's benefit, a prudent use of the pruning knife would be of service to some of the soliloquies and many of the national ebullitions. Patriotic sentiments are congenial to the best feelings of an American audience; but the palate of the public is too delicate to bear a *surfeit* of even the most sumptuous entertainment."

This criticism would hardly be deemed severe, except by a very sensitive author. The next Orrery contained a Card, of which the following is all that is necessary, to understand the complaint against the criticism: —

☞ The Author of the "Traveler Returned" presents her compliments to Mr. Paine; she feelingly regrets that she has not met with his approbation. [Some slight mistakes in the sketch of the plot of the comedy are then corrected.] These matters may be characterized as mere *bagatelle* — but a gentleman, *so critical* as Mr. Paine, will be at no loss to decipher their essentiality. With what propriety the accusation of "*pedantry*, *uninteresting solemnity*, *dullness*, &c. &c. are preferred against the Traveler Returned," the public will judge; and if they also join to condemn, the author has only to lament an ineffectual attempt to please.

To this, Mr. Paine affixed the following note: —

"Nil de mortuis nisi bonum" is an ancient maxim of philosophic humanity; and the Editor hopes he shall not flagrantly offend against the Latin idiom, should he translate it — Damn not a play, which has gone to "that bourne whence no TRAVELER RETURNS!!!"

The sting in this brief note was not, by any means adapted to soothe the agonies of irritated authorship. The Centinel, a day or two afterwards, contained a replication, the character of which may be inferred from Mr. Paine's rejoinder, a part of which follows: —

Why should calamity be full of words,
Windy attorneys to their client's woes,
Airy invaders of intestate joys,
Poor breathing orators of miseries?
Let them have scope.

The Editor of the Orrery feels no disposition to enter into a controversy with the *reverend* scribbler in Saturday's Centinel. He considers it cruel in the extreme to deny a disappointed author the liberty of railing at an unfeeling and stupid public, who had neither the sense to discern, nor the gratitude to reward, his unrivaled genius. Complaint is the prerogative of misfortune; and it certainly would be exacting too strict a compliance with the laws of *bienseance*, to refuse a poor benighted pilgrim, who had "*slumped neck and heels in a quagmire*," the privilege of saying he had *muddied his stockings!*

Parson Flummery is therefore allowed the highest latitude of newspaporial abuse; and as he has the most "*profound sensibility*" for the welfare of the "Traveler Returned," it is presumed that no one will ever dispute his right to the unlimited *patent* of "*dullness*" and buffoonery!

The Editor's first critique was generally acknowledged to be too lenient in its strictures. The public universally condemned the comedy *in toto.* The editor, at the sacrifice of his taste, endeavored to diminish the odium. Some of its defects he found indefensible; and had the author been of any order of animals above an incorrigible blockhead, he never would have provoked a public reprehension. * * * The substitution of *dullness* for *pathos* is not conceded by the advocate of the play. The tame interest of its serious scenes is attributed to the "profundity" of the editor's feelings! The only vindicatory plea, which the editor can make, is, that the charge, if true, was equally incurred by the whole auditory:

> Who every scene, with aching eye-string wept;
> Then *lolled*, and most PATHETICALLY SLEPT!

The vindicator of our dramatist next endeavors to obviate the charge of pedantry. * * * The accusation of pedantry was founded on the general complexion of the author's style. From her dialogue she has carefully excluded every species of colloquial ease; and, from beginning to end of her comedy we continually meet with turgid phrases, stale Hibernianisms, filched ribaldry, and forced conceits, without one single solitary SPARK of wit, to cheer, with a momentary TWINKLE, the immense vacuum of Dullness.

The next thrust in this memorable controversy, and the last on the part of Mr. Paine, was the following, which appeared in the Orrery of March 24: —

TO THE REVEREND JOHN MURRAY.

SIR,

The lenity, which marked the first critique of the editor of the Orrery on YOUR comedy, "The Traveler Returned," evidently militated with the public judgement, and his own impartiality. His ingenuous comments and candid strictures would have been thankfully received by any man of more *understanding*, or less VANITY, than yourself. But the commerce of disgusting adulation, which you have been long accustomed to hold with mankind, has banished from your intellect the small degree of purity, it naturally possessed. Perhaps, too, your ridiculous affectation might have led you to anticipate, that the various classes of citizens, whom you have indiscriminately DOGGED and BUFFOONED with your "SMOOTH CONFECTIONARY STYLE," would gorge the glutton maw of your ambition, by returning the same fulsome praise.

Under the shock of so severe a disappointment, you resorted to other means to gratify your ungovernable appetite of dramatic fame. The editor of the Orrery had not, agreeably to your preposterous wishes, extended your eulogium to the utmost limits of panegyric, "ON THIS SIDE OF ADORATION." His judgement must, therefore, be combated; and, if in your power, demolished. The "Card," which appeared in his paper of Thursday last, was delivered by yourself. You requested its publication in your own person. He had a right, therefore, to believe you the author of it. When the editor gave it a place in his paper, from a motive of humanity, he declined the severity of retort. He believed that your comedy was DECEASED, and that it had died of a NATURAL DEATH. But as it had not given up the ghost in the CHRISTIAN FAITH, there was no hopes of its glorious RESURRECTION. He therefore felt no pleasure in being a PALL-BEARER at its interment, nor in dancing over the grave of the poor unfortunate! With respect to the benefit night, which you expected from it, he wished you all imaginable success. But, as the "TRAVELER RETURNED," while he lived, was not one of the favorites of fortune, a "POST OBIT," he thought, might not be of the greatest possible value.

It has been repeatedly said, Sir, in the Mercury and Centinel, that you were not the author of the paragraphs, addressed to the editor of the Orrery, in those papers. I neither know that you dictated or transcribed them. But where is the public difference between the REAL and the OSTENSIBLE author? If it can be proved that you carried those articles to the press; — if it never has been said that you lodged the name of any other person with the printer; — and if it is well known that you acknowledged and read the last Saturday's publication in the Centinel-Office before strangers and apprentices, with all that antic grimace, for which, it is reported, you were so famous, as a strolling player in Ireland; — if all these contingencies can be substantiated, is it not indubitable, that you have not only "SEEN DOUBLE," but have SPOKEN so; and that "——— ——— When we have said ——— as false,

"As air, as water, or as sandy earth;
"As fox to lamb, as wolf to heifer's calf;

"Pard to the hind, or step-dame to her son;
"Then might we say, to stick the heart of falsehood,
"AS FALSE AS"—MURRAY!

Paine's connection with the Orrery terminated on the 18th of April, 1796, when he addressed the following

To the Public. The subscriber, having sold the Proprietary right of the Federal Orrery to Mr. Benjamin Sweetser, takes this opportunity of returning his sincerest thanks to his friends and the Public, for the liberality, which they have been ever pleased to extend him; and hopes, in retiring from the publication of a paper, whose existence has immediately emanated from their benignity, that he may safely bequeathe to his successor a continuance and extension of their patronage and favor.

The public's most obedient servant,
Thomas Paine.

The sale of the Orrery was fatal to its existence. Scarcely an original paragraph can be found in its columns after it passed from the possession of Paine. It was made up, in a great measure, of extracts from the Farmer's Museum and other popular gazettes. Sweetser, its new proprietor, in company with William Burdick, had published a paper in Boston, called the Courier, the office of which was destroyed by fire just before his purchase of the Orrery. In November following, he changed the title of his publication to "The Courier and General Advertiser," by which change the Orrery became extinct in name, as it was before in essence.

Thomas Paine was born at Taunton in the county of Bristol, Ms. December 9, 1773. He was the second son of Robert Treat Paine, "an eminent lawyer; well known as one of the patriots of the American Revolution; one of the delegates in Congress from Massachusetts, his native state, who signed the Declaration of Independence; for many years the attorney-general, and afterwards one of the judges of the supreme judicial court of the commonwealth." When Thomas was about seven years old, the family removed to Boston. He was prepared for college at the Public Latin School; entered the University at Cambridge in 1788; and graduated in 1792. Soon after leaving college, he entered the counting-house of a merchant in Boston, intending to pursue a mercantile profession. This purpose was soon abandoned; and he commenced the publication of the Orrery, with a degree of encouragement from the merchants and professional gentlemen in Boston and the vicinity, which had not then, nor has it since, had any parallel in the history of Boston newspapers. After disposing of the Orrery Mr. Paine studied law in the office of Theophilus Parsons, who was afterwards chief justice of the supreme court. In due time he was admitted to the bar, opened an office in Boston, and obtained a reasonable share of business. His passion for dramatic literature interfered with the practice of his profession, his clients were neglected, and his business diminished, till about the year 1809, when he gave up his office and removed his name from the door. He died on the 13th of November, 1811.

In 1812, Mr. Paine's works, in prose and verse, were published by J. Belcher, Boston, in an octavo volume of near five hundred pages. To the volume is prefixed "Sketches of his Life, Character, and Writings." These sketches are brief, but beautifully written. The criticisms might have been extended, with pleasure and profit to the reader, and with justice to the character of Mr. Paine as a scholar, a poet, and a writer of prose. For some unaccountable reason, some of his productions, worthy of the most conspicuous place in the collection of American poetry, have been treated with undeserved neglect. His Poems, entitled "The Invention of Letters" and "The Ruling Passion" are far superior to many poems, that, of late years, have courted the public favor in silk binding and gilt edges, and been illustrated with costly engravings. Some of his lyrical compositions enjoyed great popularity. "Adams and Liberty" was in favor with the public for many years, and was sung at almost every festive occasion, where politics could find admission. The Ode, written for the festival of the Faustus Association, was deservedly popular with the printers, and ought to be adopted by all typographical societies as peculiarly *their* household song.

As a theatrical critic, Mr. Paine's opinions were received as judicial decisions, that were not to be disputed. After he disposed of the Orrery, he wrote criticisms on plays and players for several other papers, but his articles of this description, after Russell & Cutler's Boston Gazette was established as a literary and miscellaneous journal, were generally published in that paper. Some of these articles were republished in the volume of his works before referred to.

Mr. Paine married the daughter of an actor by the name of Baker, — a young lady of fine accomplishments, amiable manners, and unblemished reputation. But such was the prejudice then existing against plays, theatres, and actors, that this marriage caused an alienation of parental affection, and, for many years, it is believed, he was excluded from the paternal roof, — although the lady never appeared on the stage after her marriage, but always sustained the character of a wife and mother with dignified propriety.

About the time that President Jefferson invited the noted Thomas Pain, the author of the Age of Reason, to revisit this country, *our* Thomas Paine petitioned the Legislature of Massachusetts for a change of name, assigning as a reason, that he was desirous of being known by a *Christian* name. His petition was granted. He took the name of his father, Robert Treat, and was ever, afterward, known by the name of Robert Treat Paine, jun.

THE BOSTON GAZETTE.

On Monday, September 5, 1795, J. & J. N. Russell commenced the publication of "The Boston Price Current and Marine Intelligencer, Commercial and Mercantile." It was a small quarto of four pages, published at the price of three dollars a year. Its contents strictly corresponded with its title. It was published in this form till March 7, 1796, when it was enlarged to a crown folio. At the end of June following, the partnership was dissolved. The publication was continued by John Russell; the paper was issued twice a week, on Monday and Thursday; and the price was raised to four dollars a year. Without any material variation in the character of its contents, except occasionally an official document concerning trade or navigation, and, now and then a paragraph sufficient to identify the editor's politics with those of the leading Federalists, it was continued in this form and size, till June 7, 1798. It was then enlarged to the size of the Centinel, Chronicle, and Mercury, and took the name of "Russell's Gazette; Commercial and Political."

In his address to the public, on introducing this change, Russell said, — "The portentous aspect of our political horizon, connected with the important events, which are daily passing on the great theatre of the European world, designate the present period as one, which *loudly calls* for the virtuous energies of all good citizens; and ought to inspire, in the breast of every man, a solicitude to contribute his efforts in support of the cause of virtue, freedom, and independence. Under this persuasion, and influenced by the advice of many valuable friends, the editor, in the humble hope of being able to extend the sphere of its utility, has deviated so far from the plan which he adopted in originating the Commercial Gazette, as to enlarge its dimensions, thereby to afford an opportunity of rendering it an important and useful vehicle of *political* information, as it is admitted to be of *commercial* and *maritime* intelligence. He confesses to have been stimulated to this alteration by the ambition he feels to take a share (he hopes it may be a conspicuous one) in the dissemination of those important political truths and opinions, which the fertile genius and talents of our countrymen, urged by the critical state of the times, daily produce in such rich exuberance. To the friends and supporters of the constitution, and those who administer it, he declares his paper exclusively devoted. To the *enemies* of either he avows himself an *enemy*. These are his sentiments; and, on these terms does he solicit the patronage of the public; for, on no other, does he think himself deserving it, or could he expect it to be permanent."

At the beginning of the year 1800, in consequence of ill health, Russell resigned the printing and publishing department into the hands of James Cutler, a young man, who had been in the office from the commencement of the paper. The next October, Russell and Cutler formed a partnership, published the paper and carried on job work on an extensive scale as joint and equal partners. The paper was thenceforth called simply the BOSTON GAZETTE.

From the day when the Gazette was enlarged and assumed the character of a political paper, it adhered, with religious firmness, to the federal party. It defended in the most able manner, the administration of John Adams against the attacks of the Chronicle, and all the republican papers of New-York and Philadelphia. Russell was, himself, a good writer of *paragraphs*, and he had the aid of able and educated correspondents. For fifteen years no paper in the country was more prompt and decided, as a watchman on the bulwarks of Federalism. It presented itself, twice a week, charged to the muzzle, with argument, invective, and ridicule, against the French Directory, Napoleon, Jefferson, Madison, the Chronicle, the Aurora, and all the host of Jacobins, Democrats, Republicans, or by whatever name the adversaries of Federalism chose to be called. Occasionally Russell allowed his opposition to French politics to betray him to the use of exceedingly offensive language. This was resented by citizen Mozard, then the French consul in Boston, and consequently, the whole artillery of vituperation was poured upon him through the columns of the Gazette. The contest was so warm that the selectmen and the school-committee of Boston were harshly censured by Russell for inviting Mozard to attend the examination of the public schools. Mozard defended himself and his native country, — or was defended by some other person, — in the Chronicle. Russell expected a personal assault, and gave notice in his paper, that, if the consul should appear at his office, he should be saluted with a shower from the *professional tub.** But I believe no rencontre ever took place.

Russell was much attached to theatrical performances, as means of innocent and elegant entertainment; and the Gazette was, for many years, a kind of official link of connection between managers and the public. The play-bills were printed at the office of the Gazette, and it generally furnished its readers with a programme of forth-coming exhibitions. It not only supplied the public with the "puff preliminary," but was the organ of the critics, who were paid for their criticism by free admission, as well as for those, who had no such temptation to influence their judgement. Thomas (afterwards Robert Treat) Paine wrote, for the Gazette, many of his most elaborate dramatic criticisms and reviews; and several other of the play-going writers made it the receptacle of their critical decisions. Russell himself was a man of taste in such matters, and could write a rebuke or a compliment as occasion might require; but he was too good-natured to be severe, and never allowed a remark to escape from his pen, that could excite the anger of the boisterous, or grieve the sensibility of the timid. Whenever his correspondents were harsh in their language towards performers, — especially those of an inferior rank, — Russell was ready with his sympathy to soothe their feelings by some kind word, as an offset to the severity of his correspondents.

Russell was a great admirer of the British essayists,

* Every Printer of the old school, knows that this was once an indispensable article in a printing-office. Modern improvements have rendered it unnecessary, and, of course, it is *out of use.*

novelists, and poets. For many years he was in the habit of placing at the head of each column of advertisements, on the last page of the Gazette, a short extract from some of those writers, embracing a sentiment, an anecdote, or some pithy remark. How large a part of these were of his own selection is not known. His friend, Mr. Samuel Gilbert, assisted him in the selection of those articles, which added much interest to the paper, and attracted the attention of a considerable number of readers.

The Embargo and the War of 1812 were topics of constant remark in the Gazette. During the war, several young men engaged in writing for it, and some of the political articles are written with great power and elegance. The Gazette had a large circulation in Maine, and was eminently influential in sustaining the federal party in that district, then a part of the state of Massachusetts. The interest its conductors took in politics did not, however, diminish its value as a vehicle of commercial and marine intelligence. This department was under the superintendence of Cutler, and was managed with proverbial talent and industry. About the close of the war, or soon after, Simon Gardner, a young man of extraordinary activity, was taken into the business as a partner, and the whole was conducted in the name of Russell, Cutler & Co. Cutler died, after a short illness, on the eighteenth of April, 1818. The firm being thus dissolved, the business was continued by Russell & Gardner, till the end of the year 1823, when Mr. Russell withdrew from it, and took leave of the public, as an editor, in the following valedictory address : —

More than forty years have passed away, since the undersigned commenced the duties and labors of editor and publisher of a periodical paper. It has been an eventful period of the world. As a nation we have gained our Independence, and established those great political institutions, which, we trust, will support our freedom, and give it perpetuity. Our government was an experiment in political history, on which admiring nations gazed, and for whose result, the lovers of liberty, and advocates of the rights of man, hoped and trembled. The timid, the ambitious, and the wicked, were against the trial; and when they saw it waking, broke out in the voice of prophecy, on the left; but it did not dishearten us; and full success has attended the endeavor. Persevering honesty has been amply rewarded. The glory may be given to a few, but, in truth, the effort was made by many.

Scarcely had we breathed from our own revolutionary struggles, before we were again excited by the convulsions of France: — This people, suddenly broke from the thraldom of unlimited power, and delirious with the thoughts of liberty, waged war against morals and man. This to us was indeed a trying time; they had taken the spark from off our altar, but the flame became unhallowed in their hands; they offered it in impurity to the genius of liberty, and the incense was rejected as strange fire. Those who have come up since, and have taken a part on the stage, can partially realize what we feared, and suffered. We felt many evils and forboded more. Party rancor sprang up among us, and separated kindred and friends. The household gods were profaned by angry discussions; around the family fireside, where nothing, even in the darkest day of our revolutionary contests, had before been heard but the accents of domestic harmony, or prayers to avert evils, or praise for blessings and protection, discord made her entry, with her usual train of miseries — fathers were arrayed against sons, and sons against fathers. These calamities, if not destroyed, were at least softened, by the persevering efforts of those patriots, who labored from love of country, and the good of mankind. At this portentous period, our columns, were fearlessly opened to, and filled with the productions of great spirits, engaged in a great cause; many of whom are remembered with tears of joy. They strengthened our hands, and encouraged our hearts. Many of them are still living, and do not wish to hear of their victories; but it will not be deemed invidious to mention one who has gone to reap the rewards of the patriot-martyr: — FISHER AMES, will ever be remembered, by the lovers of their country, of all times, and all political creeds. His soul was full of the cause of his country, and he manfully poured out the light of his mind, to dissipate the mists of political fanaticism, and to purify the world from that dreariness of thought and feeling, which grew from infidel philosophy. The cool and wary, we know have often said that his zeal was too ardent, and his fears unfounded; this may have been true, in some degree; but his sincerity was never doubted, and it is delightful now to recollect, that we were often guided by a mind so noble, in a cause so glorious.

When we look back and contemplate the events which have transpired in our short period of activity and bustle; short, we mean, when the growth of a nation is considered, it seems as it were a dream — a people increased from four millions to ten millions, and those, contrary to what has generally been the fate of nations, grown wiser and better as their number advanced. Thirteen chartered colonies, but little known to each other, have been supplanted by twenty-four independent republics, bound in an indissoluble union, possessing the power, energy, and celerity of action, of one great people, — and the knowledge, necessary to wield this great political machine, become familiar to all her citizens. We have not reached the ordinary length of a single reign of an European monarch, yet the gristle has become bone, the youthful muscle gained strength and hardihood, and the whole colossal body adorned with manly grace and comeliness — and politics and philosophy have been brought down to the common business of life.

Modesty allows him, who putteth off the armor, to speak of himself — yea, even to boast; but we wish not to boast, nor even to say much of ourselves, or the establishment in which we have long been senior; but the most fastidious and unfriendly, will permit us to say, and believe the assertion, that our end and intentions have been honest, and the means used, to bring them about, candid and fair — that we have never sacrificed our independence by time-serving, nor jeopardized our integrity by avarice. To name the events which have succeeded each other, or to mention the institutions, which have grown up, and flourished in our day, were to fill a volume. We wish not to do it; but they have been to us like so many mile-stones on the high-way of life — they shorten, or seem to shorten, the road we travel, and assist us, in calling to mind, what we have suffered, and what we have enjoyed.

It is hard for a politician, and especially an editor of a newspaper, to have pursued a long course, without offending some, and wounding others; but he only should be condemned, who continues in error, when he knows what is right, and persists in telling falsehoods, when he has discovered the truth.

We leave our duties as an editor, in peace with every one, feeling a conscious pride that we have never made the Gazette a vehicle of malice, or a chronicle of pitiful slanders. In truth, we ask no praise, but this, which no one, we think, will deny us, *our enmities were easily appeased, and our friendship seldom forgotten.*

In taking leave of the public, as the founder and conductor of the Boston Gazette, whose arduous, laborious, and responsible duties, are found to be incompatible with that degree of rest, and ease, which age, and long-tried services, require, he begs leave to express the warm gratitude, which still glows in his heart, for the repeated instances of kindness, friendship, and assistance, he has received from the hands of his political and personal friends. He would say more on this subject, but the paper, on which he writes, is too moist to receive the impression of his pen.

* * * * * * *

In surrendering the Gazette to my junior partner, the public may confidently expect that his wonted zeal and activity, will be fully exercised, in rendering it a continued vehicle of the earliest intelligence, both commercial and political, and that, in every instance, where its services are required, to aid a good cause, no selfish considerations will debar him from the prosecution of a public duty.

In taking farewell of the public, I cannot but express my acknowledgements to JAMES L. HOMER, a young gentleman, who has been long engaged in this establishment, and for several years, last past, the assiduous collector of the marine department; and in every instance, where my editorial labors, from sickness, depression of spirits, or unusual accumulation of labor, required it, has proved himself not only capable of, but most generously lent his aid in, performing those duties, expected by a reading and intelligent public. JOHN RUSSELL.

Boston, Dec. 29, 1823.

Soon after this, Mr. Russell removed to the state of Maine, and resided there with his relatives till his death, the precise time of which I am not able to record.

Mr. Gardner had been connected with this establishment from early boyhood, and had served in the capacity of errand-boy, carrier, apprentice, and clerk. Being now the sole proprietor of the Gazette, he engaged, as editor, SAMUEL L. KNAPP, a member of the Suffolk Bar, a gentleman of acknowledged literary taste, and a fine writer. By the union of the talents of Mr. Gardner as supervisor general of the whole concern, — of Mr. Knapp as the literary director, — of Mr. Homer as news collector, and Mr. William Beals as accountant and treasurer, it was expected that the Gazette would have a long day of prosperity, sufficient to satisfy the reasonable hopes of its proprietor. But an unlooked-for event was at hand, and the brilliant prospect was overshadowed with a misfortune, fatal to at least one of the partners. Mr. Gardner died on the nineteenth of April following. The following obituary notice, written by Mr. Knapp, contains no exaggerated representation of his character: —

Died on Thursday last, Mr. SIMON GARDNER, publisher and proprietor of the Commercial Gazette, in the thirty-fourth year of his age, sincerely lamented by all who knew him; for he had properties of mind and heart, worthy the fondest recollection. He was a dutiful son, a kind husband, a warm-hearted, generous friend. From childhood he was distinguished for industry, enterprise and integrity — he feared no labor, nor spared any pains in the discharge of his professional duties. He had an extraordinary tact for business; but even in his zeal to do much, he never assumed to know and to do what he did not understand, but looked at what he was engaged in, with a good share of that common sense, which leads to correct conclusions and successful results. He was desirous of accumulating wealth, and dwelt upon his plans with enthusiasm; but in every dream of opulency, he united some delightful scheme of benevolence and friendship. When perplexed, as he sometimes was, by stepping forward to serve an acquaintance, who afterwards failed to make good his promises, he felt grieved, and was chafed for a moment, but instantly set about framing apologies for his creditor, and would not believe that want of gratitude or honesty was the cause of disappointment. The death of such a man is a public loss — there is much taken from the stock of industrious exertion when he dies. Mr. GARDNER had just purchased out the share of his former partner, and had the control of a large printing establishment, and was conducting it successfully, when he was called to leave it, and finish his earthly labors. He was happily united to an excellent woman, whose prudence and good sense, assisted him in carrying into effect every judicious arrangement. The ways of Providence are mysterious, for often the useless are continued, while the active, industrious and generous, who bring their talents to produce many fold for the good of the community are taken suddenly away. But it is wise, brave and pious, to meet these afflicting events with resignation, knowing that infinite wisdom directs all things for the best.

The business was conducted by Messrs. Knapp, Beals, and Homer, for and on account of the widow of Mr. Gardner, till July, 1826. The two gentlemen last named, then purchased the whole establishment. Mr. Knapp resigned the chair editorial to ALDEN BRADFORD, Esq. and bade farewell to the customers and friends of the Gazette, as follows: —

TO THE PUBLIC.

My labors as editor of this paper ceased on the transfer of the property in it from Mrs. Gardner to Messrs. Beals and Homer. I commenced my duties in assisting in conducting the Boston Commercial Gazette, January, 1824, pursuant to an engagement made with the late Mr. Simon Gardner, the proprietor and publisher of it. His lamented decease happened in a few weeks afterwards, and his widow became sole owner of the establishment; and being advised by her friends to continue it, temporary arrangements were made for that purpose. The same agents her husband had employed were continued by her to the present time.

It will hardly be necessary to add, that a property so situated, required the utmost care and circumspection to increase its value, or, in fact, to prevent a deterioration of it. This statement is made to excuse the agent, if, at any time, the patrons of the paper thought there was a want of decision and independence in the course pursued. To him who, in any measure, assists in influencing public opinion, many things of a doubtful result will present themselves, from which, supported by pure motives, and a true moral courage, he will not flinch when his own reputation or interests only are concerned, but which he ought, and must evade, when the happiness and security of another, having no participation in the responsibility, may be involved. I make these remarks not from a wish to be excused from sins of *commission* — these I have ever been ready to answer for — but in apology for sins of *omission*, in often shunning, in the best manner I could, subjects which an editor, differently placed, should have met and discussed in an open and fearless manner. If a licentious press is a curse, a timid time-serving one is a greater. The duties of an editor are full of responsibility, both political and moral. Nothing should escape his attention, from the movements of associated nations to the petty neglects of a town corporation. He should take upon himself to watch the manners and morals of the community, and comment fearlessly, in the spirit of justice. If in the political world, he, like the prophet, deems it his duty, at the altar of freedom, to call down the fire of heaven upon the sons of Belial to consume them, it is equally his duty to return to scenes of humble life, and to bless, as far as he is able, the cruise of oil to preserve the orphan from bondage. It is much easier, I know, to tell what should be done than to do a tenth part of it; but one is certainly allowed to offer a reason for not attempting to do what might seem to have been his duty, and the public are the judges of its sufficiency. The present editor will be relieved from all such embarrassments by a union of interests and duties with the proprietors, with the intervention of other individual interests. The industry and business talents of the proprietors are well known to the public, and these are at all times the best earnests of success, for which success they have my most hearty wishes. I relinquish my duties, in conducting the journal, to my successor with great cheerfulness; and could any observation from me extend his influence, it should not be withheld — but it might savor of vanity to suppose, for a moment, that one so well known by his long public services and numerous literary productions as Mr. Bradford, could possibly be aided by any remark of one so much his junior.

SAMUEL L. KNAPP.

This was followed by a short advertisement from Messrs. Beals & Homer, giving notice that they had become the proprietors of the establishment, and assurances of their entire devotion to the service of the public, and their intention to preserve the well-established character of the Gazette. To this succeeded the salutatory of Mr. Bradford, giving an exposition of the principles, which would guide him in the discharge of the duties he had undertaken; and it runs thus : —

In addition to the remarks of the proprietors and publishers of the Gazette, the editor has only to observe, that its political character will remain unchanged. This, since its establishment, or revival in 1798, has been Federal Republican. And by this we mean *distinctly*, that it has been the advocate of the policy of the first administration of the national government under George Washington and his associates. If it has ever been a *party* paper, it will be so no longer. We do not admit it ever was such, only in so far as it supported the measures of Washington and of his political friends. If it has pursued a straight-forward course, and that originally a correct one, the error, if there be any, is with those who have *changed*. But we are not tenacious of names; principles only are important. And these, however particular measures may vary with the varying condition of the nation or of the world, never change. The great doctrines by adhering to which, our glorious revolution was effected, our state constitution was formed and adopted, a rebellion suppressed in the heart of the Commonwealth, the Federal Compact established, and the national government administered by Washington, (and *generally* by his successors) — these doctrines must still guide and direct us as a people, in order to insure our welfare and prosperity. The first and the most essential of these truths are, that the people are the source of all political power; and that civil government is formed and supported for their sole benefit. That rulers are their agents or servants, and not their masters; and that the provisions of the Constitution, adopted by the people, are to guide and control their representatives in all their public conduct.

In these principles, we all agree, at least theoretically. And while it is alike the duty and interest of the people to support their agents in the exercise of all legitimate authority, it is the dictate of wisdom and prudence to examine their conduct, lest abuses creep in and usurpations take place, and precedents are established unfavorable to the rights and liberties of the citizens. That there is danger of such evils and abuses, the history of all other times and people abundantly proves. *We* have no security against them, but in the intelligence, the virtue, and the wakeful, independent inquiry of the great body of the people themselves. *A predetermined opposition to any administration is dishonorable and unjust; and can only bring disgrace on those who are engaged in it. A blind, time-serving submission to men in office is equally dishonorable, and tends to strengthen the power of the government to the injury of the governed.* In seasons of election of rulers, the most perfect freedom of inquiry, of discussion and of opinion, is justifiable, if truth and candor be observed. The voice of the majority and the provisions of the Constitution are to be respected and obeyed. But the conduct and policy of rulers are still the proper subjects of attention and examination. Nor is the cry of "opposition" to fetter the spirit of inquiry or stifle the voice of censure, either of the past or the present, if there are reasons for disapprobation. With the truly patriotic, however, this will always be done with decency and in good temper; not by personal reproaches or misrepresentations. If those *who are in power are to be supposed corrupt*, and those *who are out of power to be selfish*, in all cases, there will be no end to criminations; and, instead of uniting for the welfare and improvement of our common country, we shall but degrade and dishonor it.

Our motto will be, "principles rather than men." Constitutional maxims should be followed by all classes of citizens; and though party distinctions may not be wholly done away, they may be less strongly marked than in former times and greater union of sentiment prevail. In a free government, there will be some diversity of opinion respecting men and measures. But if a spirit of patriotism be paramount to all other considerations, we need not despair of the common weal. Rulers must be judged by their opinions and their measures; and when the people become dissatisfied with them, they must retire to private life, and those who are more patriotic or more *popular* will take their places.

We are aware that the present is an age of inquiry and improvement in philosophy, in science and in the mechanic arts. We shall endeavor to collect all the useful intelligence furnished by foreign papers, as well as those published in this country, and present it to our readers in the most concise manner. But we mean not to be too liberal in our promises. We will only give assurances of attention and industry. The character and worth of our paper will be best learnt from the matter contained in its columns from time to time. And when we can find a space not necessarily devoted to political intelligence and the passing news of the day, we shall gladly occupy it with an article on morals, theology or literature.

The present editor feels his responsibilities increased in the labors he has undertaken, by the consideration of succeeding a gentleman of talents and general information, who was able to furnish matter for the columns of the Gazette, at once interesting and amusing. If he cannot expect to equal the former editor in a flowing style and in sporting classical allusions, he will endeavor to imitate him in the candor and magnanimity of his sentiments.

Beals & Homer continued the publication of the Gazette a few years, when a new arrangement of proprietors took place. Mr. Beals sold out his interest to Joseph Palmer, and formed a partnership with Charles

G. Greene, editor and proprietor of the Morning Post; —a partnership, that still exists, — profitable, no doubt, to all parties concerned; for Mr. Greene is *one* of the best of editors, and Mr. Beals is *the* best financier, that has ever been connected with a newspaper.

Homer & Palmer, after carrying on the Gazette for a year or two, disposed of it to Adams & Hudson, who were already proprietors of the Palladium and the Centinel. In process of time, — not a long one, — the whole united stock was purchased by Nathan Hale, and thus four semi-weekly papers,* which had, for an average of more than forty years, been important, popular, and well-established organs of intelligence, — political, commercial, social, and literary, — were merged in the Boston Daily Advertiser, and became extinct.

Soon after the enlargement of the Gazette in 1798, it assumed quite a literary character. John Russell attracted around him a number of young men, who were ready with their pens to assist him with comments on politics, literature, the drama, &c. Of these, R. T. Paine, jun. after he relinquished the Federal Orrery, was one of the most constant. John Lathrop, jun. a son of the venerable pastor of the second church in Boston, and a graduate of Harvard College; — Thomas O. Selfridge, another graduate of the same institution, a man of talent, a lawyer with increasing patronage, and who gave early promise of eminence in his profession, but who was, afterwards, unhappily involved in troubles arising from an incident that clouded the brightness of his early career and infused bitterness into the ingredi-

* The Independent Chronicle had been previously sold to Mr. Hale, *after* its union with the Boston Patriot. See vol. i. p. 266.

ents of his anticipated cup of satisfaction; — David Everett, well-known for a number of years after, as a political writer, and first editor of the Boston Patriot; — these, and some others not so well known, were constant contributors, and did much to render the Gazette an agreeable miscellany of literature as well as political discussion.

Samuel L. Knapp, who had charge of the Gazette while it was owned by Mr. and Mrs. Gardner, was a native of Sanbornton, N. H. and a graduate of Dartmouth college. He practised law some time in Newburyport, and represented that town in the Legislature of the commonwealth, in 1814. After the war he removed to Boston, and continued to practise in his profession. He assisted, for about a year, in the editorial department of the New-England Galaxy. He was a fluent and popular writer, and published several books, among which were Biographical Sketches of eminent Lawyers, and a Life of Daniel Webster. When he left the Boston Gazette he lived a while in New-York, and removed thence to Washington, where he continued his professional pursuits, and wrote letters for various newspapers. Declining health induced him to return to New-England. But the hand of death had laid hold of him, and soon placed him among the unnumbered millions of the departed.

Alden Bradford, who succeeded Mr. Knapp, was more devoted to politics than literature. He was a native of the "Old Colony," and graduated at Harvard college in 1786, in the class with the late Judge Parker and Mr. Timothy Bigelow. Mr. Bradford was educated for the office of a clergyman, and was ordained pastor of a church in Maine. I have not been informed of his reasons for leaving the profession; but, after quitting it, he was in the office of clerk of the courts in one of the counties in that part of the state. About the year 1809, he removed to Boston, and was connected with a publishing and bookselling house, till he was chosen secretary of state, an office which he filled for several years, while there was a majority of Federalists in the Legislature. Under his control the Gazette was a respectable and dignified advocate of the political doctrines which had been the creed of the federal party, before "the Era of Good Feelings," — or, in other words before the union of parties to elect Mr. Munroe to the Presidency. Mr. Bradford received, by the appointment of the Governor, the office of notary public, and held it till his death, which occurred in 1843. He had published several valuable works, of which the Life of Rev. Dr. Mayhew, a History of Massachusetts, and a History of the Federal Administration are the principal. He also collected, and published in an octavo volume with notes, the essays of *Novanglus* and *Massachusettensis*, (John Adams and Jonathan Sewall) originally published in Edes & Gill's Boston Gazette, — for which his name is entitled to grateful recollection.

John and Joseph N. Russell were printers, by profession. I believe that neither ever served any regular apprenticeship, but were employed by Benjamin Russell, — who was their brother, — in the office of the Centinel, some years previous to the commencement of the Boston Price-Current and Marine Intelligencer, from which originated the fourth newspaper in Boston, with the title of the Boston Gazette.

THE RURAL REPOSITORY.

In the autumn of 1795, Charles Prentiss commenced the publication of the Rural Repository, at Leominster, Mass. The first number was issued on Thursday, October 22, and was published weekly, on *crown* paper, at one dollar and fifty cents a year. In his prospectus Mr. Prentiss says, — "It has long been a general and just complaint that too large a proportion of most of our papers has been devoted to uninteresting intelligence and political altercations — or advertisements, useful perhaps to the man of business, but no dainty to the literary epicure. In the proposed paper, from the locality of its publication, advertisements will be, in a considerable degree, avoided. Most of its pages will be filled with *original* essays, moral and humorous, biographical anecdotes, criticisms, &c. together with selected pieces, calculated to improve and embellish the mind. The multiplicity of periodical papers, and the editor's own '*mediocritas ingenii*' considered, nothing would have induced him to the trial, but a safe dependence on a number of literary friends, and his conviction that most would be willing to patronize and encourage so laudable an attempt. But if his utmost exertions are unable to preserve it from the *Syrtes* of Dullness and the *rocks* of Disapprobation, he requires nothing more than what they will readily grant, namely, a discontinuance of their favors."

This is rather cool and philosophical. Whether Mr. Prentiss's philosophy reconciled him to the early death of his Repository, or not, is not known to the writer; but the paper was short-lived. One cannot avoid smiling at the simplicity of a youth, fresh from college, with no experience of the many nameless expenses, that, in a printing-office, swallow up an income, promising himself success in the publication of a merely literary paper in a small country village, and seemingly resolved to exclude advertisements, — the best and surest source of profit, — even if they should be offered. But Mr. Prentiss stands not alone in the catalogue of those, who have indulged in this pleasing but fatal illusion.

In one of the earliest numbers of the Repository, Mr. Prentiss, following the example of his friend Biglow, published his will. Paine immediately transferred it to the Orrery, with an introductory note, saying — "Having, in the second number of 'Omnium Gatherum' presented to our readers the last will and testament of Charles Chatterbox, Esq. of witty memory, wherein the said Charles, now deceased, did lawfully bequeath to Ch——s Pr——s, the celebrated 'Ugly Knife,' to be by him transmitted, at his college demise, to the next succeeding candidate; * * * * and whereas the said Ch——s Pr——s, on the 21st of June last, departed his aforesaid college life, thereby leaving to the inheritance of his successor the valuable legacy, which his illustrious friend had bequeathed, as an *entailed estate*, to the poets of the university — we have thought proper to insert a full, true, and attested copy of the will of the last deceased heir, in order that the world may be furnished with a correct genealogy of this renowned *Jack-knife,* whose pedigree will become as illustrious in after time as the family of the 'ROLLES,' and which will be celebrated by future wits as the most formidable *weapon* of modern genius."

For reasons, which will probably be obvious to the reader, a few lines are omitted in the following copy of the article.

A WILL:

Being the last words of Ch——s Pr——s, late worthy and much lamented member of the Laughing Club of Harvard University, who departed College life on the 21st *of June,* 1795.

I, Pr——s Ch——s, of judgement sound,
In soul, in limb and wind, now found;
I, since my head is full of wit,
And must be emptied, or must split,
In name of *president* APOLLO,
And other gentle folks, that follow:
Such as URANIA and CLIO,
To whom my fame poetic I owe;
With the whole drove of rhyming sisters,
For whom my heart with rapture blisters;
Who swim in HELICON uncertain
Whether a petticoat or shirt on,
From vulgar ken their charms to cover,
From every eye but *Muses' lover;*
In name of every ugly GOD;
Whose beauty scarce outshines a toad;
In name of PROSERPINE and PLUTO,
Who board in hell's sublimest grotto;
In name of CERBERUS and FURIES,
Those damned *aristocrats* and tories;
In presence of two witnesses,
Who are as homely as you please,
Who are in truth, I'd not belie 'em,
Ten times as ugly, faith, as I am;
But being as most people tell us,

A pair of jolly, clever fellows,
And classmates likewise, at this time,
They shan 't be honored in my rhyme.
I — I say I, now make this will;
Let those, whom I assign, fulfil.
I give, grant, render and convey,
My goods and chattels thus away;
That *honor of a college life,*
That celebrated UGLY KNIFE,
Which predecessor SAWNEY* orders,
Descending to time's utmost borders,
To *noblest-bard* of *homeliest phiz,*
To have and hold and use, as his;
I now present C——s P——y S——r, †
To keep with his poetic lumber,
To scrape his quid, and make a split,
To point his pen for sharpening wit;
And order that he ne'er abuse
Said ugly knife, in dirtier use,
And let said CHARLES, that best of writers,
In prose satiric, skilled to bite us,
And equally in verse delight us,
Take special care to keep it clean
From unpoetic hands — I ween.
And when those walls, the muses' seat,
Said S——r is obliged to quit,
Let some one of APOLLO 's firing,
To such heroic joys aspiring,
Who long has borne a poet's name,
With said knife cut his way to fame.

I give to those, that fish for parts,
Long sleepless nights, and aching hearts,
A little soul, a fawning spirit,
With half a grain of plodding merit,
Which is, as heaven I hope will say,
Giving what 's not my own away.

* William Biglow, known in college by the name of Sawney — and by which he was frequently addressed by his familiar friends in after life.

† Charles Pinckney Sumner, — afterwards a lawyer in Boston, and for many years sheriff of the county of Suffolk.

Those *oven baked* or *goose egg folded*
Who, tho' so often I have told it,
With all my documents to show it,
Will scarce believe that I'm a poet,
I give of criticism the lens
With half an ounce of common sense.

And 'twould a breach be of humanity,
Not to bequeath D——n* my vanity;
For 'tis a rule direct from Heaven,
To him that hath more shall be given.

Item. Tom M——n,† College Lion,
Who'd ne'er spend cash enough to buy one,
The Boanerges of a pun,
A man of science and of fun,
That quite uncommon witty elf,
Who darts his bolts and shoots himself,
Who oft had bled beneath my jokes,
I give my old *tobacco box*.

My *Centinels* for some years past,
So neatly bound with thread and paste,
Exposing Jacobinic tricks,
I give my chum *for politics*.

My neckcloth, dirty, old, yet *strong*,
That round my neck has lasted long,
I give Big Boy, for deed of pith,
Namely, to hang himself therewith.

And ere it quite has gone to rot,
I. B—— give my blue great coat,
With all its rags, and dirt and tallow,
Because he's such a dirty fellow.

Now for my books; first *Bunyan's Pilgrim*,
(As he with thankful pleasure will grin)
Tho' dogleaved, torn, in bad type set in,
'Twill do quite well for classmate B——

* Theodore Dehon, afterward a clergyman of the Episcopal church, and Bishop of the diocese of South-Carolina.

† Thomas Mason, a member of the class after Prentiss,—said to be the greatest *wrestler* that was ever in College. He was settled as a clergyman, at Northfield, Mass.; resigned his office some years after, and several times represented that town in the Legislature of Massachusetts.

And thus, with complaisance to treat her,
'Twill answer for another Detur.

To him that occupies my study,
I give for use of making toddy,
A bottle full of *white face* STINGO
Another, handy, called a *mingo.*
My wit, as I've enough to spare,
And many much in want there are,
I ne'er intend to keep at *home*,
But give to those that handiest come,
Having due caution, *where* and *when*,
Never to spatter *gentlemen.*
The world's loud call I can't refuse,
The fine productions of my muse;
If *impudence* to *fame* shall waft her,
I'll give the public all, hereafter.
My love songs, sorrowful complaining,
(The recollection puts me pain in.)
The last sad groans of deep despair,
That once could all my entrails tear;
My farewell sermon to the ladies;
My satire on a woman's head dress;
My epigram so full of glee,
Pointed as epigrams should be;
My sonnets soft, and sweet as 'lasses,
My GEOGRAPHY of MOUNT PARNASSUS;
With all the bards that round it gather,
And variations of the weather;
Containing more true humorous satire,
Than 's oft the lot of human nature;
(" Oh dear what can the matter be,"
I've given away my *vanity;*
The vessel can't so much contain,
It runs o'er and comes back again.)
My blank verse, poems so majestic,
My rhymes heroic, tales, agrestic:
The whole, I say, I'll overhaul 'em
Collect and publish in a volume.

My heart, which, thousand ladies crave,
That I intend my wife shall have.
I'd give my foibles to the wind,

And leave my vices all behind;
But much I fear they 'll to me stick,
Where'er I go thro' thin and thick.
On WISDOM'S *horse*, oh, might I ride,
Whose steps let PRUDENCE' bridle guide.
Thy loudest voice, O REASON, lend,
And thou PHILOSOPHY befriend.
May candor all my actions guide,
And o'er my every thought preside,
And in thy ear O FORTUNE, one word,
Let thy swelled canvas bear me onward,
Thy favors let me ever see
And I 'll be much obliged to thee;
And come with blooming visage meek,
Come, HEALTH and ever flush my cheek;
O, bid me in the morning rise,
When tinges Sol the eastern skies;
At breakfast, supper-time, or dinner,
Let me against thee be no sinner.

And when the glass of life is run
And I behold my setting sun,
May conscience sound be my protection,
And no ungrateful recollection,
No gnawing cares nor tumbling woes
Disturb the quiet of life's close.
And when Death's gentle feet shall come
To bear me to my endless home,
Oh! may my soul, should heaven but save it,
Safely return to GOD who gave it.

CHARLES PRENTISS was born in Reading, in the county of Middlesex, Mass., in October, 1774. He was the son of the Rev. Caleb Prentiss, the minister of that parish in Reading, which has since been incorporated as a separate town by the name of South-Reading. He graduated at Harvard College in 1795, commenced the publication of the Rural Repository, in October (as before stated) and married in November of the same year. The publication of the Repository was continued but a short time — I think not more than two years. Afterward, in company with a relative, John Prentiss, he published a paper in the same town, called "The Political Focus," but this had also a brief existence. In 1798 or '99, he went to Georgetown, in the district of Columbia, and, in partnership with A. Rind, published the "Washington Federalist." Afterwards he published, in Baltimore, a political paper, called the "Anti-Democrat," and edited another in the same city, called the "Child of Pallas." This was exclusively a literary paper. In 1804, he visited England, — for what particular purpose, I have not been informed. In 1809, we find Mr. Prentiss again in Boston, and about this time he published a few numbers of a paper entitled "The Thistle," which, if I remember aright, was devoted exclusively to dramatic criticism and reviews of theatrical performances. He was at sundry times a correspondent of John Russell's and Russell & Cutler's Boston Gazette. For two or three years succeeding 1810, he lived in Washington during the sessions of Congress, and reported the proceedings of that body for several newspapers, — edited a paper, called "The Independent American," — and wrote Letters for Relf's Philadelphia Gazette. In 1813, he wrote the Life of General Eaton, — a work, which, from the popularity of the subject, had considerable notoriety, but which is now rarely to be found in a bookseller's shop. In 1817, and 1818, he was the editor of the Virginia Patriot, published in Richmond. At the same time he also contributed a number of articles, — critical reviews of the publications of the day, — for a Magazine, which was published in New-York by Horatio

Bigelow and Orville L. Holley. He died in Brimfield, in the county of Hampden, Mass., October 20, 1820.

This barren sketch of dates and " local habitations " exhibits a melancholy picture of the precarious emolument derived from an attempt *to live by literature alone.* Mr. Prentiss was a scholar, a good writer, a judicious critic ; he studied no profession, and relied entirely on the exercise of his pen for support — a reliance, which many, to their sorrow, have found unsafe, delusive, and ineffectual. Had Prentiss lived half a century later, he might have seen his literary offspring dressed in scarlet and gold, and died, leaving the copy-right to his heirs.

THE VILLAGE MESSENGER.

THIS paper was published at Amherst, N. H. by Biglow & Cushing, and the publication began with the year 1796. It was very neatly printed on a new type; its general appearance being much more attractive than most of the country newspapers at that period. Its motto was, — "Whatsoever things are pure — whatsoever things are honest." And no sentiment could have been selected more truly indicative of the moral character of William Biglow, who was the principal, if not the sole editor, and to whose taste and talent it may be concluded the paper was indebted for its popularity; for after he left it, it became a meagre record of the passing events of the day.

Mr. Biglow was born in Natick, in the county of Middlesex, Mass. on the twenty-second day of September, 1773. The rudiments of his education were obtained at the common school in that town. He was fitted for college by "Old Parson Brown" of Sherburne, in the same county, — entered Harvard College in 1790, and graduated in 1794. While in college, he was distinguished for his wit, and a peculiar talent for writing poetry of a playful and innocent character. He graduated as the second scholar in his class, though he and most of his classmates thought he should have been placed first. After he left college, he taught a school in Lancaster, and commenced a course of study with the Rev. Nathaniel Thayer of that town, — intending to follow the profession of a clergyman. While here, he wrote "Omnium Gatherum," for the Federal Orrery. To add to his "slender means" of support, while pursuing his preparatory study, he engaged in the management of the Village Messenger, and subsequently wrote for the Massachusetts Magazine, published in Boston.

I have not been able to ascertain the precise time when Mr. Biglow began to preach; it must have been in 1799, or 1800. About this time he settled in Salem as a teacher, and had a private classical school of great celebrity, — preaching occasionally, as circumstances favored his disposition for that employment. He was frequently called upon to preach at the church in Brattle-square, Boston. He removed from Salem to Boston to take charge of the Public Latin School. This place he held several years, and a part of that time supplied the pulpit of the meeting-house in Hollis-street, after the death of the Rev. Dr. West, and previous to the settlement of the Rev. Horace Holley. Several of his pupils at the Boston Latin School are living to testify to his worth. Among these are the Hon. Edward Everett, Rev. N. L. Frothingham, Charles P. Curtis, Esq. and Dr. Edward Reynolds. A propensity to convivial indulgences, — first acquired, no doubt, at college, — brought on infirm health, which compelled him to leave the school, and retire to his native village. He passed some time in Maine, keeping school and writing for newspapers, but Natick was his home, and there he always found a refuge when pursued by poverty and sickness. He was accustomed to walk to Boston — sometimes to ride with people who followed the marketing business, — and spend a day or two in the newspaper printing-offices, write poetry for his friends the editors, and then return to his rural retreat. The latter part of his life he passed chiefly at Cambridge, where he was employed as a proof-reader at the University printing-office. This was an employment suited to his age and his taste. He was often heard to say, — "I have tried hard to correct my own errors, but not always so successfully as I can correct the errors of others."

While he was engaged in school-keeping, Mr. Biglow published several books for the use of pupils preparing for a collegiate education, which were approved and much used. In 1830, he published a History of Natick, and afterwards a History of Sherburne. But it is by his poetical pieces of wit and humor that he will be most delightfully remembered. In 1844, he was engaged in proof-reading at a printing establishment in Boston, which had then just been removed from Cambridge. On the morning of January 10, he was seized with an apoplexy, and lingered until the evening of the 12th, when he died. His remains were interred at Natick.

Whatever were the errors of Mr. Biglow's early years, they involved no dereliction from honesty and truth. Social indulgence in youth grew into a habit, which was the bane of life in subsequent years; — a habit, which it was hard to conquer, but which he did conquer, though at a period when physical vigor was prostrated, and mental energy enfeebled, and the "genial current of the soul" not frozen, but humbled under a painful sense of errors, which no regret could relieve, and the consequences of short-comings in duty, which no repentance could fully repair. A friend, who, I believe was once his pupil, wrote the following character of Mr. Biglow, — to the truth of which I give my personal testimony, — which was published in the Boston Courier a few days after his death: —

. . . . He was in the first place a scholar, "and a ripe and good one," possessed of a mind, which mastered much with apparently but small effort, imbued deeply with the fine elegance of classical literature, and possessed beside of an attic wit, which was the perpetual delight of his friends — a wit "that loved to play not wound." Had his mind been disciplined or enured to any thing more than desultory or occasional effort, he might have done much more. As it was, every thing that he wrote, and at various times published showed great power. His sermons were serious and devout, and distinguished by strong sense. He compiled several reading books for children, which gained him high reputation, and an excellent Latin Reader. He was, however, most known for his poetry — full of good humor, knowledge of character, a ready and original style of wit, and occasional pathos, which came over the soul with a stronger influence, because it came from a heart rich with all the sympathies of a most kind and generous spirit.

After all that can be said in praise of his mental attainments, or the strength which gave them birth, it is still on the qualities of the heart which his friends must now dwell with the most delight. He carried through life that true test of real talent, simplicity and buoyancy of feeling, which did not dread degradation from the company of children — which loved to lay itself open to their often acute examination; a heart favorable to all the influences of nature and of truth. My first remembrance of him is as a sort of commander of a military corps, composed of his scholars in Salem, which he called the Trojan Band; and the untiring assiduity and kindness with which he marched and counter-marched this miniature company, first made me love him. From this time, for forty years I scarcely saw him. In the retirement of Natick, it was my fortune once again to meet him during the last summer, his health evidently somewhat impaired by time, but his spirits still elastic and playful, almost as in the days of infancy. Playful indeed; but still, ever and anon through its play would glance the influence of a spirit somewhat saddened by misfortune and time, but still open to all good influences, with no shade of misanthropy or discontent to sully its purity, which still proved its communion with heaven, by loving all that was worthy of its love on earth. I have spoken of his intemperance, because he himself would not have wished it corrected. He was, indeed, very far from boasting of his recovery from it, and still farther from calling public attention to it, or making it a source of profit by lectures. He knew, indeed, that those who knew him must have felt the evils of intemperance, with a force stronger than any words could utter. He was loved by all; with a strong mind, and perhaps somewhat proud by nature, distinguished by his attainments, known but not feared for his wit. What such a being might have been, had his mind been tasked to it, all could see. The comparative obscurity of his later days, must have pained him; but if so, the pain did not make him harsh or unkind, and the consequences of his improper indulgence, though so nobly redeemed, would "still make themselves felt with utterance."

He was, indeed, a true-hearted and most kind man. It was delightful to meet with him during the last summer, relieved for a few weeks from the drudgery of his daily avocation, surrounded by his friends, and to recall with him the traditions of such a place as Natick; to stand with him under the oak from which the Apostolic Eliot called the wild Indian to repentance and to Christ; to wander forth through the deep shades, and the still pastures, tracing the dwelling places of those sons of the forest, or kneeling over the grey stones which marked their last resting places on earth. Here, too, he recalled to me the memories of the loved and lost, whom we had known in early life; and here, too, he spoke of one whose soul was even then stretching her wings for immortal flight.

Of Biglow's poetical performances while in college, that, which gave him the greatest notoriety, was an imitation of the old English Song, — "Heathen Mythology," — written for a convivial meeting of his class. He was surprized, a few months after, to see it with some variations, in the Columbian Centinel, introduced by the following note to the editor: —

Mr. Russell, — The votaries of the Semelian god have been generally celebrated rather for the Epicurean conviviality, than the Horatian acumen of their festive carols. The following, we think, is an honorable exception; still, it is unfortunate for the poet, that the nature of the subject involves him in a degree of obscurity, which renders him less pleasing to those, who are removed from the sphere of locality and anecdote. But, thus much may with propriety be observed, that the phiz-hitting pencil of Hogarth could not portray the features of this academical group with a more striking justness of coloring than this Bacchanalian muse has described them.

The publication of this piece caused an attack upon its author, which was published in the Mercury, and this produced a retort from Biglow, which may be found in the Centinel, under the title of "Assology, inscribed to the well beloved 'Squire Laureat Tobey." Biglow had been familiarly called by his class "Sawney," and in this retort on his antagonist, he adopted the signature, "'Squire Sawney." 'Squire Tobey came out in the next Centinel with a rejoinder, the bitterness of which was paralleled only by its vulgarity. Biglow rather laughed at the ill-nature of his opponent, and took no further notice of his spiteful ebullitions, than to publish the following: —

'SQUIRE SAWNEY TO 'SQUIRE TOBEY.

The scurrilous dirt you have kicked up at me,
To the public demonstrates you are nettled to see
A figure so true in "Assology glass;"
"Where a coat fits," the say is, "there let it be worn;"
Where the ass's skin suits, by the same be it borne;
So farewell to squibbing — bray on, Mr. Ass.

This "imitation" was frequently reprinted, under the title of "Junior-Classology." In 1843, the author himself had it printed for distribution among his college friends. This edition of it, with his introductory notice, is here given: —

The following Anacreontic was written in Harvard University, in the Autumn of A. D. 1793, for the amusement of the class whose names it bears, and of their cotemporaries. It soon found its way into a newspaper, and extended the amusement beyond the walls of college. It is now reprinted at the particular solicitation of many — some of whom are mentioned by name in the production. The last stanza in this edition was added by the author, A. D. 1842.

CLASSOLOGY.

Songs of scholars in reveling roundelays,
Belched out with hickups at bacchanal GO,
Bellowed, till heaven's high concave rebound the lays,
Are all for college carousals too low.
Of dullness quite tired, with merriment fired,
And fully inspired with amity's glow,
With hate-drowning wine, boys, and punch all divine, boys,
The Juniors combine, boys, in friendly HIGH GO.

ABBOTT, contemplative, never refusèd
From silence to rise and with humor be blest,
And AINSWORTH awhile from his books was amusèd,
And both in good spirits conjoined with the rest.
Then modest TIM ALDEN came eager, when called in,
Without being hauled in by Arabic's foe,
Witty GEORGE APPLETON, high-blooded ATHERTON,
Rigadoon ATKINSON joined the HIGH GO.

Then *little high* Sawney, called BIGLOW, appeared in view,
Mid the full chorus distending his lungs,
And BOWERS, sage president, whom Jove continue
With pleasure ecstatic to rant at our BUNGS.
Here too I might tell how TOM BOWMAN, hale fellow,
Did blubber and bellow, but won't stoop so low,
While BRAMAN *split-razor* the Plutus of pleasure,
Exhausted his treasure to enrich the HIGH GO.

With long pipe well filled Master BROOKS was here seated,
And looked, like himself, a true good-natured soul;
But the charge of all charges to BROWN was committed,
To mix with discretion the nectareous bowl.
Then jovial CHANNING, fired merriment fanning,
Was never for ganging, while liquor should flow,
And CROSBY, the blood, would be doomed if he would
Sneak away, if he could, and not join the HIGH GO.

Buck CUSHING, who ne'er to high fellow knocked under,
Full widely awake now engaged with the throng,
And all-eating, omnimouthed, all-smiling DUNBAR
Deep base loudly thundered to mirth-sounding song.

Nor did EMERSON lag, of his beauty to brag,
But with calm *Coggy* FLAGG, boys, himself he did show;
Fat FLINT was scarce able to clear the sixth table,
Ere with the pleased rabble he met in HIGH GO.

Next GEYER, eldest author, though youngest in years, came,
And blew the high flame of high jollity higher,
And HOWE, loudly welcomed with three sounding cheers, came,
And JACKSON, the orator, joined the glad choir.
Then KENDALL from high metaphysical sky
Condescended to fly on a visit below;
From Pike's learned page came McKEAN in glad rage
The full vessels to gauge and to bless the HIGH GO.

Grave OLDS next the steady *puellarum magister*,
And placid PEABODY commixed with the rest,
And PERKINS, of mirth and good cheer brave assister,
With his doctorship's presence the rapture increased,
And STEARNS, the new-comer, left Euclid and Homer
And joined with the former, while TRASK, the new beau,
Drest out alamode, with uneasiness glowed,
Till himself he had showed in the midst of HIGH GO.

HALL TUFTS the *Monsieur* came, with burlesque French phrases,
Bon sketer, ji nesse pa, en verité;
Young poet WHIPPLE, high mounted on Pegasus,
Galloped full speed to the loud "Hark away."
Then wine, sweetest treasure, and punch without measure,
Blythe parent of pleasure, the waiters bestow,
Wherewith infusèd and, faith, almost boozied,
This song I producèd in praise of HIGH GO.

Come on, merry lads, toss the bumper and bowl round,
Throw follies and quarrels of schoolboys away;
Let malice no longer becloud the glad soul round,
But friendship enlighten with heavenly ray.
With hearty compliance we 'll form an alliance,
And bid bold defiance to sorrow and wo;
We 'll ne'er be afraid, boys, though tutors parade, boys,
Here 's health to the blade, boys, who loves a HIGH GO.

In the midst of the row Senior PIERCE was invited
In mirth and in song with the Juniors to join;
He gladly complied — but was awfully frighted
At sight, on the tables, of punch and of wine.

"O murder and slaughter!" he cried out in torture,
"Bring, bring me cold water, and I'll not be slow;
Place water the nighest, — I'll drink with the driest,
And soon be the highest in all the HIGH GO."

The senior, mentioned in the last stanza, was the late Rev. John Pierce, of Brookline, an advocate of temperance from his earliest years. His whole life was a practical evidence of the sincerity and utility of his principles.

The following Anacreontic was written the next year, 1793, and was handed down from year to year, and from class to class, and sung at festive entertainments, for a long succession of years. Probably the "temperance reform" has banished it from the college rooms, and substituted something more congenial to the fashion of the age: —

THE BUMPER OF WINE.

A New Song, calculated for the meridian of North Entry, [*Famous for "High Fellows,"*] *Hollis Hall, in Harvard University; but will serve without any sensible error for our Colleges throughout the United States.*

Ye lovers of liquor, of friendship, and joy,
Let Greek and let Latin no longer annoy;
Dull epics of Homer and Virgil resign;
Our song is in praise of *a bumper of wine.*

The deep metaphysics serve only to show
How little their studious votaries know;
We ask not if matter and spirit can join, —
We find them unite in *a bumper of wine.*

For Pike and for Euclid not one of us cares;
Farewell to their angles, lines, circles and squares;
Plain nature will teach us to form a curve line,
Or a circle of friends, round *a bumper of wine.*

Let Enfield investigate physical laws, —
For every phenomenon guess at the cause;
Suffice it for us, that the fruit of the vine,
When pressed, will produce us *a bumper of wine.*

Physicians may swear to secure us in health,
They care for no more than a gripe at our wealth;
Emetics and opiates they may enjoin,
But these are contained in *a bumper of wine.*

Our good-natured revels no contention shall draw
Around the drear mazes of labyrinth law;
On quarrels let lawyers and judges refine,
But we'll drown all ours in *a bumper of wine.*

May bards ne'er be wanting to furnish a song,
To make life draw easy and smoothly along;
Yet these need no longer invoke the coy Nine,
For Helicon's fount is *a bumper of wine.*

Here 's a bumper to ours and plain honesty's friend,
May health and contentment for ever attend,
And let him be lawyer, physician, divine,
May he ne'er want a friend, nor *a bumper of wine!*

While he was editor of the Village Messenger, Biglow wrote a number of articles, — much in the style, which Noah Webster had rendered popular by his essays, called The Prompter, — taking for a motto or text, some passage of scripture, of which the following is a sample: —

" *Ye blind guides, who strain at a gnat and swallow a camel.*"

There are many of these blind guides, even in these days of wisdom and refinement — many more than will either own or believe themselves of this description.

I know one Dick Instability, who is ever crying down novels, when in company with the ladies, as though it wounded his conscience to have such vile productions perused; and yet I have seen this same Dick at the loo table as late as twelve at night, with as much brandy in his head as he could carry, and more than he ought to carry. The truth is he *strains at a gnat and swallows a camel.*

There is old Moses Moneycatcher would sooner have the plague brought into his house, than a pack of cards, even for his children to take a sober game of whist. Yet it is not a week since I found him exulting in his good luck at a shooting-match, where he had gained three turkeys for a quarter of a dollar. The man is certainly *a blind guide, who strains at a gnat and swallows a camel.*

When a young lady hides her face behind her fan at a double *entendre*, even where none was meant, and afterwards sits up all night to read Tom Jones or Tristram Shandy, she most assuredly *strains at a gnat and swallows a camel.*

Our good country people, who most conscientiously avoid an oath; but will *sniggers*, *swampit*, and *fags*, and give the devil a thousand nicknames, and affirm *by the living jingo*, by *George*, &c. do not consider that these are substituted for the most awful oaths, and that, in addition to the wickedness of them, they are most abominably silly. Persons of this description *strain at a gnat and swallow a camel.*

After he left the Messenger, Biglow sent a number of articles to his friend Dennie, for publication in the Farmer's Museum, which, as they were "composed of a farrago of materials, intended to effectuate the destruction of those enemies of mankind, spleen, immorality, and irreligion," he proposed to call "Olio." The following is the first number: —

EXTRACT FROM A MANUSCRIPT POEM.

In ballads first I spent my boyish time;
At college, next, I soared in doggerel rhyme;
Then of a school the master and adorner,
I scribbled verses for a Poet's Corner.
But when, ere while, I strove, with *slender means*,
Newspapers to edite, and Magazines;
The public frowned, and warned me, at my peril,
To drop the pen, and reassume the *ferule*.

. . . .

And now, enchanting poetry, adieu!
Thy syren charms no longer I pursue.
Past are those days of indolence and joy,
When tender parents nursed their darling boy,
In Harvard's walls maintained me many a year,
Nor let one dun discordant grate my ear.
For love of thee I quitted love of gold,
My Pike neglected and my Euclid sold;
On fancy's wings from Poverty upborne,
Saw not my coat was patched, my stockings torn;
With childish creep approached Pieria's springs,
Nor, when a man, could *put off childish things.*

Still by some *ignis fatuus* led astray,
I 've wandered on through many a dismal way:
Have seen my golden prospects end in dross;
Fought for a myrtle crown, and gained a cross.
Too proud to court the little or the great,
Thy votaries never rise in church nor state;
Not all thy power from bailiffs can secure,
Nor coax our wary fair to "marry poor."
Farewell! On others inspiration flash,
Give them eternal fame — but give me cash.

. . . .

Adieu, thou busy world! I quit thy cares;
Thy luring smiles I 've viewed, and found them snares;
Thy towering hopes pursued, and found them vain;
Thy pleasures tasted, and have found them pain;
Far other objects, now, my heart shall bind
With sacred truths to store my youthful mind,
The lessons learn, by godlike reason given,
And trace religion's path, which leads to heaven.

. . . .

Charles Chatterbox.

The following was probably written while he was engaged for the Massachusetts Magazine: —

RECEIPT TO MAKE A MAGAZINE.

A plate, of art and meaning void,
To explain it a whole page employed:
Two tales prolonged of maids deluded;
Two more begun, and one concluded;
Life of a fool to fortune risen;
The death of a starved bard in prison;
On woman, beauty-spot of nature,
A panegyric and a satire;
Cook's voyages, in continuation;
On taste a tasteless dissertation;
Description of two fowls aquatic:
A list of ladies, enigmatic;
A story *true* from French translated,
Which, with a *lie*, might well be mated;

A mangled slice of English history;
Essays on miracles and mystery;
An unknown character attacked,
In story founded upon fact:
Advice to jilts, coquets, and prudes:
And thus the pompous Prose concludes.

For Poetry — a birth-day ode;
A fable of the mouse and toad;
A modest wish for a kind wife,
And all the other joys of life;
A song, descriptive of the season;
A poem, free from rhyme and reason:
A drunken song, to banish care;
A simple sonnet to despair;
Some stanzas on a bridal bed;
An epitaph on Shock, just dead;
A pointless epigram on censure;
An imitation of old Spenser;
A dull acrostic and a rebus;
A blustering monody to Phœbus;
The country 'gainst the town defended;
And thus the Poetry is ended.

Next, from the public prints, display
The news and lyings of the day;
Paint bloody Mars & Co. surrounded
By thousands slain, ten thousand wounded:
Steer your sly politics between
The Aristocrat and Jacobin;
Then end the whole, both prose and rhyme, in
The ravages of Death and Hymen.

I will add but one more specimen of Mr. Biglow's off-hand poetical productions. It is a New Year's Address, written for the Carriers of the New-England Galaxy, January 1, 1826. As will be perceived, it is written after the manner (it cannot be called a parody, nor an imitation) of an old English song, called "The Prophets." This form I recommended to him, and the poem was finished the day after it was ordered: —

FEAST OF THE EDITORS.

Nil ego protulerim jucundo sanus amico.—Hor. Sat.

Last night, 'tis reported, our Editors met
In the Hall of the News-room, their whistles to wet,
Determined like friends of good *metal* and cheer,
To drink out the old and drink in the new year.

The meeting to *form*, they at once all agreed,
And then to their business in order proceed;
But first it was voted, their glee to prolong,
Each should tell a good story, or sing a new song.

Mr. Senator Russell was called to the Chair,
And he soon dispensed mirth and maccoboy there;
The meeting he thanked for his lofty promotion,
And chanted his song with heart-felt devotion.

TUNE.—*Miss Bailey.*

I am an older editor, than any on the stand, sirs;
Legitimacy I'll maintain in this, and every land, sirs:
Our rulers here we always choose, all by the people's voice, sirs;
If others like another mode, pray let them take their choice, sirs.
Legitimate Adams! Fortunate Adams!
He is our lawful President, then wherefore make a noise, sirs.

The *Centinel*, for many years, upon the watch has stood, sirs;
And still shall stand firm at its post, to guard the public good, sirs;
And while for faction's wounds it aims to find effectual healings,
It shall proclaim the Union's laws, to regulate your dealings!
O the Centinel! The watchful Centinel,
Long as *it* lasts, shall celebrate the era of good feelings.

Brother Knapp then arose, mid the good-humored set,
To do what he could for the widow's *Gazette*;*
But he thought that he best might succeed in a story,
Since he ne'er in his skill, as a singer, could glory.

But 'twas voted, nem. con. that they all would excuse
The defects of his wind and his music and muse:
He confessed that his stories were apt to be long,
Yet he looked rather *black*, as he chanted his song.

TUNE.—*We'll aprons put on.*

The *Commercial Gazette* shall never forget
The duties we owe to the nation;
And though we may *nap*, we will dream in the trap
Of no faction to suffer starvation.

* See Knapp's Valedictory, p. 260.

When Adams was named for the office he claimed
  By the greedy for loaves and for fishes,
'Tis true, we began by abusing the *Man*, —
  But the *President* has our best wishes.

The song was scarce finished when Greene,* in a rage
For himself and his partner, was prompt to engage;
And he threw a stout look of defiance among
All the brothers and bottles around, as he sung.

TUNE. — *Battle of the kegs.*

Oh! ye may grin and laugh who win,
  And at your triumph chuckle;
The *Statesman* will be saucy still,
  And ne'er to Adams knuckle.

Ay, lowly bow in worship now
  Before the rising sun, sirs;
Let come what may, ye ne'er shall say
  We strike at the first gun, sirs.

Now by the powers! this land of ours
  Its name for freedom loses,
When such a man as Adams can
  Pluck all our beards and noses!

Crawford, we're told, was begged to hold
  The purse-strings of the nation;
But * * * * * *

Much more had he sung, but the chairman seemed vext
And told Young and Minns 'twas their turn to sing next;
They winked at each other, and fashioned their strain
To promote, in the meeting, good humor again.

TUNE. — *Jolly Millers.*

In titbit paragraphs we tell the news of every sort;
And, like Procrustes with his bed, we dock long tales to short:
For sects and parties 'tis our aim to make but little fuss;
And if we care not for the world, — the world cares not for us.

The chairman then nodded to classical Hale,
Who regretted the dignified *Daily* should fail;
But to make his apology took him so long,
'Twas voted a story, and saved him his song!

Next, Fessenden rose, with 'a round face and body,'
Declaring, although it might seem very odd, he

* Nathaniel Greene, editor of the Statesman.

Could not, for the life of him, give them a song,
Unless he should make it as he went along.

TUNE. — *O dear! what can the matter be?*

Since I have turned *Farmer*, if one of the muses
I woo to my service, the coy jade refuses,
And old friend Apollo my corn-field abuses!
"Non sum qualis eram."
O dear! what can the matter be?
Since dairies began to succor and spatter me,
The nymphs of Parnassus are deaf to my flattery, —
So fine me a *hot-toddy* dram.

His finger the chairman then pointed ☞ to CLAPP,
Who snored o'er the *Evening Gazette*, in a nap;
He said he ne'er sung, but in notes most sonorous
He *hummed* a brisk tune, and all joined in the chorus.

TUNE. — *Saturday night still comes.*

The next, that came forward, were BALLARD and WRIGHT,
Both cleaning their throttles and bowing polite;
But they feared they should 'buy no opinions of gold,'
As one seldom sung, t'other had a bad cold.

TUNE. — *Yankee Doodle.*

The *Chronicle* from able hands,
Ye know to us came down, sirs;
And still its credit firmly stands,
In country and in town, sirs.
Yankee Doodle, keep it up —
We stick to the old-school, sirs;
So here's for liberty! a cup,
And may the people rule, sirs.

The only learning freemen need
Is democratic knowledge,
And while they can the *Patriot* read
A fig for Harvard College!
Yankee Doodle, keep it up, &c.

In vain for power the tories try,
And all their virtues mention;
We stop their mouths, whene'er we cry
The watchword of *Convention!*
Yankee Doodle, keep it up, &c.

The chairman then called upon HALLOCK and WILLIS,
Whose *Recorder* has long been *a warning*, and still is!
And this is the Hymn, they with emphasis thundered,
By a few others joined, to the tune of Old Hundred.

HYMN.

Great Calvin! with humility
We dedicate our Press to thee;
Oh! may it bid thy doctrines roll
From sea to sea, from pole to pole.

By "awful warning" we would keep
Within the fold thy straying sheep!
And we would guard the orthodox
From anti-christian wiles and knocks!

Then BADGER and PORTER,* all *booted* and *spurred*,
Like Castor and Pollux, sprung forth at a word;
Though *jaded* with *speed* and *high-pressure*, they swore
They would *whistle* an air, but could do nothing more.

TUNE.— *Wayworn Traveller.*

With an air then arose great Brother Ballou, †
As much as to say, 'Sirs, who but I, who?'
And he thought that his doctrines were so *Universal*-
Ly known, that they hardly required a rehearsal.

TUNE. — *Peas upon a trencher.*

My lads it is all folly
To yield to melancholy;
For there 's no hell,
But where we dwell,
Then wherefore not be jolly?
Mankind are all mistaken,
Who think the vile forsaken;
For though we stray
From Virtue's way,
We still shall save our bacon!

The chairman next called upon good Dr. COTTON, ‡
Whose *Medical* paper could not be forgotten;
He preluded his dirge in a bumper of water,
And beat his own time with a pestle and mortar.

TUNE. — *Pleyel's Hymn.*

The life of man 's a life of wo!
We live to die, — to die we grow;
To-day we laugh, to-day we cry,
To-morrow take a cold and die!

Whate'er the doctors say or think,
There 's death in all we eat and drink,

* Editors of the American Traveller.

† Rev. H. Ballou, editor of a Universalist paper.

‡ John Cotton, publisher of the Medical and Surgical Journal.

Death, in each pill-box they have got,
Death, even in this pewter pot!

Oh! when will quacks their arts throw by,
And men, secundum artem, die?
How long must we be dosed with jugs
And gallipots of Conway's drugs?

Should I while singing, not avoid
To trill with "process condyloid"
At edge of "glenoid cavity,"
My jaws would break thus — eh! — eh! — eh!

When a story or song was demanded from REED,*
He modestly doubted how he might succeed;
But still he was willing to sing with his brothers,
And hoped for that candor, which he showed to others.

TUNE. — *St. Helen's.*

On others' faith we 'll not intrude,
Nor with their practice be too rude,
  Whate'er their creeds, or ours, may be;
While in our hearts we feel the flame
Of love and charity, a name
  Can never make us disagree.

Then BUCKINGHAM stood half-erect in his place,
With a reprobate leer on his sanctified face;
He said not a word, but his looks seemed to say,
I will sing my own ditty, and in my own way.

TUNE. — *Adams and Liberty.*

The rights of the Press let us firmly maintain,
  Though foes should deride and friends should forsake us;
Neither favor nor fear shall our freedom restrain,
  For if patrons will pay, the banks cannot break us.
      Let Noah ne'er hint,
      With a villanous squint,
That a Yankee dares think what he dares not to print;
  Though libels *are* libels because they are true,
  We care not, and, ———, there 's no danger for you.

The chairman here bolted a deep pinch of snuff,
And cried, "By Apollo! we 've heard songs enough!
For the clocks to *strike small ones* already begin,
So the Old Year is out, and the New Year is in."

Then all having pledged, "Long life and success
To the friends of a free and a liberal Press" —
Three bumpers! — three cheers! — in good humor they parted,
And each for his dwelling, well-satisfied, started.

* David Reed, publisher of the Christian Register.

AND

BOSTON DAILY ADVERTISER.

The publication of a daily paper with this title was begun in Boston, October 6, 1796. The imprint stated that it was printed by Alexander Martin for the proprietors, but no proprietors' names are mentioned. The editor was John Burk, a fugitive from Ireland, where he had exposed himself to the vindictive power of the government, by his connection with James, Napper Tandy, and others of the band, called United Irishmen. The first few numbers were on a crown sheet. It was then enlarged, and printed on demy; and, in about six weeks, appeared on a sheet of royal size. This, I believe, was the first attempt to establish a daily paper in Boston. The editor's opening address, — and, in fact, all his editorials, — indicate that he was master of a fervid style, and wrote with feelings intensely opposed to every thing that was hostile to the liberty of speech and the press. After expressing his gratitude for the patronage his paper had received in advance, and descanting on the advantages of a daily paper, he proceeded to say : —

This, *Fellow-Citizens!* is a proof of the advantages arising from a daily publication. I call you FELLOW-CITIZENS! for I too am a citizen of these states. From the moment a stranger puts his foot on the soil of America, his fetters are rent in pieces, and the scales of servitude, which he had contracted under European tyrannies, fall off; he becomes a FREE MAN; and though civil regulations may refuse him the immediate exercise of his rights, he is *virtually* a *citizen.* He sees a moral, intrepid, and enlightened community ranged under the banners of equality and justice; and, by the natural sympathy, that subsists between the mind and every thing that is amiable, he finds his affections irresistibly attracted; he resigns his prejudices on the threshold of the temple of liberty; they are melted down in the great crucible of public opinion. This I take to be the way in which all strangers are affected when they enter these states; that I am so, will be little doubted, when it is known how much I am indebted to their munificence and liberality. I shall give better proofs of it than words — there is nothing that I would not resign for your service, but what there is little fear I shall be ever called on to surrender, — my GRATITUDE and LOVE of LIBERTY.

The election of a successor to President Washington was a subject of great interest at that time. With more modesty than was exhibited by some foreigners, who had the control of presses in New-York and Philadelphia, Burk refrained from the use of vulgar epithets and personalities. In his second paper he said : —

Of the election of President we shall say nothing. We have promised impartiality — we will keep our word. From an attachment to public liberty, we hope the future President may be as good a republican as Washington. Never has that venerable patriot been known to utter a sentiment favorable to royalty. The simile of the sublime Longinus may be applied to his resignation; he appears like the sun in his evening declination; though it loses its splendor, it retains its magnitude, and pleases more though it shines less.

People of America! with this great example of genius and patriotism before your eyes, you will be without excuse if you err. Let the man of your choice be a man of talent, information, integrity, and republican modesty; a lover not only of your constitution but of liberty in general. He ought to be a friend of the revolutions of Holland and of France; he ought to be a hater of monarchy, not only on account of the danger, but the absurdity of it; he ought not to be willing to divide the people by any distinctions. Americans should have but one denomination, — THE PEOPLE.

Burk's feelings were naturally strong against the British government, and perhaps almost as naturally in favor of France. "FRANCE (he said) goes on in the uninterrupted career of victory. On one side she is employed in regenerating the degenerate sons of the old Romans. In Germany she trails the Austrian eagle in the dust, while the eye of the Directory, like that of Alexander, is thrown with anxiety for worlds to conquer. ENGLAND, under the iron sway of a profligate administration, exhibits the melancholy example to nations of the dangers resulting from the too great security in the people. She fights like a desperate gamester, doubling stakes as she loses. The game is almost run. The people are generous, brave, honest, and unsuspecting; when they open their eyes, the delusion vanishes."

Burk's impartiality, — at least so far as foreign politics were involved in controversy, — is fairly illustrated by what follows: —

The republic of America was scarcely ever placed in so critical a political situation as at this moment — her commerce on one side invaded by a Machiavelian government, which in defiance of the most solemn treaties, continues to take their vessels and impress their seamen; — on the other side, menaced by a people, who, from the nature of their government, ought to be, and we hope still are, the friends of America, but who conceive themselves injured and insulted by the treaty with England; we hope and believe that the men, who voted for and against this treaty, are alike friendly to the constitution of America and the liberties of mankind; and we abhor that gloomy and monastic system of politics, which condemns to the Inquisition and Bastile those, who happen to differ in opinion. The Polar Star, like a stern and impartial tribunal of criticism, shall be open to the *reasoning* on both sides; but it will hear only REASONING. It will curb the spirit of faction; silence the clamors of revenge; and heal the wounds of the unfortunate, who have been, or shall be, under the delusion of error.

In the paper succeeding that, in which the preceding extract appeared, after half a column of prudent and judicious remarks, upon the neutrality and impartiality of the Star, he says, "Two compositions were sent to the office for insertion: the one 'A FEDERALIST,' the other a 'PATRIOT OF '76.' Both were party pieces. Both were violent. We excluded both." He states that the authors took umbrage at the neglect, and sent impudent letters, one calling him a *royalist* and the other a *Jacobin*. He says, — "*Both lie.* One threatens to attack the editor in the Chronicle: the other means he shall be banded about in the Centinel. . . . We probably have done them a service by refusing them a place in our paper, as they were grossly and shamefully deficient in *orthography*, *etymology*, *syntax*, and *prosody*. Their behavior appears to us the surest proof of the Star's impartiality."

In some of the early numbers of the Star, Burk published an account of his trial and defence before the Board of the University of Dublin, on a charge of Deism and Republicanism. The writings, which were the cause of this charge, were published in the Dublin Evening Post, a paper of great reputation, which strongly advocated the cause of the People against the Crown. The agents of the government discovered that he was the author of the pieces, and used their influence with the Board to remove him from the university, and he was, consequently, expelled.

The Polar Star and its editor were not treated with any superfluous degree of courtesy by their Boston cotemporaries. Whether this was owing to jealousy of its engrossing the public favor, or dislike to the intrusion of a foreigner into the pale of American editorship, — or from some other cause, is not known. From some of its editorials, it appears that it was attacked by the Chronicle, Centinel, and Mercury. In the course of a few weeks the editor published several articles, addressed "To the editors of the several newspapers in Boston," concerning "the vices that existed in newspaper establishments." He said "the period of election is ushered in by bickerings, by personalities, by squabbles and scurrilities, by feuds, by heart-burnings and heart-scaldings, by animosity, by contentions and quarrels, which reflect a disgrace on the amiable character of Liberty, and are unworthy the literary advocates of a free people." Perhaps his neighbors did not relish this rebuke (doubtless a very wholesome one) from one, who had just left his native country to escape the consequences of too much freedom of speech. There is nothing, however, in the editorial columns of the Star, which merits a similar rebuke.

Like many other editors, — some not unknown at the present day, — the publishers of the Star boasted, frequently, of the great amount of public patronage bestowed on their labors. This may, some times, be a successful finesse to procure support, but it is rather a dangerous, and hardly an honorable, experiment. The Star of October 25 said, — "The Polar Star has gained by its impartiality, in fourteen days, two hundred and thirteen new subscribers. It has lost two, because it supported the federal constitution, and did not *rave* in favor of the ridiculous and absurd establishments of royalty and aristocracy; and it has lost one, because, to use the *philosopher's* own elegant language, it is a *milk-and-water* paper, wants tone, and does not flatter one party more than the other. Majority for the Star two hundred and ten." In another paragraph it is said, — "A great *philosopher*, who inherits the science of Newton, the humanity of Rousseau, and the reasoning powers of Locke, was asked by a gentleman to subscribe for the Star, and refused, *because the editor was an Irishman.*"

Burk was evidently chagrined at the silence of the Boston press in regard to him and his paper. Two months after its first appearance, he said, — "Whenever a new paper makes its appearance in Europe, the established papers make honorable mention of their infant brother. They have at least the liberality to say, *Such a paper made its appearance on such a day, of such a month, of such a year.* But the sublime sages and politicians who compile the Boston papers, scorn to imitate such vulgar liberality; they preserve the most profound and edifying silence on such occasions. If the parents of the Star had not been careful to register its birth regularly, and according to the rules of the church, in the Temple of Liberty, before its godfathers and mothers, the people, it might have died, and its existence been forgotten, before these statesmen would have deigned to notice the *existence* of such a *reptile.*"

Encouraged by prospects of success, and, probably, by promises of assistance, the proprietors of the Star proposed to publish a semi-weekly paper, in connection with their daily publication, to be entitled "The Columbian Citizen; a Gazette for the Continent," but the project was never executed. Notwithstanding all their self-congratulations, and assurances to the public of gratitude for unprecedented favor, they were obliged to call upon their subscribers for a fulfillment of the conditions of subscription, in order to enable them to keep the Star *above the horizon.* But all was ineffectual. I cannot tell the exact date of its *setting*; but the date of the last I have seen is February 2, 1797. If this was not the last number, the publication was discontinued in a short time after, and Martin, the printer of it, was engaged in the printing of another newspaper in Philadelphia.

While in Boston, Burk wrote a tragedy, called "The Battle of Bunker-Hill, or the Death of General Warren," which was performed a number of times at the Haymarket theatre. For many years the managers of the Boston theatre used to bring it forward on special occasions, to gratify the patriotism of the pit and gallery. The tragedy had not a particle of merit, except its brevity. It was written in *blank verse,* if a composition having no attribute of poetry could be so called. It was as destitute of plot and distinctness of character as it was of all claim to poetry. Burk, afterward, was the editor of a political paper, in New-York, called "The Time-Piece," and was arrested on a charge of publishing a libel, contrary to the provisions of the "Sedition Law" of 1798. The issue of the affair I never knew. About the year 1800, it was reported that he was killed in a duel in one of the southern states.

FEDERAL GAZETTE

AND

DAILY ADVERTISER.

On the first day of January, 1798, Caleb P. Wayne issued the first number of a daily paper, in Boston. In his opening address to the public he referred to the title as announcing the character of his politics — "Federal, by which he meant highly favorable to our present excellent constitution, and to its administration." His sentiments were more definitely described in another paragraph: —

As the editor is an American, he shall avoid as much as possible all partiality towards any foreign nation; and shall speak favorably or unfavorably of each, in proportion to the injuries of which it may be guilty, or the good faith it may observe, towards his own country. No private scandal or defamation will ever find a place in his paper; but public men and public measures, he conceives, are fair subjects of public animadversion. Jacobinical principles he detests, and shall omit no opportunity of exposing their dangerous tendency, though he shall not soil his page with illiberal censure on the individuals who propagate them, as long as they keep within the bounds of decorum and personal respect; but he will not pledge himself always to treat with tenderness the notorious revilers of our government and its officers. This is the only impartiality which the editor professes, and these are the only sentiments he thinks a real American should entertain.

In the second number of the paper is a note expressing the editor's pleasure, that the decisive and candid manner, in which he had announced his principles, had met with general approbation; and that but *one* subscriber had deemed his address *as unpardonably offensive*, and withdrawn his name as a subscriber. He adds, "If to express a detestation of Jacobinism, and a sincere love and admiration of our country, its constitution and administration thereof, be considered as 'unpardonably offensive,' we shall with pleasure erase the name of those who may wish to 'go to the Chronicle,' and there obtain as much of Jacobinism and subterfuge as they may wish for."

The editorials of this paper were not written in a much more scholarly style than those of the other Boston papers. They were generally short, but spicy and ill-natured. In following out to their utmost length the principles announced in his opening address, the editor was not sparing of reproof to any of his own party, if he found one in the slightest degree timid or wavering. He availed himself of an occasion to abuse Mr. Russell of the Centinel (whose attachment to the Federal Administration was undisputed) in the following style: —

☞ Having read the remarks in yesterday's Centinel, respecting our Ministers, France, &c. we declare them such as should make the Editor of that paper (allowing him to be a true American) blush with shame. The language of imbecility in a mealy-mouthed tone, is not such as at this period should issue from a Federal press. Firmness alone will repress audacity. The Editor of the Centinel says — "IF the French Directory has forgot the dignity which is attached to a sovereign and independent State," &c. "IF!" a good one, truly! Why does the Editor of the Centinel query, with his "IFS" and "ands!" Is he turning into a Jacobin, forgot he was a Federalist, or was he . . . crazy? He knows, and for certain, or he certainly ought to know, that the French "Powers that be" HAVE forgot the respect due to the United States, as a sovereign and independent nation: The insult offered the United States through our Ministers only is sufficient to do away all

"*Ifs & ands*" in the opinion of every one but the Jacobins. But the editor of the Centinel "is a delicate fellow, says Tom Bolin," and like the Jacobins always glosses over insult offered the United States with an "IF," &c. Real Federalists will never use such milk-and-water queries as does the Editor of the Centinel; — when their nation or government IS insulted, true Americans will never sneak-in-the-corner, nor be afraid to proclaim that justice demands reparation for the insult in other places than "up the chimney" — any thing the IF Editor of the Centinel says to the contrary notwithstanding. — The comparison drawn by the Editor of the Centinel, between the treaties negociated by France with Spain, and between the United States and Great-Britain, is rank Chronicle Jacobinism — as he plainly insinuates much against our treaty with Great-Britain as it affects France — and says, "*If*" the Directory of France will break their treaty with Spain, *it is not to be doubted* that their *example* would go further than their precept! Intimating as *if* France will break her most solemn and sacred obligation with Spain, that the United States *will* follow their *example* and break with England! An insinuation more degrading to the spirit of true Americans, more encouraging to the French faction, than all the doltisms and falsehoods that as yet have issued from the French presses, the Chronicle, the Aurora, the Argus, &c.

Having given a specimen of the manner in which the Editor of the Gazette behaved towards his cotemporaries of the federal school, when they did not rise to his standard in the political thermometer, let us see how he treated his opponents: —

Newspaper War!

THE FEDERAL GAZETTE.

vs.

Bache's AURORA, *Carey's* RECORDER, *Holt's* BEE, *Pierce's* ORACLE, *&c.*

The Editor asks pardon of his readers for devoting a part of the Federal Gazette to the *business of warfare* — he loves *peace* as sincerely as they do — yet when repeatedly attacked by the *papers of sedition* it might be a crime to let them always pass unnoticed. He expected that the candid politics of the Federal Gazette would arouse the minions of sedition, from North to South; and make them desperate in their endeavors to crush it — he is not surprized at the many attempts of the Jacobins, to injure the circulation of a paper tending to expose their party to merited contempt; but it is astonishing that printers, professing themselves federal, should unite with a certain vehicle of sedition in this town to prevent it being universally read — he shall make no comments on such conduct — but proceed —

Among the first of his opponents, ranks the notorious Jacobin

BACHE,

Editor of the Aurora, Printer to the French Directory, Distributor General of the principles of insurrection, anarchy, and confusion — the greatest fool, and most stubborn Sans Culotte in the United States. He attacks the Federal Gazette's *elegance of diction*, a thing that he knows as much about as *Lyon* does of common decency, and which his paper is as destitute of as the Boston Chronicle is of truth. No sooner had this Chief of Anarchy given the signal for attack, by a discharge from his feathered cannon, than to work went all his understrappers in the different parts of the United States.

Next appears the insipid and detestable Editor of the *Recorder*,

O'CAREY,

who so generously supplies all the pastry-cooks in Philadelphia with his paper *gratis*, for their various uses; a general pedler in French arguments; and who, after having been four or five times sent to oblivion, has lately been permitted by the Devil to come forth again and wage war with virtue and order. His attacks, however, are but second editions of Bache's — with this exception, that they are, if possible, still more pitiful. *O'Carey* is at a loss to know, what can be meant by the term, "milk of human kindness." So destitute is his soul of sensibility and virtue! After the above, follows one

HOLT,

of New-London, Editor of a little vehicle of sedition, called the BEE — for which he will accept "*pay in any thing.*" This fellow's words are — "*Peter Skunk* has *gained* an ally, and Federalism another prop, in the Federal Gazette published at Boston by one *Wayne*;" and then asserts that *Cobbet* has no friends *left* except *Fenno*, the aforesaid *Wayne*, and *Dennie*, the erudite Walpole Fire-brand." Mark, reader — First he asserts that *Peter* has gained an ally and Federalism a prop, and in the same breath says, *Peter*, and consequently, Federalism, has *no friends left*, but *Fenno*, *Dennie*, and *Wayne* — this is equal to the Irish General who told his men they *advanced* one step *backward!* Notwithstanding he "*takes pay in any thing*" he cannot obtain even the praise of one Jacobin, nor the subscription of the "*meanest hostler*" — an incontrovertible truth this, that Connecticut is not the democratic state represented by *M. Lyon*, any thing he or *Holt* says to the contrary. He called his paper the Bee, very properly, but he ought to have told what kind of a *bee*, as it is evidently one of those called *Drones*, that are as devoid of any sting as *Holt* is of common sense, and who live on the sweets of society, without adding to the common stock, and are always kicked out of the hive for *stupidity;* which fate he richly deserves. He concludes with advising *Mr. Bowen* to get the skin of the Editor together with *Peter Porcupine*, and have them stuffed, and placed in the museum, and no doubt this would be as gratifying to this Sans Culotte as the sight of the guillotine reeking with blood is to the sanguinary French populace. If this *Holt* was placed in a niche of some public corner, he would immediately become the reservoir for all kinds of ejection, and would then be in a very appropriate *honey-hive.*

Next, with majestic stride, appears a member of the new order of Jacobin Chivalry, arrayed with the Wooden Sword and other insignia,

CHARLES PIERCE,

the irredoubtable Editor of the Portsmouth *Oracle*. The readers of the Federal Gazette will recollect that some time ago this *Pierce* was mentioned as having refused to publish *Scipio* — Instead of justifying himself, he has prated chiefly about the term *we*, which the Editor uses instead of the singular *I;* a practice almost universally adopted by Editors of newspapers, and which he himself uses. *Pierce* the Sans Culotte being now *compelled* to publish the numbers of "FEDERAL SCIPIO," has (to keep back the real truth from being known) asserted that he has published them to evince his *impartiality!* What his Jacobin friends will think of his inconsistency, of his deviation from their party, is, probably, that he is a mere dish-water-fop, unworthy the confidence of *any* party.

Mr. Pierce tells his readers that he is ignorant of the *meaning* of the word Jacobin. Poor man! why did he not consult the "Book of Knowledge" he printed some time ago? he has, to exculpate himself from the charge of *Jacobinism* asserted, (or a *writer* has asserted for him) that "the tenor of his life has been neither base, wicked, nor nefarious," and that "he keeps his stone steps free from ice! consequently, he cannot be a Jacobin." Well said, most grave Sir *Charles!* But all this whining will not convince your readers of your impartiality — no, no, Mr. *Pierce*, while whole columns are inserted from the *Aurora*, *Argus*, and *Chronicle*, together with the piece signed VERITAS, (an infamous Jacobin as ever lived, and whom I strongly suspect to have written the card for you, addressed to me) are admitted with alacrity — and pieces in justification of our government are placed in the back ground as your friend *Monroe* wished to place the United States with respect to foreign countries, not one of your patrons (unless they are as destitute of candor as you are of sense) will believe you.

But *Charley* seems to have been seized with the *horrors*, the natural consequence of a guilty mind, as he begs to be excused from my "*shaving* hand," dreading a "*federal cut throat*" no less than a "*Sans Culotte guillotinist*" *! !* Leave off this whining, supplicating cant; gird on your wooden sword and other insignia of your order, *Pierce*—call VERITAS and all your Sans Culotte friends to your assistance; for be assured that all your begging will have no effect. You shall not be freed from the lash of Truth and Federalism, until you prove by your actions that you are a virtuous man and no Jacobin. If you have one grain of candor within you, an idea of justice, or the most trivial pretensions to what you profess, give this a place in your paper; if you do not, every man will despise you no less than I do your infamous political tenets.

Such was the style of the political *war documents* of 1798.

The articles here alluded to, signed "Scipio," were first published at Philadelphia, in the United States Gazette. They were entitled "Reflections on Mr. Monroe's View of the conduct of the Executive on the foreign affairs of the United States, connected with the mission of the French Republic, during the years 1794, 5, 6." They extended to ten or more numbers, and were republished in the Federal Gazette.

At the end of three months from the commencement of his paper, Wayne found himself under the necessity of abandoning the experiment of a *daily* publication, "for want of sufficient encouragement." Unwilling, as he says, "to desert a cause in which he felt himself warmly interested," he continued to publish, twice a week, on Mondays and Thursdays, for one month longer, when the publication was discontinued.

The failure of this enterprize could hardly have been avoided. The income from advertising customers was small, and could not have been worth naming, in comparison with the necessary cost of a daily publication.

The original communications were not numerous, and what few there were, were chiefly on the politics of the day, — subjects on which the editor himself exhausted all his powers. Most of his paragraphs are similar in style and temper to the specimens already given. The paper was apparently conducted with industry; but industry without judgement is not all, that is required to render a daily paper worthy of extensive support.

Wayne came to Boston from Philadelphia, and returned to that city soon after the discontinuance of the Federal Gazette.

THE CONSTITUTIONAL TELEGRAPHE.

THE first number of this paper was published in Boston, October 2, 1799, by SAMUEL S. PARKER. Common rumor said that the editor was instigated to the enterprize by a belief that the Chronicle did not quite satisfy the wishes and expectations of some of the most ultra of the republican party. The editor himself, in his salutatory, gave some reason to suppose that such a cause might have existed. He said, — " Exclusive of the common motive, by which every effort of industry is stimulated, the editor is induced to believe that a new paper, in this town, would be cheerfully received and zealously patronized by those federal Republicans, who constitute the great mass of real American citizens, men attached to no faction, who prefer the interests of their own to those of any other country ; who comprehend and revere the principles of civil liberty, as recorded and established in the Declaration of Independence, and in the constitutions of the states and federal government ; who will support these illustrious monuments of the American revolution with their fortunes and their lives ; who, to a just sense of their obligations to maintain these institutions and the laws of the land, made in pursuance of them, unite a belief that " the liberty of the press is essential to the security of freedom in a state ; " &c.

It was a semi-weekly paper, published on Wednesday and Saturday.

The editor was aided by several writers, but none of surpassing excellence. "Democritus" wrote a series of essays, — one on the duties of a republican editor, in which there seems to be a sly hit at some of those of its own party: and others on "American Aristocracy." This writer had been a correspondent of the Chronicle, but had been silent for a time. His reappearance was greeted with great enthusiasm by other writers, in the Telegraphe. Another series of communications were entitled "Standing Army," by "A friend to the President."

The editor appears to have been indebted mainly to correspondents for original matter. The paper contains nothing of his composition, but short summaries of news, with an occasional attack upon some cotemporary federal paper. The Aurora, the Chronicle, and other leading republican papers, are liberally drawn upon for political discussion. Both editor and correspondents opposed, with all their power, the election of Caleb Strong to the chief magistracy of the commonwealth in the spring of 1800. Their whole artillery of satire and abuse was discharged at Alexander Hamilton, — who visited Boston in June, 1800, — and those, who showed him any marks of respect.

Parker was a physician in the county of Worcester, and, I believe, resided there most of the time while the Telegraphe was published in his name. That name disappeared from the imprint on the tenth of July, 1800. Previously no printer's name had been attached to it. The paper of that day purports to be printed "by Jon-

ATHAN S. COPP, for the proprietor, at his printing-office, south side State-street." The typography and mechanical execution were miserable specimens of mechanic art. While the Telegraphe appeared with Copp's name as publisher, there was much more of what may be called editorial matter, than at first; from which it may be inferred that he filled the office of editor as well as printer. He was a native of New-London, and though he served his apprenticeship with a decided federal printer, he was a bitter reviler of every thing that had the odor of federalism.

At the end of the first volume, September 27, 1800, Parker gave notice that he had "sold out his proprietorship" to JOHN S. LILLIE, "who had agreed to carry it on in support of the republican *interest*, for which it was sincerely instituted." He added,—"When the proposal for printing the Telegraphe was offered to the public, the proprietor conceived there was not a republican paper printed in this commonwealth; which was one principal occasion of his coming forward, to endeavor to advocate and defend the constituted RIGHTS of his fellow-citizens, which was ever dear and precious to him; but finding his domestic circumstances and avocations such, that he could not pay that personal attention to the office, which the nature of the business required, he thought best to sell out to some person, that would pay more particular attention to it than was practical for him to do."

The following are specimens of Doctor Parker's paragraph writing:—

The Centinel of Wednesday last says, that in two hundred papers published in the United States, only twenty are Jacobin: (but mark,

Americans! Jacobin and republican are synonymous terms with the federal tories.) That only twenty republican newspapers are published in the Union, is "a shameless and insolent lie;" the fact is, more than that number have been established in the short period of the last six months, and at least fifty decidedly republican papers since the GAG bill, &c. have been in force, any thing which Ben Russell may say to the contrary notwithstanding. That falsehood and deception have long been conspicuous traits in the character of the *knowing* editor of the Centinel, we will not at present spend time to demonstrate.

December 21, 1799.

Ben Russell's remarks on that independent and republican member of Congress, Mr. Randolph, are so smutty and *black*, as to be even below contempt; issuing from a polluted fountain, which is continually casting up mire and dirt, they would, of course, have been unworthy our attention, did we not conceive it a duty, sometimes, to expose to the view of our republican fellow-citizens, this paragon of Billingsgate, this pretended advocate of "Washington federalism." Instead of coming forward and endeavoring to confute the arguments of Mr. Randolph against the standing army, this cowardly assassin contemptuously calls him a "smock-faced youth," "master Randolph," and describes him as certainly "black." This is argument! This is the dernier resort of aristocratic federalism, of our pretended friends of good order and energetic government. This is conclusive reasoning; it is emphatically federal logic. *February* 8, 1800.

It is suspected that the Charlestown Granny had two projects in view when he undertook his late journey to Philadelphia. The ostensible and *public* object was said [to be] to use his influence to have the Dock Yard established at Charlestown. The other object is said to be the appointment of *himself* by Bushrod Washington to be the writer of George Washington's Life. Joe Dennie, who is paid for writing in Fenno's Gazette, has let the "Pig out of the bag." He says that the Doctor applied to Bushrod Washington for the papers and the job, but was refused both. The remarks by Dennie are rather severe, particularly as the Doctor has declared himself of the same politics and sentiments as Joe. . . . . . The Doctor is a most extraordinary man; his wisdom is a *compound sublimation* of illuminati plots, Ocean plots, Tub plots, Taylor plots, Pig's feet, ears, and tail plots; in short, he is like the word *Hannah*, for you may spell him at each end, and find him out on all sides; he ought to obtain complete success, for his arduous efforts for the public *good;* it is infinitely more laudable than speculations in Georgia Lands. *April* 5, 1800.

Let these suffice.

The Telegraphe was seldom, if ever, noticed in the other Boston papers — a fact, which, it is evident, greatly annoyed the editor, and he referred to it, in rather querulous terms, more than once; but his complaints produced no response from his cotemporaries.

Mr. Lillie began his editorial career with a pledge to conduct the Telegraphe on the principles adopted by his predecessor, and a promise that nothing should be admitted, in opposition to the equal rights of man. The political paragraphs were more numerous, and more severe in their tone, and as the presidential election soon after terminated in favor of Mr. Jefferson, the writers in the Telegraphe assumed a more triumphant and defiant style towards their political opponents.

In the Telegraphe of February 18, 1801, the editor informed his readers that, "being unprepared to meet the *common law of England,* in its full extent and rigor, prefers to remain for a short time *incog.* Conscious of his own integrity of heart, he will not, (when prepared) shrink from a fair and impartial trial by a jury of his own countrymen." How long he kept himself secreted, is not now recollected. His paper of March 31, 1802, contains a circumstantial account of his trial and the cause of it, of which the following is an abstract, — chiefly in his own language: —

The editor of the Telegraphe, to satisfy his numerous correspondents and the public, communicates the following statement of facts, as it respects his fine and imprisonment, for a libel on the "Lord Chief Justice of the Common Law of England." At the opening of the Supreme Judicial Court in this town in February 1801, His Honor Judge Dana, after giving a charge to the grand jury, in his usual manner, observed to them, that "he had in his hand a paper, called the Constitutional Telegraphe, in which was contained the following piece, under the head of communications: —

"A dirty piece appeared in the chaste Palladium of Tuesday, 27th ult. dated at Washington, but undoubtedly fabricated here, either by the illuminati Doctor, one of the pious editors, or the Lord Chief Justice of the common law of England. The author of the paragraph endeavors to blacken the character of that great and benevolent man, Thomas Jefferson, Esq. whom the people delight to honor. It likewise attempts to degrade Governor M'Kean and Judge Brackenridge. Now know ye, that Gov. M'Kean, when chief justice of the supreme court in Pennsylvania, nor Judge Brackenridge, now chief justice of that state, never set aside the verdict, of a jury of twelve honest men, upon a promise of receiving one thousand acres of land in the province of Maine — and endeavored to obtain an impeachment of an attorney-general, for disclosing such corrupt conduct. Know ye, therefore, that the very lengthy piece on the first page of said immaculate paper, containing as much matter as a common law judge's charge to a grand jury on libels, is artfully designed to reconcile the minds of the citizens to that execrable engine of tyrants, the common law of England, in criminal prosecutions; and that they may rest easy under it, and embrace it as their birth-right. But, know ye, that whenever a republican Senate and House of Representatives convene, purged from those locusts to society, aristocratic lawyers; then this ten-headed monster will be slain, and its remains sunk in the unfathomable gulf of everlasting forgetfulness, and tyrant party judges will weep and wail, and gnash their teeth, because their reign of terror is at an end — such tyrants exclaim '*hoc me mali habit.*'"

Here his Honor, it is said, exclaimed, very *emphatically*, (at the same time pointing to himself) "That means ME, gentlemen." . . . This libel, as it was called, was handed to the grand jury, who, after a long and arduous struggle, found a bill, which, when the editor had notice of, he absented himself, not knowing who the author was, and being unprepared at that time to answer to its responsibility, and meet the vengeance of the judiciary, it being in the height of the reign of terror. . . . At the opening of the supreme court last August, the editor was summoned to appear, and was arraigned before the bar, to answer to an indictment for the above libel, as it is called. He applied to George Blake, Esq. as his counsel, who plead in his behalf, guilty of *publishing*, and consequently threw himself upon the lenity of the court. . . . His Honor Judge Bradbury, after making his remarks on the heinousness of the crime, observed that the court would indulge me till next term, in order that I might have an opportunity to discover the author. In the mean time, the original manuscript was handed round to different persons, who said they could recognize it as the hand-writing of John Vinal, Esq. Accordingly, at a meeting of the grand jury, a complaint was entered against him, as the author of the supposed libel. The grand jury, after a comparison of hands, were fully satisfied of Mr. Vinal being the author, and were unanimous in finding a bill against him. This gentleman was therefore arraigned, and plead not guilty; he was tried, — and from a comparison of hands not being legal evidence, was acquitted. The editor and his friends then expected that the honor as well as justice of the court would be satisfied with a severe reprimand, for his inadvertency, particularly at the present period, when false, malicious and scandalous libels are continually issuing from the federal presses against the President and government of the United States — instead of which, a fine of one hundred dollars, and three months imprisonment, was the award of the court. The above, to the editor's best recollection, is a true and faithful statement of the facts which he cheerfully submits for the consideration of his friends and the public. JOHN S. LILLIE.

Boston Gaol, March 30, — 19*th day of Imprisonment.*

This article was followed by another, acknowledging his obligations to friends and customers, and calling on delinquents to settle their accounts. Presuming that the person to whom he had entrusted the care of the Telegraphe, would conduct it on the principles he had himself practised, he "relinquished the arduous duties which had heretofore devolved upon him."

The Telegraphe of April 14, came out in the name of J. M. DUNHAM, as printer and editor. No essential change took place in the character or appearance of the paper, except, that, a few weeks after, the title was changed to Republican Gazetteer, and was decorated with a cut, representing Hope leaning on an anchor, holding in her right hand a staff with the cap of liberty, and in her left, a scroll, bearing the word *constitution.* Underneath was the motto, —

O Liberty! expand thy vital ray;
O'er the dark globe diffuse celestial day;
Thy spirit breathe, wide as creation's space;
Exalt, illume, inspire the human race.

John S. Lillie, after passing through the usual course of education in the common schools of Boston, was apprenticed to Benjamin Sweetser, an extensive and respectable dealer in English goods. For a while he kept an English or dry goods store in Union street. Mr. Sweetser, who, I believe, was a relative, aided him in the purchase of the Telegraphe. After the term of his imprisonment expired, he held the office of a clerk in the United States Loan-Office, and subsequently in the United States Branch bank. He died in 1842. He was an invincible disciple of the Jeffersonian school of politics, and endured the reproaches of his federal cotemporaries with a firmness and perseverance, which his most inveterate opponents could not but admire.

John Moseley Dunham, who succeeded Mr. Lillie as the publisher of the Telegraphe, was a printer by trade. He published the Republican Gazetteer some two or three years, and afterward established a manufactory of Printing Ink at Cambridge, from which he supplied most of the Printers in New-England. He went to Ohio, after the war of 1812. His subsequent history is to me unknown.

The editorials of the Telegraphe, under its several conductors were chiefly short paragraphs, indicating that the writers had a familiar acquaintance with the vocabulary of vituperation and a readiness to use it on all occasions. Many of them are mere *squibs* aimed at the federal papers and their editors, variegated with fulsome epithets applied to the leaders of the republican party. Mr. Jefferson was seldom referred to but in terms little less than idolatrous, and every incident that occurred, in the remotest degree tending to show the devotion of his partisans to him or his administration, was eagerly sought and published. The history of a singular tribute of affection to him is now but little known. It appeared in the Telegraphe in the summer of 1801, — and thus it runs : —

REPUBLICANISM:

Or, a tribute of Respect from the Ladies of Cheshire, Mass. to the President of the United States.

In the town of Cheshire, state of Massachusetts, the Ladies of the Rev. Mr. Leland's church and society agreed to make a cheese * to present to His Excellency Thomas Jefferson, as a mark of the exalted esteem they had of him, as a man of virtue, benevolence, and a real, sincere friend to all Christian denominations, and their full confidence in his being placed in the executive chair of the American nation, and their full assurance of his wielding the government at much less expense than his predecessor, and as well, and it is hoped much better. Accordingly they requested Mr. Leland to procure a cheese vat, at their expense, six feet diameter, and twenty-one inches thick, to press the cheese in; and, on a certain day, they were to assemble at Mr. David Brown's with the curd. The vat held fourteen hundred weight of curd, and they had three hundred weight left. This cheese was made from the milk of nine hundred cows at one milking. When our informant left Cheshire, the cheese had not been turned, but would be in a few days, as the machinery for that purpose was nearly completed. . . . . This cheese is to be sent, in the spring of 1802, to the seat of government, under the care of Mr. Leland, who was formerly a neighbor to Mr. Jefferson fifteen years in the state of Virginia. The motto on this cheese is, — "*Rebellion to Tyrants is obedience to* GOD."

From J. M. Dunham, the Republican Gazetteer passed into the possession of Benjamin True, and Benjamin Parks, who gave it another new name, — The Democrat. These gentlemen employed as editor, an Englishman, by the name of John Williams, — an author by profession, better known by his assumed signature, Anthony Pasquin, — a name, on which William Gifford conferred immortality, in his celebrated poem, The Baviad. In the first edition of that poem, Gifford had applied the lash of satire to the productions of Williams

* See page 167.

with an unsparing hand. In the second edition he thus refers to him : —

It has been represented to me that I should do well to avoid all mention of this man; from a consideration that one so lost to every sense of decency and shame, was a fitter object for the beadle than the muse. This has induced me to lay aside a second castigation, which I had prepared for him, though I do not think it expedient to omit what I had formerly written.

Here, on the rack of Satire, let him lie, —
Fit garbage for the hell-hound Infamy.

I am told that there are men, so weak as to deprecate this miserable object's abuse, and so vain, so despicably vain, as to tolerate his praise. For *such* I have nothing but pity; but should there be a man, or a woman, however high in rank, base enough to purchase the venal pen of this miscreant, for the sake of traducing innocence and virtue, then —— I was about to threaten, but it is not necessary; the profligate cowards, who employ Anthony, can know no severer punishment than the support of a man, whose acquaintance is infamy, and whose touch is poison."

For this satire, Williams prosecuted the publisher of Gifford's Poems; but, on the exhibition of his own writings, by the defendant, — who set up no other defence than the truth of the libel, — Williams was nonsuited. Williams, at one time, was employed as a writer for the Chronicle, — but whether before, or after, his connection with the Democrat, is not recollected.

The Democrat was discontinued in 1808.

THE GREENFIELD GAZETTE.

In January, 1792, a paper was first published at Greenfield, in the county of Hampshire, (now the shire town of Franklin county) by Thomas Dickman, entitled the Greenfield Gazette, or Massachusetts and Vermont Telegraphe. Its editor, Thomas Dickman, was a native of Boston, and served a regular apprenticeship with Benjamin Edes, — for whom he always entertained a high respect. He was a good printer, — a much better one, mechanically, than ever his master was, — but never undertook to write for his paper any article of greater length than the statement of an ordinary occurrence. In politics, he was a republican, and held to the sentiments he had imbibed in the office of Edes's Gazette; but he never obtruded his views, offensively, on his subscribers, a majority of whom were disciples of the federal school. He was a man of sound judgement and good taste, and if there was not much in the editorial department of his paper to excite either applause or dissatisfaction, there was nothing that could reasonably give offence.

In 1798, the second title of the paper was struck out, and in place of it was put "An Impartial Register of the Times."

William Coleman, afterwards the originator and editor of the New-York Evening Post, came to reside in Greenfield about the year 1794, and occasionally wrote for the Gazette an article concerning the political affairs of the day. He intended to make Greenfield his permanent residence, and laid out plans for improvement, which, if they had not been defeated by the want of means to effect them, would have added much to the attractions of that pleasant village. The mansion-house, which he erected, and nearly completed, was one of the most magnificent, in the style of its architecture, which then existed in that part of Massachusetts. Mr. Coleman was celebrated for his skill in the amusement of skating; and, it was said that he had *skated* on Connecticut river, from near Greenfield to Northampton, — twenty miles, — in an evening; but of this fact I have no knowledge. He represented the town two years in the Legislature. He gave up his residence there in the latter part of 1797.

James Elliot, then a clerk in a variety store in Guilford, Vermont, frequently contributed both prose and poetry. This gentleman, in 1793, enlisted as a non-commissioned officer in the army, under General Wayne, and was with it two or three years. He returned in 1796, and published a volume of his "works," in poetry and prose. This volume was printed at the Greenfield press. Mr. Elliot studied law at Brattleboro', and afterwards was elected a representative to Congress. He resided a short time in Philadelphia, and edited a paper called the Freeman's Journal. He returned to Brattleboro', where he established himself in the practice of the law, and held several important offices under the state government. He has been dead a number of years.

Of Elliot's poetry the following piece is probably as fair a specimen as any that was published in the Greenfield Gazette. It was written at Greenville, in the Territory N. W. of the river Ohio, November, 1795. He was then, probably about nineteen years of age.

INVOCATION TO MEMORY.

Descend, fair Nymph, from thy aerial throne,
  Aid me to string the long neglected lyre;
Dispel my griefs, make all thy joys my own,
  And kindle fancy's recollective fire.

Emerged from realms obscured by Lethean glooms,
  The Muse, inspired by thee, renews her lays;
Beneath thy fostering hand fair Science blooms,
  And Art to thee its humble homage pays.

Come, gentle Genius of the sacred scene
  Of arts and wisdom — authoress of fame;
Come with sweet aspect and celestial mien,
  Assist the bard, and animate his flame.

Lead me to the retreats of early youth,
  The seats of pleasure and the bowers of ease —
Where, clothed with native innocence and truth,
  Beneath the shelter of umbrageous trees, —

I listened to the sound of the soft gale,
  That wafted odors o'er the verdant plain;
Or sighed responsive to the red-breast's tale,
  And Philomela's sweetly plaintive strain —

Recall, sweet Nymph, those scenes of silent peace,
  And social joy, which graced my earlier hours;
When, in colloquial charms, the mind sought ease,
  Or roved through Contemplation's awful bowers, —

Or when I dared on Truth's bright wings to soar,
  By Rollin guided, by thy spirit fired,
Traversed the regions of historic lore,
  And Fame's immortal monuments admired.

Yes, I have, oft, when evening's silent reign
  Hushed the gay world to sleep, explored the page;

Viewed the bright list of chiefs (a godlike train,)
  Who graced the Grecian and the Roman age:

Conversed with virtuous Socrates, — admired
  The classic, eloquent, and generous flame,
Which Tully's pure and patriot bosom fired,
  And followed Pompey o'er the plains of fame, —

Beheld, with rapture, the Athenian youth,
  Cimon, illustrious on the embattled heath,
And Phocion, ardent in the cause of truth,
  And glorious in the trying scene of death, —

Wept o'er the fallen liberty and laws
  Of Rome, with Cato, — joined the dauntless band
That armed with Brutus to revenge her cause,
  And slew the tyrant of his native land.

Since such the brilliant harvest Memory yields,
  Of mental joys, surpassing sensual charms,
Why should I longer till those sterile fields,
  Fruitful alone in ominous alarms?

Why seek seclusion's uninviting shade
  And give my heart a prey to causeless fears?
Why roam, forlorn, the solitary glade,
  And drown my sorrows in a sea of tears?

Memory, with thee I'll pass the vacant hour,
  An humble votary at thy sacred seat;
Thy charms surpass luxurious pomp and power —
  E'EN THE REMEMBRANCE OF PAST PAINS IS SWEET.

Mr. Elliot was, in the true sense of the phrase, a SELF-TAUGHT MAN. Of humble but respectable origin, he had no advantages of what is called a liberal education. I have understood that his father died when he was quite young, and that he was early placed in a situation, where some compensation could be obtained for his services. The store, in which he was a clerk before he enlisted into the army, like all country stores in thinly settled towns, (and Guilford was then hardly a village) was not a very favorable situation for acquiring a knowledge of literature or science; yet young Elliot so improved his leisure hours, as to make an acquaintance with the best English classics, and to lay a foundation for the attainment of a distinguished position in society. While preparing himself for admission to the bar, he wrote for other newspapers than the Greenfield Gazette. In January, 1797, a paper called the Federal Galaxy, was started at Brattleboro', by Thomas Dickman and Benjamin Smead, (a young man, who had been one of Dickman's apprentices,) to which he contributed a number of articles. When the Farmer's Museum was enjoying its brightest day of fame, Elliot was a constant correspondent, and one whose contributions were highly valued by Dennie. Such men are worthy of remembrance. In honoring them the country honors itself.*

Another correspondent, whose writings gave some celebrity to the Greenfield Gazette, was the Rev. John Taylor, the minister of the church in Deerfield. He furnished a long series of papers, entitled "The Proverbialist," an imitation, — and by no means a bad one, — of Franklin's "Poor Richard."

The late judge of probate in Franklin county, Richard E. Newcomb, frequently aided the editor with his advice and some times with his pen. But the files of the Gazette exhibit no extraordinary effort to acquire a literary character. It was a respectable record of intelli-

* This Mr. Elliot had a brother, (Samuel) some years younger, who succeeded him, in the store at Guilford — a youth of similar disposition and taste, and who also became somewhat distinguished as a writer in the newspapers. He wrote for the Federal Galaxy, a series of numbers under the title of the Rural Moralist. He also studied law, and was for many years, in successful practice in Brattleboro'. He also held some public offices, the duties of which he discharged with fidelity; and HE, too, has been dead some years.

gence, and an entertaining and useful repository of matters interesting to the population of the rural districts in Massachusetts and Vermont, to which its circulation was chiefly confined.

In June, 1798, Dickman sold his printing apparatus, bookstore, and subscription books for the Gazette, to Francis Barker, — a young man, who had served a short apprenticeship at book-printing, in the office of Messrs. Thomas & Andrews, Boston. He knew nothing about conducting a paper, and had not patience to learn. Having inherited some property, he had visited Europe and South-America, and had just enough of his patrimony left to enable him to purchase the establishment. He enlarged the paper; — expunged from the head the second title of it, and inserted, in its place, "A Register of Genuine Federalism." Though he had no experience as a printer of a newspaper, he had some very just notions of the responsibility of an editor. In his address, at the opening of his new career, he said, — "The office of a conductor of a political print, in its operation on the public mind, is, perhaps, of more importance to the political opinions of a nation, than the occupation of any other individual in the community. By promulgating *error*, he becomes a *noon-day pestilence* to society; but, by diffusing *truth*, he is, in effect, a powerful instrument of general utility and happiness. Fully impressed with these sentiments, the present editor does not shrink from a public avowal of his firm determination to publish, at all times, and on all occasions, a *truly genuine American Gazette*, exclusively devoted to the propagation of *federal principles* and the vindication of his country's honor; in opposition to all the clandestine artifices of *party*, the insidious cant of Gallic *fraternity*, and the open menaces of unblushing *sedition*. The editor believes that the constitution of United America combines the greatest portion of *liberty* with the best security of *law*, that any nation ever experienced since the first institution of civil government among mankind; he therefore does not hesitate to declare, that he, who is unwilling to support this form of government, with all his physical and moral energies, commits a *sacrilege on his nature*, by rejecting the greatest possible *human* good, that regenerated man has ever enjoyed since the introduction of the Christian Religion."

With all this patriotic resolution, Barker never wrote a political paragraph of ten lines, during the ten months which he held possession of the Gazette. He made two or three visits to Boston, in the mean time, of several weeks each, and left the whole charge of the paper, and the post-office also, (he having obtained the appointment of postmaster,) to his oldest apprentice. Sick of his bargain, in May, or the beginning of June, 1799, he made an arrangement with Dickman, to take back the paper, printing-office, bookstore, post-office, and all. He then applied for a commission in the army which was raised by a law of Congress, in consequence of the difficulties with the French Republic. He obtained the commission of a lieutenant, and was stationed at Oxford, in the county of Worcester, till the army was disbanded.

Dickman carried on the business again for some years, when he relinquished it in favor of John Denio, — an excellent, good-hearted fellow, who had been his apprentice. This gentleman, after several unsuccessful experiments in business, at sundry places, is now — or was, quite recently, — the publisher of a paper at Albion, Orleans county, N. Y., and in the enjoyment of a public office, which, I sincerely hope may afford, for the remainder of his life, a quiet and happy independence.

The Gazette has since passed through the hands of several proprietors, and is still published under the title of "Gazette and Courier" — a paper called the Courier, began at a much later period, having been united with it.

Mr. Dickman removed to Springfield, where he published a paper some years, and then changed the business of printer and editor for that of a retailer of dry goods, groceries, &c. Relinquishing that employment, he opened a reading-room, which, for a while, was a favorite resort for his fellow-citizens and neighbors, but was never a source of much income. He has been dead some years. It may be said of him, as of many other printers, that he was industrious and intelligent — honest and faithful — worked hard and died poor.

THE POLITICAL GAZETTE.

In April, 1795, the first number of the Political Gazette appeared, published in Newburyport, by William Barrett. It was very neatly executed, and contained many excellent original articles, though none of them seemed to be the production of the editor; whose labors appeared to extend no further than to the selection of news and to recording the deaths and marriages that happened within the circle of his townsmen and their neighbors. Some of the poetical compositions of "Peter Quince," (Isaac Story,) were written for this paper, before that writer had been laid under contribution by Dennie, of the Farmer's Museum. One of Peter's Odes, published in the Political Gazette, was dedicated to the Green Dragon Tavern, — a well-known public house in Boston, and famous as the scene of caucuses of the republican party. Thus the ode commences: —

Hail, place of refuge — kind resort — all hail!
  Like Rome's fair consecrated mount,
    Called Sacer:
That is, a holy and becoming jail,
  Where each sad *state-menacer*
Fled, when the laws were calling to account, —

Whither resorted every sinner's son,
Where any mischief vile the rogues had done,
  So Livy says, and he 's a man of parts,

A man who tells a crooked story straight;
Who gives to every little sentence weight,
  And wins with pleasing style his reader's hearts.

Yes, *thou* art such a place — but of an humbler kind;
  That is, thou art of lower, meeker nature;
Being for meaner purposes designed,
  Though the snug nest-hole of each factious creature.
In thee Rebellion, with her turtle feet,
And fell Contention, groveling, growling, meet.

Thou art no Dragon, like those mentioned by
  The holy patriarch, in a holy place,
  Nor wouldst thou show so fierce, so grim a face,
Or issue flame from thy meek, modest eye.

No, lovely Dragon, well I know thou 'dst not;
  'Tis not thy nature — nor wouldst thou affright
From his dull sleep one Jacobinic sot,
  Who courts thy bowels by the rays of night,
Thinking, when safe within thy liquored tomb,
The eye of Reason cannot pierce the gloom.

. . . .

Hail, thou, whose color putrefaction suits:

. . . .

No flaring tail waves round thy scaly form,
  No paw terrific — or red darting tongue: —
  No — thou art yet in thy sad train but young,
Knowing but just the name of stately-storm.

Hadst thou a flaming tail, or griping claw,
You 'd never use it 'gainst our steady Law;
No, you 'd not do so — nor would you admit
  A man of merit, or a man of praise,
A worthy fellow, or an honest cit,
  Within thy maw his frowning head to raise.

Thou knowest better, ay, art wiser,
Hast, too, a good adviser,
  Yclept the cut-throat, cramp-eyed *Faction*,
Who recommends, with lengthened face,
To thy important useful place
  The vile projectors of each traitorous action.

. . . .

. . . .

Long may you stand, the sign-post of state-evil,
And keep poor feeble patriots from the devil:
Long may you — — is good Peter's wish.
Peter 's thy friend; thou knew'st it, long ago,
He serves thee in the clouded day of wo,
And offers to thy palate this small dish.

. . . .

The Gazette contained a series of papers, chiefly on moral subjects, under the title of The Camelion; another called the Literary Syphon; and still another, under the head of Dishes from the Table of Momus. Among the "dishes" served up by this writer were "The character of a mighty good sort of a Woman," and "The character of a mighty good sort of a Man," — articles well seasoned with wit and sarcasm. I am not quite satisfied that these two articles were originally written for the Political Gazette; but of the originality of the following, "From the Desk of Beri Hesdin,"* there can be no doubt: —

"THE GOOD MAN IS NOT AT HOME."

So *Beri Hesdin* thought, or Deacon Graves would surely have let in the maimed soldier, who, in the last beating storm, stood knocking at his door. The wind whistled through his tattered raiment, and hunger pinched him within; but, the door opened not. "And why?" says the mild form of Pity, "why did not the deacon make haste to let him in?" I will tell thee, thou inhabitant of some brighter world: he was sitting by his fire-side — not studying "the whole duty of man," or "the Christian's guide;" but calculating by compound interest; how rapidly he was rising to estate, from the purchase of that poor petitioner's notes, at the low rate of two shillings on the pound; and now the brave veteran has no insignia of having served his country, but wounds and poverty — *the good man is not at home;* he hath gone a long journey, even to the land of hard-heartedness, having taken *a bag of money* with him.

* This writer became, afterward, a regular correspondent of the Farmer's Museum.

When in our smaller courts of *judgement*, we behold the man, who hath sworn to do justly, and act according to law and evidence, taking the length and weight of the parties' purses, instead of listening to the voice of reason and justice, — If instead of rendering to Cæsar the things that are Cæsar's, he is balancing the rich man's fee against the poor man's right, — we may exclaim, with the son of David, *the good man is not at home.*

Dick Dashaway and Peter Rednose, never would have drank a dozen of Madeira at Sir Simon's house, and played with spotted pieces of paper till the crowing of the cock — *had the good man been at home.* Madam's chairs would not have been broken, nor the fine wrought fringe of her best bed been trodden under feet. The porter would not have pocketed his half joe for conveying Dick on his shoulders, nor surgeon Cancer a bill of sixty pounds for drawing broken glass from Peter's shin.

* * * * * * * * *

Beri Hesdin fears that long indeed is the journey of the good man; for as he passed by the doors of his temple, he beheld, and lo! in the midst thereof were those, who robbed the widow of her dower, and eat up the portion of the fatherless — sitting — veiled with the form of Christianity, and in a tone of godliness making long prayers. There also was he, who taketh from the way-faring man his purse, and from the pilgrim his socks; who letteth not the beggar pass in peace, but blasphemeth him because he is poor.

Ye that are slipping off the leading-strings of life, and entering the stage of action, where bustle and confusion wear the form of business; and dissipation and idleness draw aside him that hath his bag of money with him — be careful that virtue is your companion and prudence your guide; or at the close of life you will find clouds and darkness round about you; your feet stumbling on the dark mountains of despair, and when you knock at the door of mercy, will hear the voice of Peter exclaiming, "*the good man is not at home.*" BERI HESDIN.

The Political Gazette, was discontinued, as an independent publication, in October, 1797. A paper, called the Impartial Herald, had been published, some years, in Newburyport, by Angier March. The proprietors of the two papers, wisely agreed to unite their labors and expenses on one, which they issued semi-weekly, on Tuesday and Friday, and called it the

NEWBURYPORT HERALD AND COUNTRY GAZETTE.

Mr. Barrett withdrew from the concern about the first of January, 1798, and left the whole in the hands of Mr. March; who, apparently, conducted the paper with as much fairness and impartiality, as could be expected or desired by reasonable men. He was, however, annoyed by grumblers, (what editor is not?) as appears by the following article in the Herald of June 22, 1798:—

Some men who honor my paper with a perusal very seldom, frequently complain that it is a party paper, that I publish only on one side, &c. &c. I would beg leave to ask what those gentlemen want? A person this moment has the impertinence to look over my shoulder and reply to my query, *Why, the loaves and the fishes which they suppose those in office receive.* And in fact I believe it of many. But in the name of liberty, what two sides can there now be in this country—but those of America's friends and foes. Is not the government of our own formation and adoption, and has not experience proved it the best on the globe? Are not the administrators of it men of our own choice, from among ourselves, and removable at the will of the people? And is not that man a traitor to his country who vilifies and abuses so free and valuable, so independent and judicious a government, and so honest and virtuous an administration of it? Every American, every Man who has the least spark of integrity and patriotism will answer these questions in the affirmative. It is well known that the present government of France is straining every nerve to fraternize this country in the same manner that they have Holland, Venice, the states of Italy, Germany and Switzerland—and to accomplish its *virtuous* intentions, have made use of foreign agents in this country, bribery, corruption, and finally threatens, that unless we submit to their domination, to ravage our coasts and destroy our Commerce.

And yet there are found men base and mean enough to say publicly, that they are justifiable in their demands, and that the Editors of Newspapers who refuse to publish, and republish, their base and traitorous scurrility, "*publish only on one side!!!*" If this is publishing on one side, they may rest assured that on that side only shall I publish—on the side of my country. And neither French nor English bribes or threats shall ever induce me to swerve from patriotic rectitude.

Conscious that I have discharged my duty to my subscribers and country with assiduity and attention — I shall not regret the loss of a subscriber who dislikes the principles or disdains the abilities of the EDITOR.

There were some well-written political communications in the Herald, on the exciting topics of the day. But the reader has probably already seen extracts enough of this character, and I pass them over to present a specimen of the writing of one, who, fifty years ago, was quite notorious as a *writer* for the newspapers, and who published a pamphlet, containing a number of his newspaper articles, and near the end of the book, ushered in two or three other articles, with a note to the reader, saying that they were not of his writing, but "very drole." This gentleman's name was Timothy Dexter. His mansion in Newburyport, and the fences that inclosed it, were decorated with the images of all the Presidents of the United States, and with those of other individuals, and objects. The article, that follows, is an exact transcript from the original: —

Mister Printer,

WHAT is the Noys About the Lyon got down to our Congress there making A grat Noys got the art of Spiting and telling of grat things what he was Eabel to Love to turne the Corent as he was the man Capebel of so Daring and wanted to be more than A man alse & & so on Now is the grat worey ounited Stats to be Shouk in the wind A 2 Leged Lion A Anemel and wee tillers of the Leand felow mortels to Swet and tile to pay five thousan dolors to pay our worthy Congres men for this beast Lion and Likewise but two Leged halfe way basterd Life if this be put up with Corn under frace and be Shone boys and Louse all you felow mortels have won and be Com Doup but Now A wake Rouse turne out A bad man with out Cost beat the Roags march put sum fetters on them or him to transport them but Dont Let it Cost the Labering men so much to trye such Anemel it is Now good wisdum but hurst the Cose and the han Cuffs will frett the Rists some then tafe Care my felow mortels of Dubel minded men

A freethinker

This is a fair specimen of much that Timothy Dexter published, to *enlighten* his fellow-citizens. According to the doctrine of Jaques in "As you like it," he might truly be called a fool, for "heaven sent him fortune." But why heaven showers wealth so bountifully where it has denied brains, is a problem, that philosophy has not yet solved.

The Newburyport Herald, has had several proprietors. It has maintained a respectable rank among its cotemporaries, and is now a daily publication, conducted with much ability, and meriting, as I presume it receives, a good share of public support.

THE SALEM REGISTER.

On Monday, May 12, 1800, William Carleton issued a paper in Salem, under the title of the Impartial Register, which was continued semi-weekly on Monday and Thursday. Its motto was, —

> All parties here may plead an honest, favorite cause:
> Whoever reasons best on Nature's, Wisdom's laws,
> Proclaims eternal Truth — gains Heaven's and Man's applause.

A few months after its first appearance, it took the title of the Salem Impartial Register. Subsequently the title was changed to the Salem Register; then to Essex Register; and again to Salem Register, under which title it is now published.

The Impartial Register began its career as an advocate for the election of Mr. Jefferson to the Presidency. With all the ability of its editor and his friends, — among whom were the Rev. William Bentley and some of the wealthiest families in Salem, — it opposed the doctrines and the measures of the federal party. The political warfare between the Register and the Salem Gazette was carried on with great vigor and bitterness. In the autumn of 1802, Timothy Pickering, — Mr. Adams's ex-secretary of State, — was nominated by the Federalists of that district, as a candidate for representative to Congress. The Democratic candidate was Jacob

Crowninshield. Perhaps no electioneering contest was ever fought with more determined resolution to live or die with the result. Crowninshield was elected, and, to console themselves for their defeat, the Federalists prosecuted the editor of the Register for a libel on Pickering. A few days after the election, Carleton was indicted by the grand jury of the county of Essex, then sitting in Salem. The article, on which the indictment was founded, was in the following words: —

Robert Liston, the British Ambassador, distributed five hundred thousand dollars amongst the partisans of the English nation in America. Generous Tars, and honest Landsmen, do you think it likely that Jacob Crowninshield partook of these secret largesses? But can you entirely banish from your breasts the idea that our Ex-Secretary might receive from his dear friend and intimate companion some little token, some small gratuity, for all his zealous efforts against liberty and her sons, for all his attachment to the interests of England, for all his endeavors in all his transactions, to prostrate neutral rights at the mercy of every commander under the British, from his honor Admiral Harvey to the mild Matson, and from him down to the pirates of New-Providence, for all these good and loyal services? Is it at all unlikely that Squire Timothy did not receive some small trifling remembrance of the favor of his most sacred majesty of Britain — not to mention the affair of Senator Blount, Maitland, and the Black Emperor?

Carleton announced the fact, in his paper of November 18, as follows: —

SQUALLY APPEARANCES. The editor of this paper was yesterday called into Court to answer to an indictment for a supposed libel upon the ex-candidate and ex-secretary, Timothy Pickering. He forbears to make any remarks upon this transaction. He leaves it to the juries of a Republican Country to determine his crime and his punishment. His Judges, however Federal, will, he trusts, be impartial in their charges, and he shall cheerfully abide the verdict of twelve virtuous yeomen. He knows well who are the characters to whom he owes this prosecution; and the *mildness* and *modesty* of the complainants have long exemplified their *hatred* of PERSECUTION.

The trial came on in the following April, before the Supreme Court at Ipswich. Carleton was convicted, and, on the 25th, was sentenced to pay a fine of one hundred dollars, and the costs of prosecution; to be imprisoned in the county gaol two months; and to give bonds with two sureties in four hundred dollars each, to keep the peace for two years. The comments of the Register on the trial and its result were unexpectedly mild and respectful:—

> The result of the late prosecution is well known. The printer is taken from his family and is confined in gaol. His scanty means are to be taken away in fines, and he is to be treated as if he were the only offender. No indulgence is to be granted from that provocation, which the law considers in a quarrel. No consideration that he acted in his own defence, that the government of his country, which he reverenced, was insulted in the person of its first magistrate, and that all the candidates he could propose for public honors were abused and traduced. Allow that he cannot prove all his assertions. Can they who gave the provocation prove their assertions? Have any attempts been made to know whether they can? Is it not cowardly to insult a man, and then to sue him for insult, after he has been provoked? Much honor may this prosecution do the dismissed secretary, or to any of his friends.

Carleton died on the 25th of May, 1805, aged about thirty-four years. The Register states that he had endured great debility in consequence of a fever, under which he labored during his imprisonment;—that on the Monday preceding his death, he was occupied with his usual vigor till late in the evening:—and that, on Tuesday morning, a violent fever, with derangement, came on, which terminated his life in twenty-four hours. "He was born in Salem, and descended from two of the ancient families of the country. He always possessed great cheerfulness of temper and great benevolence of mind. He was distinguished by his perseverance, activity, and uprightness. To his generous zeal the public are indebted for the early information, which the Register gave of the most interesting occurrences. The friends of his youth enjoyed the warmth of his gratitude. His professions and friendships were sincere. He was an able editor, a friend to our happy administration, and an honest man."

After Carleton's death, the Register was "Printed for Elizabeth Carleton," his widow, till August 25th, when she also died, just thirty-two days after her husband. From that time, it was "published for the Proprietors;" but no name of either proprietor or printer appeared in the imprint, until it was placed in the possession of Haven Pool and Warwick Palfray, — two young men, who had been apprentices in the office, and to whom the management of the printing had been entrusted, after the death of Carleton. Mr. Bentley was the man, who contributed more than any other to keep the paper alive; but others assisted. Joseph Story, — the late Judge Story, then a practising lawyer in Salem, — wrote frequently for the Register, and his paragraphs are placed under the editorial head, undistinguished by any mark to identify them; but I am greatly deceived if the following were not from his pen: —

Who can stand before envy? The happy establishment of Mr. Jefferson in the seat of the chief magistrate of our Union, must, for several years exclude many, who expected offices under a different administration, from any hopes of promotion. In this delay of their honors, they have no other way to gratify their restless ambition, than by degrading those, who have reached the honors they could not obtain. And when we consider their number, their desperate purposes, and the power of disappointment upon ambition, what can be thought a sufficient restraint upon inflamed passions and malignant fury? The world has seen, often, the violence, which envy can purpose, and produce.

And where a comparison is made between present and past times, it may be said, we suffer little in our own times, from the worst cause of public discontents and distraction. We may well enough be prepared for the worst things, but we should remember that the fear of the public contempt can alone prevent the perpetration of them. At present, in our country, the public virtue is too active to admit the full triumph of envious prosecutors of good fame. The best rule, in the present state of things, is to suffer Time to be the interpreter of the actions of men: not to approve or condemn, till calm inquiry has done all its office, and then we may find the true value of our national benefactors. *April* 29, 1805.

The great pains taken to increase all prejudices against the French, when they had little power over the abuses which their subjects commit, while every indulgence was given to the English, too plainly discovered prejudices, which ought most seriously to be reprehended. Far should any American be from any disposition to excite needless prejudices against any nation. Far should he be from justifying an injury from one that had not the same favor from another. To preserve our Independence, we must deal justly, and be circumspect with all. If no political evils could arise, we might be indifferent on this subject. But to the French we have no attachments which interest cannot create. Of the British, we have all the partiality which can belong to customs and laws. We should cultivate favor with all, but upon the great principles which all will justify. But are we strangers to the artifices by which an undue foreign influence can be obtained? Have we never suffered from them? Is there a generous Englishman who cannot distinguish between justice to his nation, and a submission to his unreasonable claims? Is there one who does not wish to feel the distinction? Let it not then be supposed, that a love of our own nation, above any other, is a hatred of any nation. We wish the firmest affection between the two nations established upon honor and justice. But when they violate the laws of nations, when they commit depredations upon the unprotected commerce of individuals, and seize without notice upon the innocent as their prey — we must be forgiven if we say, we abhor commerce with such a nation, and withdraw from every alliance with oppression. *Sept.* 19, 1805.

It is among the last attempts to degrade the immortal President of the United States, to insinuate that his friends feared to display to the whole world the full history of Washington. Justice to the history of our country would spread a glory round our national benefactor, and discover to the nation new causes of their sincere gratitude. To the historian, no objection should be made by which he might be discouraged in his utmost investigations. We leave him not only every occurrence, but all the colors by which he could emblazon it. We hope he will not withhold a single circumstance, provided he is not disposed to leave it naked and unexplained. Let him tell the whole truth, and it will raise a monument of glory to the President of the United States. We may venture to predict all these advantages from the past success of his enemies. He is more known, more esteemed, more illustrious, by every attempt to injure his reputation. When political character is confounded with domestic anecdote which cannot be explained, scandal is confounded, and envy speechless. *Nov.* 4, 1805.

In August, 1806, an advertisement appeared in the Register, stating that "The Salem Register having been supported in its editorial department by the voluntary assistance of its friends since the decease of the late editor, Mr. Carleton, the proprietors are desirous of obtaining an editor to conduct the same in future." No new arrangement appears to have been made, however, till July, 1807, when Warwick Palfray, jun. who had been an apprentice with Carleton, formed a partnership with Haven Pool, and purchased the entire establishment. Pool & Palfray conducted the business, as partners till the decease of Pool, in July, 1811. From that time to January, 1835, Palfray was the sole editor and proprietor, when he received, as a partner, John Chapman, who had served an apprenticeship in the office. This connection was not of long continuance. Mr. Palfrey died on the 23d of August, 1838, at the age of fifty-one years.

Warwick Palfray, jun. was a native of Salem, and a descendant of Peter Palfray, the first settler in that place, — he having taken up his abode there some years before the arrival of Governor Endicott. With but slight advantages of education, from an unaided apprentice in a printing-office, he became the editor and proprietor of an important and influential newspaper. At the time of his decease, he was a member of the common council of the city of Salem, — an office, which he had held from the organization of the city government. He had represented his native town several years, in the House of Representatives of the state, where he was an active and useful member.

Mr. Palfray began his apprenticeship with Carleton in 1801. After the death of Carleton, while the Register was held as the property of Carleton's heirs, and for two years after, while it was owned by a company of gentlemen, he was one of the principal conductors. When, in connection with Pool, in 1807, he became proprietor of the establishment, he was still a minor; but such was his intelligence, integrity, and stability of character, that he possessed the entire confidence of the friends of the Register and the party of which it was the organ; and the event showed that their confidence was not misplaced.

An obituary notice in the Register, from which some of the preceding facts have been derived, — written, undoubtedly by a friendly hand, but, I believe, from personal knowledge, without exaggeration — furnishes the following paragraphs: —

Under the editorial care of Mr. Palfray, the Register has had a popularity and influence probably equal to any semi-weekly paper in the state. It was under his charge during the whole period of the Embargo and War, and all the excitement incident to that period of embittered political feeling and almost deadly party hostility; — yet, notwithstanding all the excitement of those periods, he gave as little just cause of offence as any man living could. Possessed of the most generous and honorable feelings, he never willingly gave just cause of offence to a political opponent. Personal allusions were always painful to him; and at those periods of deadly feud, when he was placed at the editorial desk, it was his greatest pleasure to take from the papers handed him for publication, the poisoned arrows; and when he could not, consistently with political duty, wholly remove personal allusions, to soften them to the utmost limit. Little, at those periods, did his political opponents, who were censuring the bitterness of the communications, know how much he had attenuated their violence, and how he had to struggle with his correspondents to restrain the madness of party.

Mr. Palfray was a firm, unwavering, and consistent politician. Success never made him assume an ungenerous attitude towards his political opponents, and defeat never discouraged from perseverance to gain the ascendency for what he deemed correct principles and measures. He never truckled to power nor sought personal advantages for himself. All the offices he held were unsought; for he was uncommonly modest and diffident of his own powers and claims. Though for years the uncompromising combatant of the old federal party, no man was more gratified than himself at that epocha of good feeling, when it was considered proper for those, who had been so long estranged from each other, by mistaken views of each other's opinions and principles, to act in concert, and no man felt less of the leaven of old party than himself.

In the private relations of life, Mr. Palfray was incapable of giving offence amounting to an insult. His heart was the abode of pure thoughts — his life the exemplar of good principles. The tongue of calumny, in the times of bitterest political animosity, never breathed a syllable against the spotless purity of his life and character.

After the death of Mr. Palfray, the Register was continued, for a year or two by John Chapman, the surviving partner. A son of Mr. Palfray, (Charles W.) then became associated with Mr. Chapman, and the paper is now published by them. Its appearance indicates that the concern is prosperous, and that those, who conduct it, intend it shall lose none of its well-founded claims to support.

The Salem Register, from its commencement, has been the favored channel, through which many good and able writers have chosen to diffuse their political opinions. Whatever offence it may have given to political opponents, it cannot be denied that its sentiments have been promulgated with great ability. In its early stages, the late Judge Story (before his appointment to the bench of the supreme court) was a liberal contributor. Andrew Dunlap, a lawyer of promising talents, was one of the writers, previous to 1825; and Joseph E. Sprague (the present sheriff of Essex county) frequently enriched its columns with political disquisitions. But it is generally believed that the writer on whom the conductors mainly relied for aid, was the Rev. William Bentley. Of the character, and career of this gentleman,—so often mentioned in the preceding pages of this volume,—the following memoir has been compiled, from such notices of him as appeared in newspapers soon after his death, and from the personal recollections of one of his intimate friends.

William Bentley was born in Boston, June 22, 1759. He was the son of Joshua and Elizabeth Bentley, and was named William in honor of his maternal grandfather, William Paine, who was a man of some property at the northerly part of Boston. This old gentleman had a strong attachment to this grandchild, attended to his early education, and paid his expenses at college. Young Bentley was early distinguished for his natural talents, and for his uncommon acquisitions in classical and general literature. He graduated in 1777, and was immediately employed as assistant teacher in the Boston Latin Grammar school, where he had been fitted for college; and, in 1779, he was the preceptor of the North Grammar school. He was appointed tutor in

Greek and Latin at Harvard College, in 1780, and while holding this office he prepared himself for the ministry. On the 24th of September, 1783, he was ordained, as colleague pastor with the Rev. James Dimon, over the East Church in Salem. His colleague died in 1788, and Mr. Bentley continued his pastoral relation, alone, with the church, till his death, December 29, 1819. He was distinguished for the position, which he took in the early part of his career, — with his friend and class-mate, the Rev. James Freeman, of Boston, — in favor of Unitarianism.

In 1794, when William Carleton undertook the publication of the Salem Gazette, he and Mr. Bentley boarded with an old lady, — a relative of Carleton's; and, to assist the young kinsman of his landlady, Mr. Bentley was induced to write a summary of news, weekly, for the Gazette. Not long after, Carleton had a long and severe sickness, and, as an act of friendship, he conducted the paper alone. While thus engaged, he opened a correspondence with Professor Ebeling of Hamburg, who was preparing a History and Geography of the United States. The German professor wanted materials, and Mr. Bentley took unwearied pains to collect and send them to him. He sent all the curious books he could procure and wrote many letters. It then occurred to him that, by writing a summary of intelligence for the Gazette, he might aid both Ebeling and Carleton, and this was the origin and motive of his labors in that department of the paper; for he was never paid a dollar for his services, which were constantly and industriously continued for near a quarter of a century. The various newspapers, received in exchange for Carleton's paper, Mr. Bentley was accustomed to pack in the neatest manner, and send to Professor Ebeling, with an index to such papers and articles as he deemed most important. In return for such books as Mr. Bentley sent to him, the Professor sent German publications, but no cash transactions ever passed between them.*

Mr. Bentley was one of the earliest members of the Massachusetts Historical Society, and was induced to write for its Collections a History of Salem; but becoming disgusted with the conduct of one of the publishing committee, (the Rev. Dr. Morse,) he abandoned the design after having made some progress. This is to be regretted; for he was minutely acquainted with every interesting incident concerning his adopted town, and retained in his iron memory, a thousand facts, which he had labored to collect, but which he had not recorded.

Nothing could exceed the labor and activity of Mr. Bentley in his profession, and in every department of social life. He left *three thousand three hundred sermons*, and *fifty-six* other manuscripts of various sizes, some quite large and elaborate, in which he had recorded the events of the passing day, and his observations in philosophy, theology, astronomy, meteorology, geology, and many other branches of science, that, in his day, were rarely attended to by the scholar. He was *expert* in at least twenty-one languages, besides having that smattering of others, which arises from a

* In 1818, Israel Thorndike, of Boston, purchased the library of Professor Ebeling, and, presented it to Harvard College. The newspapers, which the Professor had received from Mr. Bentley had been bound, making quite a number of large volumes, and they form, an interesting portion of the library of that institution. Many of the books on American History, which came from Professor Ebeling, it is presumed are, also, those he had received from Mr. Bentley.

thorough acquaintance with so many. In Latin, Greek, Hebrew, Arabic, and Persian, he probably had no rival in this country. He read all the popular languages of Europe, not excepting the Russian. He corresponded with the petty chiefs of Arabia and Eastern Africa; and it is related of him, that when the Tunisian ambassador presented his credentials to our government, no one, but Mr. Bentley, could translate them. His library contained four thousand volumes, and was the largest and best *private* library in the nation, except that of Mr. Jefferson.

His devotedness to books did not prevent an unusual attention to the concerns of the people of his parish. Besides writing such an immense number of sermons, averaging nearly two a week for thirty-six years, his visits to every member of his congregation were frequent, and his knowledge of all their concerns was such as to enable him to be their best comforter and friend.

Mr. Bentley's cabinet of Natural History was large, until the establishment of the Salem Museum, in which he took an active part, induced him to deposite his collection where it would be more useful. As many of his parishioners were ship-masters and sea-faring men, his opportunities for gaining an acquaintance with distant parts of the world were numerous and well improved; and the Summaries of the Register and the mercantile portion of Walsh's arithmetic, which he contributed gratuitously, show how he used his knowledge. Few scholars wrote so rapidly and so well as Mr. Bentley. We refer to his penmanship, of which his manuscripts in Hebrew, Greek, and Arabic, as well as in the common characters, are beautiful specimens of chirography.

The mass of useful knowledge, thus collected, he poured out liberally in his Summaries, and in conversation, which he loved, and in which he particularly excelled. The study of so many languages evidently had an unfavorable influence upon his style of writing his vernacular, which, in his latter days, was sometimes obscure, and marred by the use of words, etymologically correct, but not conformable to popular usage.

In politics, Mr. Bentley was strictly a republican, but his writings were not of the stamp to give them currency with the federal party. As the technical republican was not the most powerful party in the state of Massachusetts, however it may have been in the nation, there can be no doubt that his attainments and talents were treated with less regard than if he had belonged to the other party. Educated at Harvard, a tutor in that college for several years, unequaled as a biblical critic and a linguist, if there was any honor in an academical degree, he was, undoubtedly, entitled to it; but while degrees were liberally bestowed on men, who had not a tithe of his merits as a scholar, his claims were passed by and repudiated till there was no grace in conferring the honor. In August, 1819, the degree of D. D. was conferred upon him by the corporation of Harvard; but, if the formality of acceptance was necessary to constitute him a Doctor of Divinity, he was never one of that class by virtue of a sheet of parchment. It has been said that, some years before, those who opposed him on the ground of religious sentiment, offered to confer on him the degree of LL. D. (to which, probably, he had as fair a claim as many, who receive it,) but that one or two of his friends in the corporation objected to this as insulting to his clerical character, and, of course, the matter was dropped. His will was made a month or two before the doctorate in divinity was conferred, but the tardy honor did not induce him to alter it, and his library which was his chief wealth, was scattered among other institutions. To the last, however, he cherished a deep interest in the prosperity of his alma mater, as his Diary fully proves; and no one, it is presumed, ever heard him express disappointment or regret at the neglect, which was but too apparent to every one else.

In his editorial capacity, Mr. Bentley was always respectful, though firm. No charge to the contrary was ever brought against him; and in an attempt to "draw him in," when Carleton was indicted for publishing a libel on Timothy Pickering, his political opponents were disappointed. He was a true patriot. He loved his country and her institutions, and never hesitated to say so. He sought no distinction; and though honored with the personal regard of more than one President, nothing could induce him to ask any favor for himself. When, in 1805, Mr. Jefferson invited him to take charge of what he intended should become a national college in Virginia, Mr. Bentley promptly declined, remarking to his friends, that his people were his wife, and as he could not take them to Washington, he would never consent to a divorce. As an instance of his patriotism, it is related that when the Constitution frigate was driven into Marblehead by three British ships, and fears were entertained that she might be captured, he was performing his ordinary service in the pulpit. Some one informed him of the circumstance, and he instantly stopped the services, announced the intelligence to the congregation, and, remarking that they could worship God at all times, but could save the Constitution only by immediate action, he left the pulpit, hurried to the fort at Marblehead, reported himself to the commander, and requested to be placed where he could be of service. He was ordered to stand by one of the guns. The danger was soon over, and returning to Salem in time for the afternoon service, he delivered an extempore sermon on patriotism, from the text, "There go the ships!"

In stature, Mr. Bentley was below the middle size; he was even short, and appeared the more so, because he was always fat. At the age of fifty-two, he weighed two hundred and fourteen pounds, though hardly above five feet in height. In his personal habits, he would have done credit to the best modern teachers of physiology. Personal cleanliness was a virtue with him, and no day passed without much exercise in walking, which he believed to be the best exercise for a scholar. All his writing was done while he was in a standing posture. He never used a chair in his study; but he had one low bench, on which he sat, if he sat at all. Temperance was another of his virtues. He always retired early, and usually studied or wrote an hour or two before sunrise. His food was always simple, and very uniform at home, for he had been admonished, many years before his death, that there was some organic trouble at the heart. This, no doubt, caused his death. Having been to see a parishioner, who had just returned from a long voyage, and staying after his hour of retiring to rest, he hurried home. The night was excessively cold; and, when he entered the room, he stood with his back to the fire, apologizing to his landlady for staying out so late, and fell upon the floor, and died instantly. It was supposed that the transition from the cold atmosphere to a warm fire so increased the flow of blood as to produce suffocation.

No man, probably, was better prepared to die. A life of the most unbounded charity, of purity, innocence, and simplicity, and of active usefulness, is no mean preparation for death; but, besides being armed at all points, which have reference to the world to come, Mr. Bentley had settled up with the present world. The sums he gave away, for useful and benevolent objects, would startle one, who knew how limited his salary was and how much of it, due from poor parishioners, was never paid. It is a singular fact that, at his death, he did not owe a cent, and nothing was due to him that he would ever have attempted to collect. When his executor was called on, by the probate court, for his accounts, there were no materials from which to make one, — the legacies having been duly delivered, and the executor being the residuary legatee. In his will, Mr. Bentley requested his executor to burn all his manuscripts; but he has, prudently, kept them, until most of those persons, who were noticed in them, especially in the Diary, have passed away, and a mass of facts has been preserved for future antiquaries.

Mr. Bentley published but little beyond what he wrote for the Salem newspapers. His first publication was a small Hymn Book for the use of his society, in 1789, which passed through two or three editions. Next was his History of Salem, in the first series of the Historical Collections, — never completed. Two or three Masonic Addresses, and seven or eight Sermons, — one of which was the election sermon when Governor Sullivan was first chosen — complete the catalogue.

Mr. Bentley rode only on short excursions in his neighborhood. He was never in Rhode-Island, Connecticut, or Vermont; in Maine only once; in New-Hampshire but twice; and was never out of New-England. Yet his knowledge of every part of the world was more exact than some of the greatest travelers ever acquire. He loved home; and was so much attached to it when it had become familiar, that he changed his boarding-place only once during his whole ministry.

His antiquarian knowledge surpassed that of any other man in New-England. The notices of men and events, scattered throughout his Diary from 1783 to 1819, would form several volumes. His notices of books, of subjects in Natural History, and his statistical tables, are equally copious and extensive.

There are still living, — 1850, — one brother and one sister of Mr. Bentley, at the ages of seventy-three and seventy-seven years. His father died at the age of ninety-five, and his grandfather at eighty-four. The latter was born in England, and was brought to this country, when a boy, by his father, who was an officer in the expedition against Quebec, and perished there, leaving his child an orphan in Boston. The father and grandfather were both mechanics.

The funeral of Mr. Bentley took place in Salem, January 3, 1820. The devotional services were conducted by the Rev. Messrs. Kirkland and Prince, and a sermon was preached by Professor Everett. The funeral procession was long, composed of the members of the church and society, relatives, municipal and public characters, and a large column of Free Masons. Masonic solemnities were performed at the tomb by the officers of Essex Lodge, of which he was a member.

The obituary notices of Dr. Bentley were numerous; and those newspapers, which had been violent in their remarks on his career as a politician, were courteous and respectful to his memory. The Salem Gazette, which had probably treated him with more indignity than any other paper, after mentioning his death, said, — "As a divine he was distinguished for extensive erudition; as a preacher, he was eloquent and brilliant. His activity and industry in literary pursuits never diverted his attention from his parochial duties; he was the friend, counselor and guide of his parishioners, and always enjoyed their warmest attachment and affection. To the poor and unfortunate he carried not empty professions of sympathy, but he was their active friend and comforter. He daily sought the abodes of misery, poverty, and misfortune, and, to the extent of his pecuniary resources, administered to their relief and comfort. His influence, his example, and his most active exertions, were devoted to the alleviation of sorrow and suffering. His extensive and various attainments in literature and science, and his familiar knowledge of most of the ancient and modern languages, have given him merited celebrity among the learned of this country and of Europe. He was a principal and active member of the Historical and Antiquarian societies, and was ever an enthusiastic friend of our University and other literary establishments."

APPENDIX TO VOLUME II.

Note to page 63.

I COULD never discover the origin of the almost deadly feud, which existed between Benjamin Austin, jun. and Benjamin Russell; and it may be questioned whether any one can refer to any specific act or word, as the cause of it. It is difficult to conceive how the newspaper squibs which would now be considered harmless, or too contemptible to excite serious anger or lasting animosity, should have kindled such furious and implacable hatred. Mr. Austin began to write under the signature of "Honestus," in March, 1786, — about two years after Russell began to publish the Centinel; and not long after he is alluded to in the Centinel by the nick-name of *Honee*, an epithet which grew into common use, insomuch that many people supposed that to be the real name of the man. Whether this abbreviation of his signature, which he had adopted, was first suggested by Russell, is not, and probably never will be known. If it were so, — and if the continued repetition of it in the Centinel, and afterwards in other papers that were opposed to the Chronicle in politics, fixed it upon the individual, personally, — it seems hardly credible, that the reproach, — if it were a reproach, — should have made a wound so deep as to lead to the scene at the town-meeting in Fanueil Hall. Before that occurrence, there is nothing in either of the papers, — that, at the present day, would be thought of consequence enough to prevent a recognition of courtesy on a public occasion like that; — certainly not any thing sufficient to warrant so harsh and rude a remark as that made by Austin, in presence of their assembled fellow-citizens. Political hostility had not then risen to its burning fever; and on some points, the two combatant individuals had acted not only in perfect unison, but rather seemed to emulate each other to produce certain effects. Personalities, more disgusting, and quite as irritating in character and purpose, are to be seen almost every day in the leading political papers. I think there must have been some occurrence, the nature and history of which are lost in obscurity, to open such a fountain of bitter waters. The quarrels of editors would form a curious and not worthless volume.

After the account of the trial, which is given in the text, appeared in the Apollo, Russell was called upon by numerous friends, — probably many who had not seen that report, — to publish a statement, which one of his friends had prepared for the Centinel. He consented to the publication, although, at first, being a party concerned, he resolved to be silent. His first allusion to the affair is this: —

> It was not the intention of the editor to admit any remarks or strictures on the litigation between him and Mr. A——, into the Centinel; because he supposed his antagonist so completely mortified, that any observations thereon would appear like unmanly exultation — and he had reason to expect silence on the part of that antagonist. He has, however, been disappointed in the latter particular; and recognizing as he does, the scurrility of A—— in the Chronicle, he is necessitated to meet him in a field of scribbling controversy. If he occupies any portion of the public attention, which might have been directed to a more worthy object, his apology must be received, inasmuch as he is not *a volunteer* in the service.

In the same paper, a correspondent hinted that, if any one should vote for the Chronicle candidate for senator (meaning Austin) on the first of April, he would richly merit "the compliment of the day." Russell, in a subsequent paper, said, — "The *senatorial demagogue* has long held the *copy-right* of scurrility and abuse. To reply to his *dirt*, in kind, would be an invasion of that *right*, and entitle him to *another* action of *damage. 20s.*" This appears to be the last reference to the matter, in the Centinel.

INDEX TO VOL. II.

NOTE. On page 270, sixteenth line, by an unfortunate blunder, the word *quid* stands in the place of a much better one, — *quill.*

www.ingramcontent.com/pod-product-compliance
Lightning Source LLC
LaVergne TN
LVHW010143110826
845151LV00002B/412
* 9 7 8 1 4 2 5 5 3 8 7 8 1 *